THE MANAGEMENT OF INTERNATIONAL TOURISM

STEPHEN F. WITT, MICHAEL Z. BROOKE AND
PETER J. BUCKLEY

Volume 5

Routledge
Taylor & Francis Group

LONDON AND NEW YORK

First published in 1991

This edition first published in 2013
by Routledge
2 Park Square, Milton Park, Abingdon, Oxfordshire OX14 4RN

Simultaneously published in the USA and Canada
by Routledge
711 Third Avenue, New York, NY 10017

First issued in paperback 2014

Routledge is an imprint of the Taylor and Francis Group, an informa business

British Library Cataloguing in Publication Data
A catalogue record for this book is available from the British Library

ISBN 978-0-415-62615-6 (Set)
eISBN 978-0-203-06696-6 (Set)
ISBN 978-0-415-81268-9 (Volume 5) (hbk)
ISBN 978-1-138-00766-6 (Volume 5) (pbk)
ISBN 978-0-203-06851-9 (Volume 5) (ebk)

Publisher's Note
The publisher has gone to great lengths to ensure the quality of this reprint but points out that some imperfections in the original copies may be apparent.

Disclaimer
The publisher has made every effort to trace copyright holders and would welcome correspondence from those they have been unable to trace.

The Management of International Tourism

STEPHEN F. WITT

MICHAEL Z. BROOKE

PETER J. BUCKLEY

London
UNWIN HYMAN
Boston   Sydney   Wellington

Published by the Academic Division of
Unwin Hyman Ltd
15/17 Broadwick Street, London W1V 1FP, UK

Unwin Hyman Inc.
955 Massachusetts Avenue, Cambridge, MA 02139, USA

Allen & Unwin (Australia) Ltd
8 Napier Street, North Sydney, NSW 2060, Australia

Allen & Unwin (New Zealand) Ltd
in association with the Port Nicholson Press Ltd
Compusales Building, 75 Ghuznee Street, Wellington 1, New Zealand

First published in 1991

British Library Cataloguing in Publication Data

Witt, Stephen F.
    The management of international tourism.
    1. Tourist industries. Planning
    I. Title   II. Brooke, Michael Z., *1921*–
    III. Buckley, Peter J. (Peter Jennings) *1949*–
    338.4791

    ISBN 0-04-445124-5
    ISBN 0-04-445993-9 pbk

Typeset in 10 on 11 point Times by Fotographics (Bedford) Ltd
and printed in Great Britain by
Billings and Sons Ltd, London and Worcester

Contents

List of tables

List of figures

Preface

The rapid growth in international tourism has promoted widespread interest, including the blossoming of many educational courses. Several tourism texts have been published recently, but there seems to be a gap at the high-level end of the market, which this text seeks to fill. The book is aimed at final-year undergraduate, masters degree and post-experience courses where there is an international tourism component, as well as specialist courses in tourism. In addition, the book should be of considerable interest to managers in tourism, travel, hospitality, transportation and consultancy companies, as well as to local authorities and national tourist offices. The objective is to provide a comprehensive review of the field of international tourism with an emphasis on the management of tourism.

The authors wish to thank the two anonymous reviewers who provided most helpful detailed comments on an earlier draft of the manuscript. Their suggestions have been incorporated into this final version of the text. The authors also wish to thank the many tourism professionals who have contributed their time and resources to this book and our colleagues in the academic community who have commented on various drafts in print and at seminars. We would also like to thank the students at Swansea and Bradford who have acted as guinea-pigs for teaching purposes.

Thanks are also due to Mrs Chris Barkby, Mrs Liz Hickson and Mrs Pauline Thomas for their patience and word-processing skills on the many drafts of the text.

STEPHEN F. WITT
MICHAEL Z. BROOKE
PETER J. BUCKLEY
Swansea, Manchester and Bradford

1

The environment of international tourism

Introduction

It is clear that tourism is playing an increasingly important role in the world economy. For example, international tourism receipts already comprise 7 per cent of the value of world exports and this figure is expected to grow. Currently international tourism is second only to oil in world trade, and it has been forecast that by the turn of the century it will be the most important sector.

The scale of world domestic tourism far exceeds that of international tourism, both in volume and value terms. Total world receipts from tourism – international and domestic – exceed the gross national product (GNP) of any country in the world except Japan (where GNP is approximately equal to world tourism receipts) and the USA (where GNP is approximately twice the value of world tourism receipts).

Many countries look to international tourism as a source of valuable foreign exchange to alleviate balance of payments problems. The importance of domestic tourism should, however, not be understated; in many cases international and domestic tourism represent real alternatives, and therefore domestic tourism can have a marked impact on the balance of payments through its import substitute role.

In recent years there has been increasing emphasis on the employment-generating potential of tourism. The general decline in traditional manufacturing activities in countries such as the UK and the USA has led to a search for alternative employment opportunities. Advantages of tourism incluue the facts that it is a relatively labour-intensive industry and that many of the job opportunities lie in low-skill occupations where unemployment tends to be concentrated.

Although interest has tended largely to centre on the economic importance and benefits of tourism, more recently increasing concern has been expressed regarding the undesirable physical and sociocultural impacts of tourism. In particular, the effects of pollution, over-use of facilities, social disorder, and so on, caused by massive influxes of tourists can give rise to a 'tourism backlash' in host communities, even to the extent of resulting in open resentment of tourists. These detrimental impacts of tourism need to be taken into account in tourism planning at destinations.

Definitions, concepts and data

In order to proceed with our discussion of tourism we first need to define precisely what is meant by such terms as 'tourism', 'tourist' and so on. Wanhill (1988, p. 2) defines 'tourism' as the 'temporary movement of people to destinations outside their normal places of work and residence and the activities undertaken during the time spent at those destinations'. Conventionally, 'temporary' means up to one year when referring to international tourism, and a period of up to a few weeks or months (according to the country concerned) for domestic tourism. The generally accepted definition of a 'visitor' is a person travelling for up to this specified period 'to a place other than of his usual environment and whose main purpose of visit is other than to exercise an activity remunerated by an entity within the place visited' (Allard, 1989, p. 420). When referring to domestic tourism, a minimum distance travelled requirement is sometimes included in the definitions of 'tourism' and 'visitor', and, in addition, hospital patients are usually excluded. Visitors can be divided into two categories: 'tourists' who stay at least one night in the place visited; and 'excursionists' or 'day visitors' who do not stay overnight in the place visited. Although excursionists do not use accommo-dation facilities in the destination, they represent an important segment of the tourism market and are included within our definition of tourism.

'International' visitors are people who cross international frontiers to travel to countries other than their usual country of residence. 'Domestic' visitors are generally taken to be people travelling within their own country (Burkart and Medlik, 1981; Middleton, 1988), although the World Tourism Organization (WTO) proposes that inbound foreign visitors should additionally be included in the definition (see Allard, 1989). In the former case the terms 'domestic visitor' and 'internal visitor' are synonymous, whereas in the latter case 'domestic' visitors comprise 'internal' and 'inbound foreign' visitors. We shall adopt the more common definition in which domestic is taken to mean internal.

The definition of tourism encompasses a wide variety of visit purposes: holidays, visits to friends and relatives, business visits, attendance at conferences, visits for religious or health reasons, and so on. The WTO detailed international classification of travellers is shown in Figure 1.1.

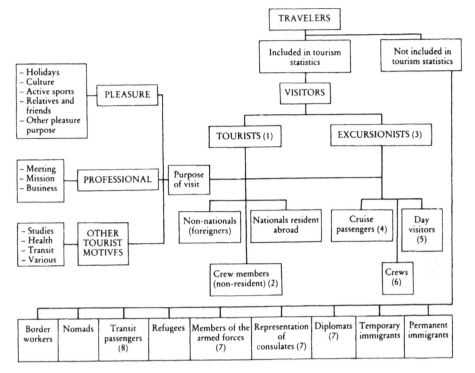

1. Visitors who spend at least one night in the country visited.
2. Foreign air or ship crews docked or in lay over and who use the accommodation establishments of the country visited.
3. Visitors who do not spend the night in the country visited although they may visit the country during one day or more and return to their ship or train to sleep.
4. Normally included in excursionists. Separate classification of these visitors is nevertheless recommended.
5. Visitors who come and leave the same day.
6. Crews who are not residents of the country visited and who stay in the country for the day.
7. When they travel from their country of origin to the duty station and vice-versa (including household servants and dependents accompanying or joining them).
8. Who do not leave the transit area of the airport or the port. In certain countries, transit may involve a stay of one day or more. In this case, they should be included in the visitors statistics.

Figure 1.1   International classification of travellers.
Source: World Tourism Organization.

Although the emphasis in this book is on *international* tourism management many of the concepts and techniques discussed are equally applicable to domestic tourism.

The measurement of tourist flows takes place in various ways. International inward tourist flows are usually recorded by frontier counts, sample surveys or registration at accommodation establishments. A problem with frontier counts is that in certain cases a substantial transit traffic element may be present, which distorts the statistics. Accommodation establishment records exclude excursionists, tourists staying with friends or relatives and those in other forms of unregistered accommodation. When different receiving countries use different measurement methods it becomes very difficult to compare arrivals data across destinations. International outward tourism flows are often measured by origin countries using sample surveys which they apply to returning residents. Other methods used to collect these data are household surveys or micro-censuses.

International tourism receipts are defined as the receipts of a country resulting from payments for goods and services made by international visitors during their stay in the country visited. In general, they exclude all forms of remuneration resulting from employment, as well as international fare receipts. International tourism expenditures are defined as payments for goods and services made by residents of a country visiting abroad, and again in general exclude all forms of remuneration resulting from employment, as well as international fare payments.

Tourist expenditures/receipts data are collected in various ways (Allard, 1989). The most common method is for central banks to assemble the data using the 'bank reporting method'. Other techniques are the 'estimation method' and the 'mixed method'. In essence, the bank reporting method is based on the registration by authorized banks and agencies of the buying and selling of foreign currencies by travellers. There are many problems associated with this method of data collection, such as the identification of a transaction as a tourism transaction, the non-reporting of relevant transactions, the possible netting of some inward and outward foreign currency transactions data and the inability to capture 'black market' transactions (which are a prevalent feature of many countries with rigid exchange control regulations). The major reservation associated with the bank reporting method is that the data are unreliable for identifying tourist receipts from a particular origin country. Any geographical breakdown provided relates to the denomination of the currency and not to the generating country; thus, for example, residents of countries with currencies that are not readily acceptable may well use US dollars on their foreign visits. The estimation method is based on sample surveys. These are usually applied to returning residents and departing non-residents. This method provides the most reliable data on tourist expenditures/receipts. The mixed method aims to improve the statistics produced by the bank reporting method. Supplementary data obtained from other sources (for example, visitor surveys) are used to weight the transactions statistics, thereby improving consistency and reliability.

The tourism 'industry' may be thought of as comprising all those sectors of the economy that contribute to meeting the needs of the tourist. Middleton (1988) breaks these sectors down into accommodation (for example, hotels, guest houses, holiday parks), transport (airlines, railways, shipping companies), travel organizers (retail travel agents, tour operators), attractions (theme parks, heritage sites, shopping facilities) and the destination organization sector (national tourist offices, regional tourist offices, local tourist offices). It is clear that tourism is a highly complex industry, and this is reflected, for example, in the problems associated with assessing the employment generated by tourism. The main complication is that the tourism industry is not defined in terms of the goods or service supplied, but rather in terms of the type of customer demanding goods and services. Thus a waiter may spend part of his time serving local customers and part of his time serving tourists, and so not all the jobs in tourism-related industries such as hotels and catering are supported by tourist spending.

The main sources of data relating to international tourism are the WTO, which regularly produces several publications containing tourism-related statistics, and the Organisation for Economic Co-operation and Development (OECD), which publishes *Tourism Policy and International Tourism* annually. The OECD is concerned with tourism in OECD member countries, whereas the WTO is concerned with world tourism. In particular, the WTO's *Yearbook of Tourism Statistics* is the most comprehensive collection of official government tourism statistics available, covering 150 countries and territories. More detailed information on individual countries is usually available directly from the country concerned; organizations such as central banks, national tourist offices and national statistical offices are often able to supply tourism-related data.

Economic environment

WTO figures show that international tourist arrivals totalled 405 million in 1989 with corresponding receipts of almost 211 billion US dollars. These receipts accounted for 7 per cent of world international trade and 18 per cent of world trade in services. When domestic tourism is also included tourism receipts rise to more than 2,000 billion US dollars. The (international plus domestic) tourism industry accounts for 12 per cent of world GNP.

Balance of payments

The balance of payments implications of international tourism are very important for certain countries and regions. The balance of receipts from inbound tourists and expenditures by tourists travelling abroad gives rise to the tourism balance, and this varies considerably from country to country and region to region. As discussed earlier, caution must be exercised when dealing with tourism expenditure/receipts data; the methods of compiling the statistics vary across countries, so the data are often not strictly comparable, and, in particular, there are serious inadequacies associated with the bank reporting method of data collection. Nevertheless, tourism expenditures/receipts data provide useful information regarding the sign and approximate size of the tourism balance.

Table 1.1 depicts the tourism balance for the major regions of the world. Europe has the most favourable balance, but there are sharp differences within this total. In fact, only Southern Europe has a large positive tourism balance (reflecting the importance of sun/sea/sand tourism). The combined deficit on the tourism account for Northern and Western Europe is more than two-and-a-half times as high as the deficit for North America, the continent with the worst tourism balance. By contrast, Central America, and, in particular, the Caribbean show healthy surpluses on their tourism accounts. For Africa as a whole tourism receipts exceed expenditures, but within the continent there are great variations. In Northern Africa there is a large positive tourism balance because some countries that border the Mediterranean attract considerable numbers of European

Table 1.1   Tourism balance in major regions of the world, 1987 (US $ million).

	Receipts	Expenditure	Balance
Africa	3,619	2,640	979
Eastern Africa	700	257	443
Middle Africa	82	440	−358
Northern Africa	1,811	695	1,116
Southern Africa	665	880	−215
Western Africa	361	368	−7
Americas	33,329	34,679	−1,350
North America	19,313	26,625	−7,312
Central America	4,014	2,654	1,360
South America	3,875	4,119	−244
The Caribbean	6,127	1,281	4,846
East Asia and the Pacific	19,190	18,382	808
Europe	95,147	85,495	9,652
Eastern Europe	2,156	943	1,213
Northern Europe	17,413	24,080	−6,667
Southern Europe	35,712	8,202	27,510
Western Europe	38,519	51,272	−12,753
Middle East	5,572	5,568	4
South Asia	1,857	1,088	769

Source: World Tourism Organization (1989).

Table 1.2 Tourism balance in individual European countries, 1987 (US $ million).

	Receipts	Expenditure	Balance
Austria[1]	7,604	4,516	3,088
Belgium	2,980	3,886	−906
Denmark	2,219	2,860	−641
Finland	791	1,458	−667
France	12,008	8,618	3,390
Germany (West)	7,716	23,551	−15,835
Greece	2,192	507	1,685
Iceland	86	213	−127
Ireland	811	814	−3
Italy	12,174	4,536	7,638
Netherlands	2,666	6,362	−3,696
Norway	1,244	3,056	−1,812
Portugal	2,148	421	1,727
Spain	14,760	1,938	12,822
Sweden	2,033	3,781	−1,748
Switzerland	5,352	4,339	1,013
Turkey	1,721	448	1,273
United Kingdom	10,229	11,898	−1,669

Source: World Tourism Organization (1989).
Note:
1   Including international fare payments.

tourists, and in Eastern Africa there is also a good positive tourism balance. In East Asia and the Pacific and South Asia tourism receipts are higher than tourism expenditure.

International tourism receipts and international tourism expenditures are far greater for Europe than any other region (Table 1.1), and Table 1.2 shows the breakdown for individual European countries. The most favourable tourism balance is achieved by Spain (US $12.8 billion), followed by Italy (US $7.6 billion), France (US $3.4 billion), Austria (US $3.1 billion), Portugal (US $1.7 billion) and Greece (US $1.7 billion). The least favourable tourism balance is achieved by West Germany (−US $15.8 billion); although tourism receipts for West Germany exceed those of both Austria and Switzerland (which have positive tourism balances), the massive tourism expenditure of US $23.6 billion gives West Germany by far the worst tourism balance in Europe. The second least favourable tourism balance is achieved by the Netherlands (−US $3.7 billion), followed by Norway (−US $1.8 billion) and Sweden (−US $1.7 billion).

Table 1.3 examines the tourism balance for selected non-European countries. The major destination in Eastern Africa for international tourists is Kenya, and here receipts from international

Table 1.3 Tourism balance in selected non-European countries, 1987 (US $ million).

	Receipts	Expenditure	Balance
Eastern Africa			
Kenya	344	21	323
Mauritius	138	51	87
North Africa			
Morocco	1,000	100	900
Tunisia	672	94	578
Southern Africa			
South Africa	587	835	−248
Western Africa			
Nigeria	78	38	40
North America			
Canada	3,939	5,840	−1,901
United States	15,374	20,785	−5,411
Central America			
Mexico	3,497	2,361[1]	1,136
South America			
Argentina	614	894	−280
Brazil	1,502	1,249	253
The Caribbean			
Bahamas	1,174	152	1,022
Barbados	379	29	350
Jamaica	595[2]	32	563
East Asia and the Pacific			
Australia	1,789	2,351	−562
Japan	2,097	10,760	−8,663
Malaysia	717	1,272	−555
New Zealand	934	784	150
Singapore	2,216	791	1,425
Thailand	1,947	381	1,566
Middle East			
Egypt	1,586	52	1,534
Jordan	580	445	135
Kuwait	100	2,505	−2,405
South Asia			
India	1,455[2]	302	1,153
Pakistan	171	248	−77

Source: World Tourism Organization (1989).
Notes:
1 Including expenditures from national and foreign resident excursionists visiting the USA.
2 For year ending 31 March.

tourism exceed expenditure by US $323 million. This is, however, considerably smaller than the positive tourism balance achieved by Morocco (US $900 million). In North America, both Canada and the USA achieve negative tourism balances. International tourism expenditures by the USA are US $3 billion below the level for West Germany and international tourism receipts are US $8 billion higher. Thus the US tourism balance of −US $5.4 billion is much more favourable than that for West Germany (−US $15.8 billion) (Table 1.2). In Central and South America only Mexico has a large positive tourism balance (US $1.1 billion), similar to that of the Bahamas, and the other Caribbean countries also show healthy positive balances. In East Asia and the Pacific, Japan has a massive negative tourism balance (−US $8.6 billion), second only to West Germany. In the Middle East, Egypt is a substantial earner of foreign exchange from tourism (US $1.5 billion); by contrast, Kuwait had a large negative tourism balance (−US $2.4 billion). In South Asia the country with the highest level of international tourism receipts and most favourable tourism balance (US $ 1.2 billion) is India.

The contribution of international tourism receipts to the balance of payments can also be assessed in terms of the percentage of exports that these receipts represent. Table 1.4 presents these figures for selected countries. It can be seen that there is enormous variation among the destination countries. In certain developing countries in Africa and the Caribbean tourism plays a vital role in exports: for example, tourism receipts represent more than 40 per cent of exports in Barbados, more than 30 per cent in Morocco, and approximately 20 per cent in Kenya and Mexico. Tourism receipts also play an important role in the balance of payments for certain European countries, representing more than 20 per cent of exports for Greece and Spain, and 18 per cent for Austria, although the latter figure includes international fare payments. For Japan and West Germany, however, tourism receipts constitute only a small proportion of total exports.

It should be borne in mind that international tourism generates balance of payments effects that are far more complex than those of the initial tourism receipts/expenditure (the *primary* effect). In particular, the extent to which tourism expenditures in a destination country generate import demand in that country will have a major impact on the foreign exchange generating ability of tourism. The *secondary* effects on the balance of payments include imports of supplies by the providers of tourism services (hotel operators, restaurant operators, and so on), expenditures on marketing abroad, and payments to overseas investors in the form of interest and dividends.

Table 1.4   International tourism receipts as percentage of exports for selected countries, 1987.

	Receipts as % of exports
Africa	
Kenya	20.9
Morocco[1]	32.3
Americas	
Barbados[1]	41.6
Canada	3.6
Mexico[1]	19.5
United States	4.6
East Asia and the Pacific	
Australia	5.7
Japan	0.7
Thailand	14.1
Europe	
Austria[2]	18.3
Germany (West)	2.2
Greece	20.2
Italy	8.9
Spain[1]	25.8
Switzerland	8.9
United Kingdom	5.8

Sources: World Tourism Organization (1989). International Monetary Fund (1989).
Notes:
1   1986 figures.
2   Including international fare payments.

Employment in tourism

The tourism industry is one of the foremost generators of employment but precise figures for jobs in tourism are difficult to obtain. As discussed earlier, the major complication is that the industry is defined in terms of the customer demanding goods and services. There are many sectors serving tourists as well as other customers; for example, a taxi driver may spend 20 per cent of his/her time transporting tourists and 80 per cent of his/her time transporting commuters. Thus, in order to obtain reasonably accurate figures for job numbers in the tourism industry, it is not only necessary to identify all those sectors that provide goods or services for tourists, but also to estimate the proportion of the working time that a person in one of these sectors spends on providing tourism-related goods and services.

Official figures on employment in tourism are generally not available on this basis. For example, Table 1.5 shows data relating to staff employed in tourism in various European countries. In many cases the figures just refer to staff employed in hotels and restaurants, but clearly many of these staff may spend some of their working time serving local customers. Staff employed in travel agencies and national tourism administrations are obviously classified correctly where they appear in the table, but the 'staff employed in other sectors of the tourist industry' component is not always an accurate classification. In the case of the UK, for example, this component includes public houses, night clubs and libraries, and for many of these sectors the tourist trade is likely to be a small proportion of total trade. The major reservation we have regarding Table 1.5, however, is its incompleteness. Many major sectors of the tourism industry, such as transport, are not represented at all.

In order to be able to make cross-country comparisons, attention merely focuses on the 'staff employed in hotels and restaurants' category, which is available for all the countries in Table 1.5. West Germany has by far the highest figure for numbers employed in this category (992,000), followed by the UK (509,400), France (301,200), Switzerland (181,100) and Austria (116,700).

The first stage in assessing tourism-generated employment is to identify which categories of employment in the official statistics are tourism related (Vaughan, 1986). Tourism affects many sectors of the economy, but the main tourism-related sectors are hotels and catering, transport (air, sea, rail and other inland transport), transport supporting services, retail distribution (food, clothing, filling stations, and so on), and tourism and recreational services. Estimates then have to be made of the proportions of employment in each of these sectors directly attributable to tourism. The official statistics often do not include the self-employed, but this group represents an important element of the workforce in tourism, and needs to be included. Estimates, therefore, are necessary for this group also.

An alternative approach to assessing tourism-related employment is through the use of economic impact studies. The essence of this method is to use visitor spending figures to derive estimates of job generation. If, say, $10,000 of visitor spending creates one job in tourism, the total number of jobs created as a result of visitor spending in an area can be estimated. The method can be refined to allow for visitor spending patterns in order that job generation in the various tourism sectors can be identified. The first stage in this approach is to estimate total visitor spending split according to sector: hotels, restaurants, retailers, and so on. The second stage involves estimating the rate at which visitor spending is converted into direct employment in these various sectors.

Table 1.5 Staff employed in tourism in selected countries.

	Year	Sector	Numbers employed
Austria[1]	1987	HR	116,700
Finland[2]	1987	HR	63,000
France[3]	1986	HR	301,200
		V	20,500
		A	400
		O	128,900
Germany (West)[4]	1986	HR	992,000
Greece[5]	1986	HR	42,000
Netherlands	1986	HR	57,500
		V	5,700
Norway[6]	1987	HR	55,000
Portugal[7]	1984	HR	32,900
Sweden[8]	1987	HR	86,100
Switzerland[9]	1986	HR	181,100
Turkey[10]	1987	HR	110,000
		V	1,900
		A	9,600
		O	1,300
United Kingdom[11]	1987	HR	509,400
		O	80,100

Sources: OECD (1987, 1988).
Notes:
HR   Staff employed in hotels and restaurants.
V   Staff employed in travel agencies.
A   Staff employed in national tourism administrations.
O   Staff employed in other sectors of the tourism industry.

1 Weighted average of peak season (August) and low season (November).
2 Weighted average of peak season (July) and low season (February).
3 Employees only; A denotes representation abroad and regional tourist offices.
4 Of which approximately 160,000 are foreigners.
5 Hotel employees insured by Hotel Employees Insurance Fund only (approximately 70 per cent of total).
6 Average of first and fourth quarters.
7 As at 31 July.
8 Of which approximately 15,000 are foreigners.
9 Of which approximately 70,000 are foreigners.
10 As at 31 December for HR and A, 31 March for O and 31 October for V; V denotes minimum number of persons that travel agencies have to employ; A includes regional tourism administrators and staff working in the Culture section of the Ministry of Culture and Tourism; O denotes licensed tourist guides.
11 Weighted average of peak season (September) and low season (March); O denotes public houses, bars, night clubs, clubs, libraries, museums, art galleries, sports and other recreational services.

Income from tourism

The importance of tourism to an economy can be measured by examining the ratio of income generated by tourism to gross domestic product (GDP). Table 1.6 gives tourism receipts as a percentage of GDP for selected countries. It is clear that Caribbean countries such as Barbados are vitally dependent upon tourism as an income earner: for this country international tourism receipts constitute one-quarter of GDP. Tourism receipts are clearly also important (albeit on a much smaller scale) to Austria, Morocco and Spain, amounting to more than 5 per cent of GDP in each case. For Australia, Japan, West Germany and the United States international tourism receipts represent less than one per cent of GDP.

Table 1.6 International tourism receipts as percentage of GDP for selected countries, 1987.

	Receipts as % of GDP
Africa	
Kenya	4.4
Morocco[1]	5.4
Americas	
Barbados[1]	24.6
Canada	1.0
Mexico[1,2]	3.4
United States	0.3
East Asia and the Pacific	
Australia	0.9
Japan[1]	0.1
Thailand	4.1
Europe	
Austria[3]	6.5
Germany (West)	0.7
Greece	4.6
Italy	1.6
Spain[1]	5.2
Switzerland	3.1
Turkey[1]	2.1
United Kingdom	1.5

Sources: World Tourism Organization (1989). International Monetary Fund (1989).
  Notes:
  1   1986 figures.
  2   Including expenditures from national and foreign resident excursionists visiting the USA.
  3   Including international fare payments.

Tourism multipliers

The multiplier measures the impact on an economy of extra expenditure introduced into the economy. Tourism multipliers refer to changes in the levels of income, output, employment and the balance of payments caused by a change in the level of tourism expenditure (Fletcher and Snee, 1989b; World Tourism Organization/ Horwath and Horwath, 1981). Tourist spending on accommodation, catering, transportation and so on in an area, tourism-related investment in the area and exports of goods stimulated by tourism generate income. Part of this income will leak out of the economy in the form of imports, savings and taxes, but the remainder will become a second round of spending in the economy, thus generating more income. The process continues, with each round smaller than the previous one owing to leakages, until the amount of expenditure becomes negligible. The concept of the multiplier is embodied in the relationship between the amount of the initial injection of tourism expenditure and the final ensuing effect on the economy.

The impact of the extra tourist expenditure on the economy can be split into the *direct, indirect* and *induced* effects. The direct effect is the amount of income (output, etc.) generated directly in the tourism sectors by the increase in tourism expenditure. The indirect effect relates to the successive rounds of inter-business transactions that are caused by the direct expenditure. It is the amount of income (output, etc.) generated by the tourism sector in purchasing extra goods and services from suppliers in the domestic economy, and by these suppliers in turn purchasing extra goods and services from domestic suppliers, and so on. The induced effect is the amount of income (output, etc.) generated by the higher level of consumer spending on domestically produced goods and services, which results from the additional personal income generated by the direct and indirect effects of the increase in tourist spending. The sum of the indirect and induced effects is termed the *secondary* effect.

The multiplier is generally expressed as the ratio of the sum of the direct, indirect and induced changes in the economy to the initial increase in tourism expenditure which caused the indirect and induced effects (the 'unorthodox' tourism multiplier).

Fletcher and Snee (1989b) identify six tourism multipliers:

1   The *output* multiplier: this measures the extra output (direct and secondary) generated by an extra unit of tourism expenditure.
2   The *sales* or *transactions* multiplier: this measures the extra business turnover (direct and secondary) generated by an extra unit of tourism expenditure. It is similar to the output multiplier, but excludes additions to inventories caused by the initial change in tourism expenditure.

3   The *income* multiplier: this measures the extra domestic income (direct and secondary) generated by an extra unit of tourism expenditure.

4   The *employment* multiplier: this measures the increased number of full-time equivalent jobs (direct and secondary) created as a result of an extra unit of tourism expenditure; alternatively, on account of the problem of differing units of measurement, it is often calculated as the ratio of the increased number of direct and secondary full-time equivalent jobs created to the direct jobs only, which result from the increase in tourism expenditure (the 'orthodox' tourism multiplier).

5   The *government revenue* multiplier: this measures the extra net government revenue generated by an extra unit of tourism expenditure, and usually includes all forms of government revenue (direct and secondary) less government expenditure on subsidies and grants to those sectors of the economy involved in the direct and indirect provision of tourism-related goods and services.

6   The *import* multiplier: this measures the value of imported goods and services (direct and secondary) generated by an extra unit of tourism expenditure. Tourist spending in a host country comprises expenditure on both domestically produced and imported goods and services. Furthermore, suppliers to the tourism industry purchase some factors of production within the economy and import the others. In addition, some induced expenditure goes on domestically produced goods and services and the rest on imported goods and services.

Multipliers can be calculated for a country as a whole, a region or a local community. In general, the size of the economy is likely to affect the size of the multiplier; for example, the tourism income multiplier is likely to be much smaller for a small local community than for a (large) country, because of the higher proportion of goods and services that will need to be 'imported' into the area (leakages) in the former case as a result of the initial increase in tourism expenditure. A small range of economic activities within an area is likely to result in a small amount of trading taking place among these activities, and hence a small value for the multiplier. Tourism income multiplier values estimated for areas of widely differing sizes are presented in Table 1.7, and it can be seen that the estimates range from 0.2 to 2.0.

Table 1.7   Tourism income multipliers.

Geographical area	Income multiplier value
Turkey	1.98
United Kingdom	1.73
Irish Republic	1.72
Jamaica	1.27
Egypt	1.23
Dominica	1.20
Cyprus	1.14
Bermuda	1.09
Hong Kong	1.02
Mauritius	0.96
Antigua	0.88
Bahamas	0.79
Fiji	0.72
Cayman Islands	0.65
Iceland	0.64
British Virgin Islands	0.58
Gibraltar	0.57
Door County, USA	0.55
Sullivan County, USA	0.44
Gwynedd, North Wales, UK	0.37
East Anglia, UK	0.34
Kendal, Cumbria, UK	0.30
Edinburgh, Lothian, UK	0.28
Brighton and Hove, UK	0.22
Winchester, Hampshire, UK	0.19
Bournemouth, Dorset, UK	0.18

Source: Fletcher and Snee (1989b).

Physical environment

The impact of tourism on the physical environment needs to be taken into consideration when planning tourism developments. A mass influx of tourists to a destination without regard to the consequences for the physical environment may well destroy the very resource that attracts tourists; the physical environment is often a powerful attraction to tourists and thus an important ingredient in the tourist product (Fletcher and Snee, 1989a).

Tourism can result in the pollution of lakes, rivers and coastlines by human waste, petrol discharged from boats, and so on. The transport of tourists pollutes the atmosphere through exhaust fumes. High noise levels can occur in previously peaceful surroundings, and litter may become a problem. Tourism on a large scale can also create congestion at, for example, airports and destinations; there is often a physical limit on the ability to absorb tourists, but before this stage is reached, the appeal of the tourist facility may well be reduced by overcrowding. Tourism can also destroy the balance of nature in an area; it can result in soil erosion, damage vegetation and wildlife, disrupt agriculture and destroy natural and manmade features. Building developments can have a marked detrimental impact on the physical environment. For example, mass tourism to coastal resorts leads to large-scale construction of hotels, restaurants, shops and so on, which often totally transform the physical environment.

In the case of natural resources, the ability of the resource to absorb tourists is an important physical constraint. Three types of carrying capacity limitation have been identified (Holloway, 1985; Lavery, 1987): physical capacity, environmental capacity and ecological capacity. *Physical* capacity is the absolute limit on tourist numbers that a resource can cope with. *Environmental* capacity is the maximum number of tourists that an area can accommodate without initiating a decline in the general perceived attraction of the area. *Ecological* capacity is the maximum number of tourists that an area can absorb before ecological decline takes place. It may, however, be possible to increase carrying capacity through the use of appropriate management techniques.

Measurement of the impact of tourism on the physical environment is a difficult task. Various techniques have been developed to try to assess this impact, but, for example, soil erosion may be a result of other land uses in addition to tourism, and it could be difficult to separate the effects of tourism from those of the other activities.

Attempts should be made to minimize the costs of tourism developments to the physical environment. In order to protect and preserve the physical environment it is necessary to instigate conservation measures, and new tourism developments, such as buildings and signposting, should be 'environmentally sensitive' (Prentice, 1989). Planning controls are necessary to balance the conflicting demands of tourism (and other land uses) and conservation – 'to protect and preserve the natural environment from unsystematic and unplanned human manipulation' (Mathieson and Wall, 1982, p. 97). These authors also point out that:

> conservation and the preservation of natural areas, archaeological sites and historic monuments have emerged as important spill-over benefits of tourism. In turn, the protection of these prime tourist resources enhances and perpetuates tourism by maintaining its very foundation. The tourist industry has as much interest in maintaining a quality environment as organizations specifically dedicated to that cause. (Mathieson and Wall, 1982, p. 97).

In fact, tourism also may well provide the economic means whereby conservation and preservation can be effected.

Finally, it should be borne in mind that *other* (alternative) industries *also* cause damage to the physical environment in the form of pollution, and so on.

Sociocultural environment

Tourism can have marked sociocultural impacts on both tourists and destination-country hosts. Many of the impacts on the host population are negative. For example, tourist–host encounters in poor countries can lead to envy and resentment on the part of hosts as they see the comparative wealth and lifestyle of the foreign visitors (the 'demonstration effect'). This may lead to dissatisfaction on the part of locals with their own standard of living, way of life and value systems, and can pose a threat to family relationships and the traditions and stability of local communities. In addition, a sizeable influx of tourists to certain Third World countries may be regarded as a form of 'neo-colonialism' by residents of the destination country, emphasized by the 'subservient' role played by local workers in the tourism industry, such as waiters, bar staff, hotel porters and taxi drivers. More generally, large numbers of tourists may cause irritation and even antagonism in the destination as they compete with the locals for the use of overcrowded roads, beaches, and so on. Increased crime levels may also accompany high influxes of tourists. These social consequences present serious problems in certain destinations.

The negative cultural effects of tourism include the dilution and trivializing of traditional arts and crafts. Given the temporal constraints faced by tourists, they want 'instant culture'. The demand by foreign tourists for authentic experiences of a different culture often results in staged displays of, for example, folk dances and ceremonies. The customs and traditions of the host population are manipulated to make the experience more enjoyable for tourists; tourist attractions are often developed which conform to tourist expectations rather than accurately reflecting the genuine culture. Works of art sold to tourists may not be authentic; as mass tourism takes over and visitors with less per capita spending power than those travelling independently arrive, the destination may react by selling mass-produced poorly made artefacts.

Although the detrimental sociocultural impacts of tourism have been emphasized, there are also beneficial impacts. International tourism can promote better understanding between people of different cultures and nationalities, particularly as far as those tourists are concerned who tend to travel independently and actively try to fall in with, meet and talk to the local population. Cohen (1972) suggests a typology of four tourist roles: organized mass tourist, individual mass tourist, explorer and drifter. For the mass tourist categories most arrangements are preplanned and prebooked in the tourist's home country through a travel agent, and these tourists have little direct contact with the host community. They tend to stay largely within the micro-environment of their home country, where familiarity is at a maximum and novelty at a minimum. The 'explorer', by contrast, arranges his trip alone and tries to get off the beaten track, but nevertheless still requires reasonable accommodation and transport. He attempts to associate with the host community and to speak their language – here novelty plays a much greater role than for the mass tourist. The 'drifter' ventures furthest away from the sphere of familiarity; he attempts to live the way the people he visits live, sharing their accommodation, food and customs, and is almost completely immersed in the host culture. Clearly, the contacts between the explorer/drifter tourists and the host community can result in considerable beneficial social impacts in terms of promoting better understanding between different nations.

Tourism also has positive cultural effects; in many cases local customs and culture have been revived in host communities because of the interest shown by foreign visitors.

Measurement of the impact of tourism on the sociocultural environment presents the problem of isolating the behaviour associated with tourism from that associated with other influences, which is a difficult task.

Political environment

The extent of government involvement in the tourism industry will depend upon the political philosophy of the ruling party, the country's history, socioeconomic conditions and level of development, and the extent to which tourism supply is already in existence (Joppe, 1989). Government actions can aim to support or control the tourism market, and can be directed towards the supply of or demand for tourism services.

Tourism supply

The government can play a role in facilitating tourism development by improving the tourism infrastructure of a country: for example, by building new roads and airports and raising the level of public services provided (water systems, sewers, and so on). The provision of adequate education and training facilities to meet the requirements of the tourism industry is a further means by which governments can support the tourism industry.

A major method by which the authorities can encourage tourism development lies in the provision of investment incentives. These have three main purposes (Bodlender and Ward, 1989):

Acceleration of realization of development. By providing incentives the government can enjoy the resultant (usually economic) benefits sooner. Although a project may eventually be realized anyway (even in the absence of incentives), the provision of incentives may hasten the development.

Satisfaction of profit motive. Investment incentives may assist in the generation of profits at a level sufficient to meet corporate objectives, and thus enable an otherwise unprofitable project to go ahead.

Project discrimination. Investment incentives can be used to increase the profitability of tourist developments in certain areas (such as depressed inner cities in need of regeneration), or of certain types. Such incentives, while encouraging developments in these areas, also make investment in locations which are not favoured (for example, holiday destinations suffering from the effects of overcrowding) relatively less attractive.

Investment incentives fall into two categories (Wanhill, 1989):

Reduction of capital costs. This may be executed through the provision of capital grants, loans at subsidized rates, interest rate subsidies, tariff exemption on construction materials, provision of land at below market value, and so on.

Reduction of operating costs. This may be brought about by the provision of accelerated depreciation allowances, tax 'holidays' (5 to 10 years), tariff exemption on materials and supplies, training subsidies, and so on.

Typically tourist projects, such as the construction of hotels, have a relatively high level of fixed costs arising from the initial capital investment and relatively low operating costs, that is, a high operating leverage. In order to reduce the business risk and encourage investment, the preferred type of financial help, therefore, is that which reduces capital costs (Wanhill, 1989). Investment incentives may be provided automatically for tourism industry projects, or be discretionary and biased to encourage developments in specific locations or of specific types.

In order to encourage foreign investment in the tourism industry, it may be necessary for the government to guarantee repatriation of capital and profits.

Legislation can be used to protect those resources which represent tourism attractions, for example, historical sites, national parks and monuments. Governments can also either use public funds to acquire such resources, or provide financial support for their restoration, maintenance and improvement.

Governments play an important role in controlling the various sectors of the tourism industry, for example, through the imposition of fire regulations on hotels and health regulations on restaurants. In many countries there is a compulsory or voluntary system of registration and classification of hotels and other accommodation establishments. Public transport companies, tour operators, travel agencies and tour guides are often controlled through a system of licensing. The major objective of the government in this sphere is the protection of the consumer.

Obstacles in relation to the foreign supply of tourism services are often imposed by governments in the form of foreign exchange restrictions, rules governing the right to establish a business, and so on. These mainly stem from concerns regarding competition. Thus, even within the European Community, national airlines have various advantages over foreign competitors. For example, foreign airlines are usually not allowed to compete in domestic air transport markets.

Tourism demand

Governments are usually involved in the stimulation of tourism demand, both domestic and inbound international, through tourism promotion. A country's national tourist office (NTO) is the organization that generally is officially responsible for carrying out this marketing function. Some of the activities of the NTO are aimed at the tourism industry and others at the consumer; with the growth in inclusive tours the marketing emphasis has had to shift from appealing merely to the independent traveller to also catering for tour operators and other sectors of the trade.

Some governments provide positive incentives in the form of subsidies to encourage their residents to take domestic holidays, for example, holiday vouchers are given to the low paid in France and subsidised holiday centres have been run by some governments in Eastern Europe.

Obstacles in relation to the demand for international tourism can be imposed by governments in generating and receiving countries. Exchange controls on outbound tourists in the form of restrictions limiting the amount of currency that may be purchased for travel abroad are in effect in many countries, and departure taxes discourage foreign tourism. Time-consuming administrative formalities also act as a disincentive to foreign travel. Entry visa requirements of the host country are an impediment to international tourism because of the costs in money and time. Destinations may also impose special taxes or minimum exchange requirements on tourists.

The nature and extent of government involvement with domestic, international inbound and international outbound tourism varies considerably from country to country; governments can pursue active or passive roles, and seek to support or control the industry and the tourists.

Further reading

Allard, L. (1989), 'Statistical measurement in tourism', in Witt, S. F. and Moutinho, L. (eds), *Tourism Marketing and Management Handbook*, Hemel Hempstead: Prentice-Hall, pp. 419–24.

Baron, R. (1989), *Travel and Tourism Data*, London: Euromonitor.

Fletcher, J. and Snee, H. (1989), 'Tourism multiplier effects', in Witt, S. F. and Moutinho, L., op. cit., pp. 529–31.

Mathieson, A. and Wall, G. (1982), *Tourism: Economic, physical and social impacts*, London and New York: Longman.

Mill, R. C. and Morrison, A. M. (1985), *The Tourism System: An introductory text*, Englewood Cliffs, NJ: Prentice-Hall.

Vaughan, D. R. (1986), *Estimating the Level of Tourism Related Employment: An assessment of two non-survey techniques*, London: British Tourist Authority/English Tourist Board.

2

The international tourism industry

Introduction

Economic activities tend to be categorized into industries according to the goods/services produced, and, because tourists consume a variety of goods and services, elements of tourism appear under various industry classifications. Thus, in economic data terms, tourism is *not* defined as an industry – it is not designated a Standard Industrial Classification (SIC) code.

Those industries serving tourists directly may be designated *tourism-related industries* (Medlik, 1988b). A major complicating factor is that for many of these industries tourist spending will only generate part of the total output of the industry, and, therefore, it is necessary to ascertain how much of each tourism-related industry's activities are generated by tourism. (Medlik (1988a) gives the following percentages for tourism-generated activity in certain UK tourism-related industries in 1985: hotels and catering 42 per cent; recreational and cultural services 25 per cent; transport and travel services 23 per cent; and retail distribution 3 per cent.) The tourism 'industry' may then be viewed as follows:

> to the extent to which particular activities supply tourist rather than other markets, the sum total of the parts represents an entity, which may be described as an industry – that part of the economy which has a common function of meeting tourist needs (Medlik, 1988b, p. 8).

The tourism industry can be categorized into the following sectors: accommodation and catering, transport, travel organizers, attractions and destination organization These sectors are now discussed in detail.

Accommodation and catering sector

Many elements are included in the accommodation and catering sector. *Serviced* tourist accommodation includes hotels, motels, guesthouses, bed and breakfast establishments, farmhouses and cruise ships. Here, staff are at hand to supply other services in addition to the provision of rooms, which may include, for example, restaurants, bars, room service and porterage. *Self-catering* tourist accommodation includes rented villas, chalets and apartments, camping sites, caravan sites, time-share properties, second homes and motorhomes. Some types of tourist accommodation can be either serviced or self-catering, for example, holiday camps/centres/ villages, and educational institutions such as universities and colleges.

Tourist accommodation can also be split into the commercial and non-commercial sectors. Whereas serviced accommodation generally falls within the commercial sector, there are many types of self-catering accommodation that do not, for example, second homes, private yachts and staying with friends and relatives (a major source of accommodation).

The purpose of visit of a tourist will often determine the accommodation used. Most visits for business purposes will entail the use of serviced accommodation such as hotels and these are often located in city/town centres. By contrast, holiday camps/centres/ villages tend to be just used by holidaymakers, as are caravan and camping sites.

As well as being *categorized* into hotels, guesthouses, caravan sites, and so on, tourist accommodation can also be *classified* and *graded* (Burkart and Medlik, 1981; Foster, 1985; Holloway, 1985). Classification denotes the splitting up of accommodation by such physical features as the number of bedrooms with and without private facilities. Grading generally relates to the number of restaurants and other facilities provided, the availability of night porters and car-parking space, and so on, although it can include subjectively assessed features such as 'atmosphere' and 'quality'.

Location is critical for accommodation units and, once established, cannot be changed. This can be a particular problem in periods of changing tastes, on account of the fairly long time-lag between the initial plans for, say, a large hotel and its actual coming into operation. Location is important with regard to both the destination and the unit's position within the destination itself. If the destination is a resort, the accommodation should appeal mainly to holiday-makers, whereas accommodation in city centres is used mainly by business tourists. These distinctions are obviously not clear cut, in that many resort areas also attract convention business and many city centre hotels, which cater largely for businessmen during the week, frequently offer highly discounted rates at weekends in order to attract holidaymakers.

The hotel sector accounts for the major part of commercial serviced accommodation. There are several very large international companies in the hotel sector, and many of the major chains are enjoying considerable growth. Concentration is increasing in the hotel industry – the potential economies of scale to be enjoyed in the areas of marketing, finance, training and purchasing provide the appropriate inducements – and the various systems whereby growth can come about (direct investment, franchising and management contracts) are discussed in chapter 5. It should be borne in mind, however, that the grouping of hotels into chains is not necessarily an indication of ownership. A recent development has been the emergence of consortia of independent hotels in order also to benefit from marketing economies of scale. In fact, most hotels graded as three-star or higher belong to hotel chains or consortia.

At the other end of the spectrum there is an enormous number of single-unit independently owned and operated accommodation establishments – numerically the small business dominates the accommodation sector. Most hotels are still run by owner-operators.

A recent phenomenon has been the increasing emphasis on market segmentation in the hotel sector. Thus we have leisure hotels, country house hotels, all-suite hotels, budget hotels, and so on.

Table 2.1 shows the number of rooms and the number of bed-spaces that are available in peak season in hotels and similar establishments in major regions of the world. The rooms and

Table 2.1 Rooms and bed-spaces in hotels and similar establishments in major regions of the world, 1987 (thousands)

	Rooms		Bed-spaces	
	Number	% of total	Number	% of total
Africa	265	3	515	3
Americas	3,681	36	7,401	37
North America	2,807	28	5,615	28
Central America	337	3	663	3
South America	428	4	902	4
The Caribbean	109	1	221	1
East Asia and the Pacific	930	9	1,944	10
Europe	5,000	49	9,810	49
Eastern Europe	319	3	671	3
Northern Europe	725	7	1,462	7
Southern Europe	1,984	20	3,731	19
Western Europe	1,938	19	3,879	19
WORLD	10,111	100	20,114	100

Source: World Tourism Organization (1989).

bed-spaces data are also expressed as a percentage of the world total. It can be seen that almost one half of the total number of rooms and bed-spaces (49 percent) are located in Europe, and another 28 per cent of rooms and bed-spaces are located in North America. Europe and North America thus account together for 77 percent of rooms and bed-spaces in hotels and similar establishments throughout the world. Furthermore, it can be seen that there is an almost exact correspondence between the percentage of rooms in the world total and the percentage of bed-spaces for the various regions.

Food and drink account for a substantial proportion of tourist expenditure. Catering services are provided for the tourist by a wide variety of restaurants (speciality restaurants including ethnic, fast-food establishments, and so on), coffee shops, bars, etc. In addition, food and drink is provided for tourists when travelling by air, rail and sea, and sometimes on coaches.

Rapid growth has taken place in the fast-food segment of the catering sector over recent years, primarily through franchising. Fast-food chains such as McDonald's, Burger King and Pizza Hut provide standardized meals in locations throughout the world, thus providing the tourist with relatively low-cost, risk (surprise)-free dining experiences.

Transport sector

The commercial transport sector of the tourism industry includes airlines, shipping lines (both cruise lines and ferry operators), coach and bus operators, railways, car-rental firms and taxi operators. The non-commercial section of the transport sector is dominated by the private car, although a few tourists travel to their destinations by privately owned aircraft or yachts.

Air transport

Air transport is by far the major form of travel to medium-haul and long-haul destinations. On the other hand, the private car is the most popular transport mode to nearby destinations, in particular for day-trips, domestic tourism and international tourism involving a land boundary.

Air transport can be divided into scheduled and charter services. Scheduled services operate on specific routes in accordance with published schedules (and are required to do so, whatever the passenger load factor). Charter services, on the other hand, can be cancelled if demand is insufficient; they are used mainly for holiday purposes, and seats are often sold as part of an inclusive tour. Charter flights operate on short-, medium- and long-haul routes, but their major concentration is in the short-haul and medium-haul high-volume markets. For example, most short-haul air travel for holiday purposes within Europe takes place on charter aircraft. By contrast, the scheduled flights which operate on short- and medium-haul routes carry mainly business tourists. On long-haul routes the large majority of transport services are provided by scheduled aircraft, which cater for all tourism purposes (holidays, visits to friends and relatives, business purposes, and so on).

Sea transport

Shipping lines comprise cruise lines and ferry operators. Medium- and long-haul sea transport has largely been replaced by air transport, but on short-haul routes ferries can provide vital access between areas. Ferry services usually link road networks and are widely used by cars, buses/coaches and goods vehicles; they provide transport for all purposes. For example, a substantial proportion of UK outbound international tourism comprises tourists travelling by private car, and this involves a sea crossing.

Cruise lines have enjoyed a revival in recent years in certain areas. The large ships usually function as self-contained resorts and are targeted at holidaymakers. They tend to operate most successfully in warm/hot climates, such as the Caribbean and Mediterranean, and the recent substantial growth in the cruise market has mainly occurred in North America, with the majority of ships sailing from Florida to the Caribbean region. Fly/cruise packages enable tourists to get quickly to the chosen destination area, and, therefore, to have a worthwhile short (one to two weeks) cruise.

Coach/bus transport

Coach and bus operators play a significant role in the provision of tourist transport for non-business purposes – they are the cheapest form of commercial transport. They can operate as either the main or sole form of transport, or in a subsidiary role to complement the main transport mode. An example of the former is a coach tour (which may also involve sea transport). An example where coach transport plays a subsidiary role is when inclusive tour travellers are transferred from the destination airport on arrival to their accommodation. Coaches are also used in destinations for excursions. In addition, scheduled express bus/coach services, mainly on inter-city routes or city-resort routes, are important in the overall provision of tourist transport.

In order to compete more effectively with other transport modes over longer distances, considerable efforts have been made to upgrade coach travel. The provision of improved on-board facilities such as toilet facilities, drinks and snacks, on coaches travelling on the longer routes is now quite common, and on some there are also video facilities.

Rail transport

Railways were at one time the major mode of travel in many countries, but with the private car coming to dominate short-haul transport and air travel competing over longer distances, railways have generally gone into severe decline. The main use of rail travel for tourism purposes is on the inter-city services, where trains can compete effectively in terms of speed, comfort and cost with other transport modes. Time savings often occur because trains usually have the advantage that their routing goes to and from city-centre locations.

The successful development and operation of high-speed trains in certain countries, such as France and Japan, has resulted in journey times over medium distances that are considerably less than those of either car or air transport (in the latter case because of the travelling time to and from airports, which are usually situated some distance from city-centres, and also the checking-in time at airports).

Car transport

The rapid rise in car ownership during the last forty years has meant that the majority of households in North America and Western Europe now possess a car, and this is the dominant transport mode for domestic tourism, as well as for much international tourism (particularly in Europe). Car travel provides accessibility and convenience that cannot be matched by other modes, but, as distances between origin and destination get longer, there is increasing competition from air transport in terms of the saving in travel time.

Car-rental firms are playing an increasingly important role in the provision of tourist transport. Clearly, rented cars may simply be a substitute for private cars, but where substantial growth has recently taken place has been in the fly/drive travel market. Here, the advantage of speed in reaching the destination by air is combined with the convenience of having a car available for use in the destination. Fly/drive travel is used by both business and leisure tourists.

Taxi companies generally provide a complementary service to other transport companies, but one that is vital in the overall provision of transport for tourists. A major role lies in the provision of local transport between, say, an airport, shipping port or railway station and accommodation units. Taxi companies also service within-destination travel by tourists.

Travel organizers sector

The two main groups of travel organizers are retail travel agents and tour operators, although other groups, such as conference organizers, also go to make up this sector.

Retail travel agents

Most travel principals (airlines, tour operators, hotels, and so on) sell their products to tourists via retail travel agents, who receive a sale commission, but travel agents do not accept liability for the services offered by the principal. This sale outlet is extremely important in the cases of airline tickets and inclusive tours abroad.

As with the retailing of services generally, the role of the retail travel agent differs from that of the retailer of manufactured goods. In the latter case, the shopkeeper makes purchases (either directly or indirectly) from the goods manufacturer, with which he stocks his shop. By so doing the shopkeeper takes some of the risk of production off the manufacturer. In turn, if the manufactured goods retailer finds that he is being left with unsold stocks of a particular product he will try very hard to promote sales in order to avoid losses. By contrast, the retail travel agent does not purchase travel to resell to his/her customers – no stock of aircraft seats, hotel beds, and so on, is carried, and so the principal bears all the risk of production. It is only when a customer has taken the decision to purchase, say, an airline ticket or an inclusive tour that the retail travel agent approaches the principal on behalf of the potential tourist. As the retail travel agent is not in the position of having to dispose of products that he/she has previously purchased, he/she tends to display less brand loyalty towards specific companies (principals) or products than is likely to be the case with other retailers, which presents a marketing problem for the principals.

As far as consumers are concerned, the lack of brand loyalty should be an advantage in terms of obtaining more impartial advice from travel agents. In addition to the provision of information and advice, and a booking service for air, sea, rail and coach transport, inclusive tours, hotel accommodation and car hire, retail travel agents often supply various ancillary services such as travel insurance, travellers' cheques and foreign exchange, and arrange travel documentation (passports and visas).

In order to receive a commission payment from the principal for selling the principal's services, the retail travel agent often needs to be a member of a particular association or some similar arrangement, which demonstrates that certain minimum standards of competence, financial responsibility, and so on, have been achieved. In the UK, for example, for inclusive tours arranged by tour operators who are members of the Association of British Travel Agents (ABTA), the travel agent must also be an ABTA member. Furthermore, travel agents must be licensed by the International Air Transport Association (IATA) in order to receive commission from ticket sales of IATA member airlines, which is crucial for sales of seats on international airlines. Formal approval is also necessary from British Rail, shipping companies, and so on.

In the USA, travel agents need to possess a 'conference appointment' to be eligible for commission payments – from the Airlines Reporting Corporation for sales of seats on domestic airlines, from the Passenger Network Services Corporation for sales of seats on international airlines, from the Cruise Lines International Association for selling cruises, and from the National Railroad Passenger Corporation (Amtrak) for sales of rail tickets (McIntosh and Goeldner, 1986).

Tour operators/tour wholesalers

Tour operators combine accommodation and transport (and possibly other services) to give an inclusive tour, which is then sold as a holiday package at an all-inclusive price (the individual costs of the components cannot be separately identified). The majority of tour operators are tour wholesalers in that the holiday package is sold through retail travel agents, but some tour operators (for example, Thomas Cook) are tour wholesalers and retailers.

The all-inclusive price for which inclusive tours (or package holidays) are sold is usually considerably lower than would be possible if an individual tourist booked the accommodation and transport separately. The bulk buying power of tour operators enables significant savings to be made, part of which is generally passed on to the consumer. Further advantages of inclusive tours from the consumer's point of view are the convenience factor in so far as the tourist merely purchases a single travel product, and possible risk reduction in terms of product assurance when buying from a reputable tour operator. In addition, in the UK, holiday-makers who book inclusive tours with ABTA member tour operators receive a financial guarantee to cover holiday payments if the tour operator should become bankrupt.

Most inclusive tours involve air travel, and, particularly for short-haul and medium-haul destinations, charter flights are the dominant form of transport used in air inclusive tours.

The basic inclusive tour comprises a combination of accommodation (usually hotel beds), transport (usually aircraft seats) and ancillary ground transport to effect the transfers between the destination airport and hotel. However, the use of self-catering accommodation, such as villas and apartments, in inclusive tours is proving increasingly popular, as are self-drive packages in the case of UK outbound tourism – here the transport element of the inclusive tour is a ferry crossing. The basic inclusive tour can be extended to incorporate excursions and various other forms of entertainment.

Holiday packages are prepared by tour operators on a speculative basis, and it is, therefore, important for tour operators to be able to forecast likely trends in the demand for inclusive tours.

The tour operator business is characterized by horizontal integration – often a few very large mass-market tour operators dominate this sector. The large mass-market tour operator business is, in turn, characterized by vertical integration, with many operators in combination with airlines and/or hotel chains.

Attractions sector

The tourist attractions sector of the tourism industry is very diverse and is made up of natural and built resources; it comprises gardens, national parks, country parks, wildlife parks, stately homes, cathedrals, castles, ancient monuments, museums, industrial heritage sites, art galleries, theatres, theme parks, amusement parks, sports facilities, scenic railways, casinos, shopping malls, shops selling tourist products, and so on. In addition to these 'permanent' attractions there are many temporary attractions such as events and festivals. Attractions possess the characteristic of being able to draw people to them, and the 'bundle' of attractions available in a destination may well have a considerable impact on its popularity.

In order to attract tourists to a destination for, say, one or two weeks, it is necessary to have a sufficient breadth of attractions. Attractions thus often tend to be clustered.

Examples of successful developments in the tourist attractions sector are the growth in skiing holidays and the huge popularity of leisure/theme parks. A leisure park can be defined generally as:

a site, uniting in a single enclosure, a series of attractions and activities and completed with a number of important side services, such as cafeterias, restaurants, shops and lodgings (Croizé, 1989, p. 459).

The very large growth rates experienced in ski holiday demand during recent years have led to the construction of more ski lifts and ski lodges, and greatly increased production of ski equipment and ski clothing.

Theme parks have been among the most successful tourist attractions ever developed, in particular, Disney World in Florida (which attracts about 20 million visitors per year) and Disneyland in California (which attracts about 10 million visitors per year). Disney World is much more than just a theme park based on the characters and scenes from the Disney cartoons – it also has a considerable number of additional displays and features, such as the EPCOT Center (Experimental Prototype Community of Tomorrow), which is themed on the future.

The types of events and festivals that can attract tourists include sporting events such as the summer and winter Olympic Games and tennis and golf tournaments, commercial expositions, and music and garden festivals.

The attractions sector of the tourism industry differs from the accommodation and catering sector and the transport sector in that it is concerned almost wholly with leisure-related tourism (although the education market can be significant for individual attractions).

Destination organization sector

The destination organization sector of the tourism industry comprises the various tourist offices and tourist associations. At the country level we have national tourist offices (NTOs); these are government-funded organizations and most of their operations are performed on a non-commercial basis. NTOs are supplemented at a lower level by regional (or state) tourist offices and local (usually town/city/resort) tourist offices. These are often reliant on local authority and/or private sector support in addition to (possibly) central government support.

NTOs are responsible for tourism matters at the national level, and their functions vary considerably from country to country. Usually the main functon of an NTO is to engage in marketing of the country in order to attract more tourists. NTOs are sometimes also involved in planning for and regulation of the tourism industry, and many perform a co-ordinating function. Some NTOs also have certain financial responsibilities.

The marketing function of an NTO includes advertising the

country internationally (and often also nationally) as a tourist destination – it aims to emphasize the various general attractions that the country offers to tourists. An NTO should also undertake appropriate public relations activities. NTOs usually also have a market research department, which enables studies to be made in order to identify appropriate policies to be pursued: for example, the markets that should be targeted for promotional activities. Further marketing activities undertaken by NTOs include the provision of appropriate literature and information centres.

The planning role of NTOs may include assessing personnel and training requirements for the tourism industry in the country, and ensuring that adequate provision is made. In addition, NTOs can be involved in the presentation and improvement of the tourist products in the destination. NTOs may also be required to assess the infrastructure requirements of a country, which would be necessary in order to cope with expected future patterns of tourism demand, and then make appropriate recommendations. The development of infrastructure is generally a public sector responsibility, and includes provision of water supply, sewage disposal, power supply (electricity, gas, etc.), communication networks (telephone, fax, etc.), roads, airport runways, railway lines, and harbours. These facilities are used by local residents and tourists alike, but must be designed to accommodate usage at times of peak demand (often at the peak of the tourist season). If the infrastructure at a destination is inadequate, then the full potential of the tourism superstructure – hotels, restaurants, entertainment facilities, etc. – will fail to be realized.

The regulatory and co-ordinating function of NTOs may include licensing of certain sectors of the tourism industry, regulation of accommodation standards and prices, co-ordination of national promotional activities with those of individual participants in the industry (airlines, hotels, and so on), and acting as the co-ordinating link between the various regional and local tourist offices and tourist associations in order to ensure maximum effectiveness.

A major financial duty of some NTOs is to contribute funds from government sources for approved projects. These NTOs are usually responsible for directing the aid towards certain types of tourism projects in order to achieve particular objectives – for example, if one objective is to extend the tourist season, this may be achieved by encouraging the construction of all-weather leisure facilities.

Regional or state tourist offices have a similar working pattern to that of an NTO. A major part of their activities is concerned with marketing the regions to potential tourists, and includes advertising campaigns, exhibitions and provision of regional literature on accommodation and attractions. They also provide development advice to private sector tourism operators within the region, and undertake market research in order to be able to disseminate more detailed local information. Local tourist offices are mainly concerned with promoting the town/city/resort.

Further reading

Burkart, A. J. and Medlik, S. (1981), *Tourism : Past present and future*, 2nd edn, Oxford: Heinemann.

McIntosh, R. W. and Goeldner, C. R. (1986), *Tourism: Principles, practices, philosophies*, 5th edn, New York: Wiley.

Medlik, S. (1988), *Tourism and Productivity*, British Tourist Authority/English Tourist Board.

3

Tourism demand

The growth and spatial distribution of world tourism

Tourism demand has grown rapidly throughout the 1970s and 1980s, with world international tourist arrivals increasing from 160 million in 1970 to 405 million in 1989. Table 3.1 shows, however, that this growth has not been steady, and in fact for the years 1982 and 1983 a decline in tourist arrivals was recorded. However, in general, tourism demand has stood up well to economic pressures: for example, international tourist arrivals continued to grow in the mid-1970s in spite of the massive oil price rises and supply shortages that occurred.

After sluggish growth followed by decline in the early 1980s (the 1983 level of world international tourist arrivals was below the 1980

Table 3.1 World international tourist arrivals, 1970–1988 (millions).

Year	Arrivals	Rate of growth (%)
1970	159.7	11.6
1971	172.2	7.9
1972	181.9	5.6
1973	190.6	4.8
1974	197.1	3.4
1975	214.4	8.8
1976	220.7	3.0
1977	239.1	8.3
1978	257.4	7.6
1979	274.0	6.5
1980	284.8	4.0
1981	288.8	1.4
1982	287.0	− 0.7
1983	284.4	− 0.8
1984	311.2	9.4
1985	325.9	4.7
1986	333.9	2.5
1987	358.9	7.5
1988	390.0	8.7
1989	405.3	3.9

Source: World Tourism Organization (1990).

Table 3.2   International tourist arrivals by region, 1988 (millions).

Region	Arrivals	% share
Africa	12.0	3
Americas	72.5	19
East Asia and the Pacific	42.0	11
Europe	251.5	64
Middle East	9.0	2
South Asia	3.0	1
World	390.0	100

Source: World Tourism Organization (1989).

level), the growth in tourism demand recovered and indeed accelerated over the 1986–88 period.

Table 3.2 presents international tourist arrivals grouped by region in 1988, together with the regions' share in world international tourist arrivals. It can be seen that Europe dominates in terms of international tourism, attracting 64 per cent of world arrivals. The Americas attract 19 per cent of world arrivals, and are followed by East Asia and the Pacific (11 per cent), Africa (3 per cent), the Middle East (2 per cent) and South Asia (1 per cent).

Although Europe and North America together account for approximately 80 per cent of worldwide international tourist arrivals, their market shares have declined during the 1970s and 1980s at the expense of developing and newly developed countries, particularly those in the East Asia and the Pacific region. Factors that have contributed to the increased market share of this region include the opening up of new air routes, the provision of relatively cheap inclusive tours and the massive increase in outward international tourism from Japan over the period (mainly as a result of the strong growth of the Japanese economy), which has resulted in increased intraregional tourism (Archer, 1989).

Most international tourism is intraregional – it originates in countries of the same region – but this varies considerably with the destination region under consideration. For example, whereas about 80 per cent of arrivals in Europe and North America are intra-regional, this figure reduces to about 25 per cent for Africa. This partially explains why Europe and North America have high market shares of world arrivals – the high levels of disposable income in Europe and North America facilitate international tourism, most of which takes place within the regions. However, country size and ease of access to other countries also affects the level of international tourist arrivals. Thus, a substantial part of the discrepancy between Europe's market share and that of the Americas may be accounted for by the following:

1 Europe contains several relatively small countries.
2 Much intraregional international tourism within Europe takes place between neighbouring countries with common land borders (or otherwise between countries that are situated fairly close to each other).

By contrast, the USA is an enormous country with great variation in climate, scenery, facilities, and so on. Hence, a domestic trip within the USA, which involves crossing a state boundary, may well be the equivalent of an international trip within Europe. The size and varied nature of the USA compared with individual European countries result in much USA *domestic* tourism being the equivalent of much *international* tourism within Europe.

The major tourism generating countries are ranked according to international tourism expenditures in Table 3.3. In 1987 West Germany was ranked first with a total expenditure of more than $23 billion, followed by the USA, the UK, Japan and France.

The major tourism receiving countries are ranked according to international tourism receipts in Table 3.4. In 1987 Spain was ranked first with total receipts of nearly $15 billion, followed by the USA, Italy, France and the UK. The USA, UK and France thus feature in the top five countries as both origins and destinations when demand is measured in terms of tourist expenditures/receipts, whereas West Germany and Japan (countries characterized in recent history by current account surpluses mainly achieved through the export of manufactured goods) are primarily generating countries, and Spain and Italy (traditional Mediterranean destinations) are primarily receiving countries.

Table 3.3 Major tourism generating countries, 1987.

Rank	Country	International tourism expenditures (US $ billions)
1	West Germany	23.57
2	USA	20.50
3	UK	11.87
4	Japan	10.70
5	France	8.61
6	Netherlands	6.42
7	Austria	5.50[1]
8	Canada	5.31
9	Italy	4.53
10	Switzerland	4.36

Source: Organisation for Economic Co-operation and Development (1988).
Note:
1 Including international fare payments.

Table 3.4   Major tourism receiving countries, 1987.

Rank	Country	International tourism receipts (US $ billions)
1	Spain	14.78
2	USA	14.78
3	Italy	12.16
4	France	12.00
5	UK	10.27
6	Austria	8.70[1]
7	West Germany	7.80
8	Switzerland	5.38
9	Canada	3.96
10	Belgium/Luxembourg	3.00

Source: Organisation for Economic Co-operation and Development (1988).
Note:
1   Including international fare payments.

Purpose of visit

The definition of 'tourist' is wide-ranging and when tourism demand
is broken down according to purpose of visit, the following categories
can be identified: holidays, business trips, visits to friends and
relatives (VFR) and miscellaneous visits. About 70 per cent of world
international tourist arrivals are for holiday purposes, and of the
remaining 30 per cent of tourist trips approximately one-half are
made for business purposes.

Holidays

Holidays are the most important tourism market overall. This
market is characterized by freedom of choice on the part of the
individual in terms of selection of destination, transport mode, and
so on, and by strong competition among the various segments of the
tourism industry (including the destinations) that supply the market.
Unlike, say, business travel, where the existence of business contacts
largely determines the destination to be visited, in the case of holiday
tourism the individual can select from among a wide variety of
destinations; thus considerations such as price become very
important.
   Holidaymakers can be divided into those who are conservative and
risk-averse and those who wish to try something new and are willing
to accept some risk. The conservatives tend to take the same type of
holiday year after year – often returning to the same country once
they have found one they enjoy (and even to the same resort or

hotel), whereas the risk-takers seek out new experiences in terms of climate, culture, scenery, and so on.

Many different types of holiday exist. For example, in terms of the mass-market, Mediterranean destinations offer 'sun/sea/sand' holidays (where the norm is to lie on a beach), whereas Austria and Switzerland offer 'lakes and mountains' holidays, which concentrate on scenic attractions in the summer and skiing holidays in the winter. There are now also many 'exotic' long-haul destinations on offer to places such as South America and Southeast Asia, where the emphasis is very much on experiencing something different. A range of special-interest holidays also exists – pony-trekking, rambling, cycling, yachting, bird watching, farm tourism, canal cruising, and so on. The short-break sightseeing holiday is also proving increasingly popular.

Business trips

Business travel is an important segment of the tourism market, and in certain sectors it plays the major role. Although only about 15 per cent of tourist arrivals are for business purposes, tourist spending on a business trip is likely to be much higher than on a holiday, so the contribution of business tourism to the total will be higher in value terms. Furthermore, as far as transport is concerned, business travellers comprise a disproportionately high proportion of air travellers (of the order of 50 per cent), and as far as accommodation is concerned they comprise a disproportionately high proportion of hotel guests, particularly in the four- and five-star range where the figure is of the order of 60 per cent (Hampton, 1989).

The business travel market is characterized by relative lack of seasonality, last-minute booking and inelastic response to price. To the extent that seasonality exists at all, the demand for business tourism is likely to be lower at times of peak holiday demand, because the businessmen themselves may well be on holiday. An important attribute of short business trips is that they usually take place during the week, so hotel accommodation tends to be little used for business purposes at weekends. As business travel is often large town/city-oriented, hotels in these business centres usually offer very attractive rates at weekends to encourage holidaymakers to stay. The facts that many business trips are booked only a short time ahead and that business travellers usually wish to spend the minimum amount of time away on their trips to achieve the required results means that business tourists require maximum flexibility – in particular, they do not want restrictive conditions attached to flight tickets – and are prepared to pay a premium for this. Furthermore, they usually require good quality accommodation, both in order to be able to function well and also to create the right image with the business contact being visited.

A particular form of business tourism is conference/congress/ convention tourism, and considerable attention has been focused on this form of tourism in recent years with the development of large purpose-built conference centres in many cities and seaside resorts. However, most conferences take place in hotels, and educational establishments (universities, colleges) also play an important role. (For a detailed discussion of certain aspects of conference tourism, see Hartley and Witt, 1990.) Conference tourism is not as predetermined as other forms of business tourism, in that the conference organizers can choose the location for the conference on the basis of facilities, price, and so on. Thus conference destinations are in strong competition with each other to attract conferences. Friel (1989) identifies the following criteria, which are considered desirable if a conference destination is to be successful:

1   It should be attractive to tourists.
2   It should have a variety of meeting facilities.
3   It should have a range of good accommodation.
4   There should be good access by air/road/rail.
5   There should be a civic commitment to hosting delegates.
6   There should be a co-ordinated approach to destination marketing and visitor servicing.

Visits to friends and relatives

Tourists visiting friends and relatives tend to spend much less per day while in the destination than do holidaymakers. They often stay with their friends/relatives and, therefore, do not make use of commercial accommodation. Similarly, daily expenditure on food and drink in restaurants, etc., is likely to be considerably lower than would be the case for holidaymakers. However, VFR tourists often stay longer than holidaymakers, and thus the total trip expenditure *may*, in some cases, be higher for the former than for the latter category of tourists. Furthermore, VFR traffic almost certainly generates additional *local resident* spending on food, drink, attractions, and so on. In addition, although daily destination expenditure is likely to be relatively low, the VFR component of the tourism market still needs to reach the destination and is likely to use similar means of transport to holiday-makers. In fact, tourists visiting friends and relatives may face higher travel costs than those incurred by inclusive tour holidaymakers, who benefit from the bulk-purchasing power of tour operators.

Miscellaneous visits

This purpose of visit includes tourism for reasons such as study, health, religion, shopping and to attend sporting events. Miscellaneous visits form a small proportion of overall tourism demand, but for certain destinations they can be quite important. For example, visits for religious reasons are dominant in the case of Vatican City, and visits to spas for health purposes form a significant segment of tourism demand in certain European countries such as Germany and Hungary.

Seasonality in tourism demand

'Seasonality' refers to the tendency of tourist flows to be concentrated into relatively short periods of the year (Allcock, 1989b). In Europe and North America, for example, the summer months of July and August are when a large proportion of the population goes on holiday. This is mainly due to natural features such as climate (the best holiday destination weather often occurs during these months), but also partly due to institutional features such as restrictions on when employees may take holiday leave and school holidays.

In recent years ski holidays have grown enormously in popularity, which spreads the tourist season into the winter months for appropriate destinations. Furthermore, many holidaymakers now go on 'winter sun' holidays.

Sesonality causes particular problems for employment, in that workers employed in the tourism industry for part of the year may have no opportunities for employment during the rest of the year, and this may cause resentment among employees. In addition, the seasonal nature of employment inhibits training and career progress.

Seasonality can result in overcrowding and overuse of facilities in destinations during part of the year, while for the remainder of the year facilities may be considerably under-used or not used at all, resulting in inefficient use of resources and loss of profit potential.

There are four principal strategies for managing seasonality: changing the product-mix, market diversification, differential pricing and encouragement/facilitation by the state of the staggering of holidays (Allcock, 1989b). Changing the product-mix involves the creation and marketing of new different attractions; thus, a summer beach resort may set out to attract the conference trade in the off-season, or it may decide to stage some special event, or to promote special-interest holidays that would be appropriate out of season. The construction of all-weather facilities, such as covered leisure complexes for year-round use are a means of extending the season.

A highly successful example in Northern Europe is the development of Centre Parcs, where accommodation is clustered around an all-weather leisure area incorporating wave-pool, water slides, and so on.

Diversification of the market to reach new potential customers may also be used successfully to counteract the effects of seasonality. North Americans, particularly from the northeast of the USA and Canada, have been travelling to Florida for winter holidays for some considerable time. The desire to escape the harsh winters for the warmth and sun of Florida has been a strong pull, and many retired North Americans spend several months there each winter. More recently, however, Florida has been marketed as a *summer* destination to UK residents, and the British have travelled there in increasing numbers.

Pricing policies can also be used to reduce seasonality. By the introduction of price reductions in the off-season, tourists can be encouraged to take holidays during this period. Similarly, if tourist resorts become overcrowded during peak periods, price rises can be used to reduce the seasonal congestion.

State-initiated measures to stagger holidays can also be successful in reducing the seasonality problem – for example, the staggering of school summer holidays over a longer period and the encouragement of the staggering of industrial holidays.

In spite of efforts to reduce seasonality in tourism, only limited success has been achieved. The prime importance attached to the weather by many holidaymakers means that only a certain amount of flexibility is possible.

Tourism demand functions

Tourism demand functions embody the relationship between the demand for international tourism and those factors that influence this demand. They are economic relationships that, when estimated, permit the impact of each of these factors on tourism demand to be identified.

Clearly, the group of variables that influences international tourism demand will depend upon the purpose of visit under consideration. For example, the demand for business travel will depend upon where major business centres are located, whereas the demand for visits to friends and relatives will depend upon where close historical, cultural, etc., ties exist, which give rise to the location of friends/relatives in foreign countries. As by far the majority of international tourist trips take place for holiday purposes (approximately 70 per cent), and it is only for holiday trips that individuals are completely free to choose the destination, transport mode, and so on, we shall just concentrate on demand functions that explain the demand for international *holiday* tourism.

The holiday demand function takes the general form:

$$Y = f(X_1, X_2, \ldots X_k) \qquad (3.1)$$

where
Y is the demand for foreign holidays to a given destination from a particular origin
$X_1, \ldots, X_k$ are the influencing variables, and
f denotes some function.

Variables which may be included in the demand function are now considered.

Demand variable

The demand for international tourism is measured in terms of the number of holiday visits from an origin country to a foreign destination country, or in terms of holiday expenditures by visitors from the origin country in the destination country. As the level of foreign tourism from a given origin is expected to depend upon the origin population (the higher the number of people resident in a country, the greater the number of trips taken abroad, *ceteris paribus*), the demand variable is usually expressed in per capita form. Occasionally, however, population features as a separate explanatory variable rather than demand being expressed in per capita form.

Income

In general, income is included as an explanatory variable. Income usually enters model (3.1) as origin country real income per capita (corresponding to the specification of demand in per capita terms). As holiday visits are under consideration, the appropriate form of the variable is personal disposable income.

Own price

Price is usually included in demand functions. For international tourism there are two elements of price: those costs incurred in reaching the destination, and those costs to be met while at the destination. Transport cost can be measured by using representative air fares between the origin and destination for air travel and representative ferry fares and/or petrol costs for surface travel. Transport cost should enter model (3.1) in real terms in origin country currency.

It may be possible to measure the cost of tourism in the destination by a specific tourists' cost of living variable if appropriate data are available. Otherwise, the consumer price index in a country may be used to represent tourists' cost of living, and Martin and Witt (1987) have shown that this is likely to be a reasonable proxy for the cost of tourism variable. Tourists' cost of living should be specified in real terms in origin currency. It is sometimes suggested that exchange rate should also appear as an explanatory variable influencing international tourism demand; although exchange rates are already incorporated to some extent in the other price variables, in practice people may be more aware of exchange rates than relative costs of living for tourists in the origin and destination countries, and thus pay considerable attention to this price indicator.

Substitute prices

Economic theory suggests that the prices of substitutes may be important determinants of demand. Potential tourists compare the price of a foreign holiday with the price of a domestic holiday in reaching their holiday decision. However, they also compare the costs of holidaying in a particular foreign destination with the costs involved in visiting other foreign countries. Thus, substitute travel costs and substitute tourists' living costs may be important determinants of the demand for international tourism to a given destination from a particular origin (Martin and Witt, 1988a). Substitute prices can be accommodated in model (3.1) through the inclusion of:

(a)   a weighted average substitute transport cost variable, and
(b)   a weighted average substitute tourists' cost of living variable.

The weights should reflect the relative attractiveness of the various destinations to residents of the origin under consideration, and are often based on previous market shares (for a discussion of weighting systems in international tourism demand models see Witt and Martin, 1987a).

Dummy variables

Dummy variables can be included in international tourism demand functions to allow for the impact of 'one off' events. These are specially constructed variables, which take the value 1 when the event occurs and 0 otherwise. For example, the 1973 and 1979 oil crises are likely to have temporarily reduced international tourism demand on account of the resultant uncertainties in the world economic situation (Martin and Witt, 1988a). Tourism flows to Greece were lower than expected in 1974 because of the heightened threat of war between Greece and Turkey as a result of the Turkish invasion of Cyprus (Papadopoulos and Witt, 1985). When governments impose foreign currency restrictions on their residents, this is likely to reduce outward tourism, as was the case, for example, in the UK during the period late 1966 to late 1969, and foreign currency restrictions can also alter the *distribution* of foreign holidays (Witt, 1980a, 1980b). Measurement of the impact of mega-events (such as the Olympic Games) on tourism flows through the use of dummy variables has been discussed by Witt and Martin (1987c).

Trend

A trend term may be included in international tourism demand models if it is thought relevant. This mainly represents a steady change in the popularity of a destination country over the period considered as a result of changing tastes, but it also captures the time-dependent effects of all other explanatory variables not explicitly included in the equation, such as changes in air service frequencies and demographic changes in the origins.

Promotional activity

National tourist offices often spend considerable sums in foreign countries on promoting the particular country as a tourist destination, as do carriers, particularly airlines. Hence, promotional expenditure is expected to play a role in determining the level of international tourism demand and thus should feature as an explanatory variable in the demand function (3.1). The appropriate form of the variable is promotional expenditure for the destination in the origin, expressed in origin country currency and real terms.

A major problem regarding the inclusion of promotional variables as determinants of tourism demand relates to difficulties in obtaining the relevant data. A further problem concerns the form of the relationship; the impact of advertising on tourism demand may be distributed over time, so that advertising in a given period is likely to influence not only demand in that period but also in subsequent periods, although the effect will diminish with the passage of time. In addition, the effectiveness of a given level of advertising expenditure in influencing the level of international tourism demand may vary across media. (A full review and discussion of the role of marketing variables in international tourism demand models is given in Witt and Martin, 1987b.)

Lagged dependent variable

A lagged dependent variable is sometimes included in tourism demand functions to allow for habit persistence and supply rigidities (see Witt, 1980a). Once people have been on holiday to a particular country and liked it, they tend to return to that destination. Furthermore, knowledge about the destination spreads as people talk about their holidays and show photographs, thereby reducing risk for potential visitors to that country. In fact, this 'word of mouth' recommendation may well play a more important role in destination selection than does commercial advertising.

Supply constraints may take the form of shortages of hotel accommodation, passenger transportation capacity and trained staff, and these often cannot be increased rapidly. Time is also required to build up contacts among tour operators, hotels, airlines and travel agencies. Similarly, once the tourist industry to a country has become highly developed it is unlikely to dwindle rapidly. The hotel industry will have invested large sums of money in the country and tour operators will have built up contacts there. If a partial adjustment process is postulated to allow for rigidities in supply, this results in the presence of a lagged dependent variable in model (3.1):

$$Y_t - Y_{t-1} = \lambda(Y_t^* - Y_{t-1}) \, , \, 0 < \lambda < 1 \tag{3.2}$$

where
Y_t is the actual level of holidays in year t,
Y_t^* is the desired level of holidays in year t, and
λ is the speed of adjustment.

The left-hand side of equation (3.2) denotes the change in the level of holidays between years $t - 1$ and t. The bracketed term on the right-hand side of equation (3.2) is the difference between the desired level of holidays in year t and the actual level in the previous year, that is, the desired change between years $t - 1$ and t. Thus equation (3.2) states that the actual change in the level of holiday taking is a proportion, λ, of the desired change. If $\lambda = 0$, then $Y_t = Y_{t-1}$, and there is no movement of the actual level towards the desired level. If $\lambda = 1$, then $Y_t = Y_t^*$, i.e. there is complete adjustment of the actual to the desired level. As we are specifying a *partial* adjustment process, λ lies strictly between zero and unity: there is some adjustment, but it is incomplete.

Equation (3.2) may be rewritten as

$$Y_t = (1 - \lambda) Y_{t-1} + \lambda Y_t^* \qquad (3.3)$$

Now Y^* is a function of $X_1, X_2, \ldots$, so the only difference between the explanatory variables present in models (3.1) and (3.3) is that the latter includes the dependent variable which has been lagged one period – hence the justification for including a lagged dependent variable to accommodate supply constraints.

Estimation and testing of demand functions

The tourism demand function (3.1) may be estimated by regression analysis using historic data. The empirical results obtained show the estimated quantitative relationship between foreign holiday demand and the influencing factors. The estimation process is as follows:

1   Specify the demand function in mathematical form (say, linear, or more commonly log-linear).
2   Assemble data relevant to the model.
3   Use the data to estimate by regression the quantitative effects of the influencing variables on demand in the past.
4   Carry out tests on the estimated model to see if it is sufficiently realistic.

When the tourism demand function (3.1) is specified in log-linear form, a resulting characteristic is that the estimated coefficients may be interpreted directly as elasticities. It is necessary to evaluate the parameter estimates obtained in a regression model in terms of both sign and magnitude in order to determine whether these estimates are theoretically meaningful. Economic theory imposes restrictions on the signs and values of the parameters in demand functions, and the estimates need to be examined to see whether they satisfy these constraints. For example, foreign holidays are 'superior' goods and thus a positive income elasticity is expected. In fact, most foreign holidays are regarded as 'luxuries' and in such cases the magnitude of the income elasticity is expected to exceed unity. Similarly, the own-price elasticity of demand should be negative and cross-price elasticities for substitutes positive. Changes in consumer tastes may move towards or away from a particular holiday and therefore the trend variable could have a positive or negative coefficient. The promotional expenditure and lagged dependent variable coefficients are both expected to be positive. If an estimated parameter has an 'incorrect' sign or does not satisfy the restrictions on magnitude it should be rejected, as it is theoretically implausible. In general, an unexpected parameter sign or size is the result of deficiencies in the model.

The empirical results may also be evaluated in terms of statistical measures of accuracy and significance of the forecasting equations. For example, the *t* test can be employed to examine the hypothesis that a particular explanatory variable coefficient is significantly different from zero, or whether the estimated value may simply have been generated by chance. If the hypothesis that a coefficient is equal to zero is true, then the corresponding explanatory variable does not influence the dependent variable and should be excluded from the tourism demand function. However, when a parameter is not statistically significant (at, say, the 5 per cent level), this does not prove that there is no relationship between the explanatory and dependent variables; the insignificance of the parameter may be a result of statistical problems. Prior belief plays a vital role in the decision regarding which explanatory variables should be retained in the equation in view of the statistical evidence. If there are strong theoretical grounds for expecting a particular explanatory variable to influence the dependent variable and a 'correct' coefficient sign is estimated but the parameter is insignificant, the explanatory variable should not be eliminated from the equation, as weak support has been obtained for the hypothesis. If the 'correct' sign is estimated for a coefficient and it is statistically significant, this provides strong support for the hypothesis that the variable has an impact on the dependent variable.

Full model specification

Martin and Witt (1988a) specify the following log-linear international tourism demand function:

$$\ln \frac{V_{ijt}}{P_{it}} = \alpha_1 + \alpha_2 \ln \frac{Y_{it}}{P_{it}} + \alpha_3 \ln C_{jt} + \alpha_4 \ln CS_{it}$$

$$+ \alpha_5 \ln EX_{ijt} + \alpha_6 \ln TA_{ijt} + \alpha_7 \ln TAS_{it}$$

$$+ \alpha_8 \ln TS_{ijt} + \alpha_9 \ln TSS_{it} + \alpha_{10} DV1_t$$

$$+ \alpha_{11} DV2_t + \alpha_{12} DV3_{it} + U_{ijt} \qquad (3.4)$$

where
V_{ijt} is the number of tourist visits from origin *i* to destination *j* in year *t*
P_{it} is the origin *i* population in year *t*
Y_{it} is personal disposable income in origin *i* in year *t* (constant prices)

C_{jt} is the cost of living for tourists in destination j in year t (constant prices)

CS_{it} is a weighted average of the cost of tourism in substitute destinations for residents of origin i in year t (constant prices)

EX_{ijt} is the rate of exchange between the currencies of origin i and destination j in year t

TA_{ijt} is the cost of travel by air from origin i to destination j in year t (constant prices)

TAS_{it} is a weighted average of the cost of travel by air to substitute destinations from origin i in year t (constant prices)

TS_{ijt} is the cost of travel by surface from origin i to destination j in year t (constant prices)

TSS_{it} is a weighted average of the cost of travel by surface to substitute destinations from origin i in year t

$DV1_t$ is a dummy variable which picks up the effects of the 1974 oil crisis

$$DV1_t = 1 \text{ if } t = 1974 \text{ or } 1975$$

$$= 0 \text{ otherwise}$$

$DV2_t$ is a dummy variable which picks up the effects of the 1979 oil crisis

$$DV2_t = 1 \text{ if } t = 1979$$

$$= 0 \text{ otherwise}$$

$DV3_{it}$ is a dummy variable which picks up the effects of the 1967–69 UK currency restrictions (applies to UK origin models only)

$$DV3_{it} = 1 \text{ if } i \text{ refers to the UK and } t = 1967, 1968 \text{ or } 1969$$

$$= 0 \text{ otherwise}$$

U_{ijt} is a random disturbance term

$\alpha_1, \alpha_2, \ldots, \alpha_{12}$ are unknown parameters.

In addition, a trend term $\alpha_{13}t$ and/or lagged dependent variable term $\alpha_{14} \ln (V_{ij\ (t-1)}/P_{i(t-1)})$ can be incorporated in the model for those origin–destination pairs where the preliminary empirical results indicate that this may be necessary.

Empirical results

The magnitudes of the various elasticities are of interest. For example, if the demand for tourism is price inelastic (the absolute value of the elasticity is less than unity), then a price reduction reduces total expenditure on tourism and a price rise increases expenditure. If, however, the absolute value of the price elasticity exceeds unity (that is, demand is price elastic), then a price reduction increases expenditure and a price rise reduces expenditure. Clearly, therefore, the impact of a price change on total expenditure on the tourism product (which is equal to the gross revenue of the suppliers) depends critically on the magnitude of the elasticity.

Martin and Witt (1988a) have estimated model (3.4) for tourism flows from four major generating countries – West Germany, USA, UK, France – to their important destinations, using data for the period 1965 to 1980. The estimated price and income elasticities for USA and UK outward tourist flows are presented in Tables 3.5 and 3.6, with the remaining coefficient values. It is clear that the importance of a particular variable in explaining tourist flows varies considerably with the origin–destination pair under consideration.

Building models for USA outward tourism proved difficult, with the result that several of these are rather simplistic, and in general contain fewer explanatory variables that the models for UK outward tourism. The main factors affecting tourism demand by USA residents appear to be income and absolute costs. Most overseas holidays seem to be regarded as luxuries with high income coefficients. The exception is Italy, which may be on account of strong ethnic/family ties or the pull for Roman Catholics to visit the

Table 3.5 Elasticities for USA outward tourism.

Explanatory variable	DESTINATIONS					
	Canada	France	FRG	Italy	Mexico	UK
Constant	−5.989	−44.313	−42.163	−9.432	−35.979	−25.659
$\ln \dfrac{Y}{P}$	0.372	4.683	4.058	0.421	3.523	2.431
$\ln C$	−0.364	−1.299	−1.345			−0.428
$\ln CS$		4.898				
$\ln TA$		−0.078				−0.198
$\ln TAS$	0.156					
$\ln TS$	−0.355					
$DV1$		−0.173		−0.154		
$DV2$	−0.042					
TREND	−0.018	−0.182				

Source: Martin and Witt (1988).

Table 3.6 Elasticities for UK outward tourism.

Explanatory variable	DESTINATIONS					
	Austria	France	FRG	Greece	Italy	Spain
Constant	-47.819	-18.619	-20.482	-28.863	-37.077	-23.563
$\ln \frac{Y}{P}$	4.550	1.952	2.387	0.387	4.394	1.775
$\ln C$	-0.235	-0.946	-0.361	-5.605	-1.608	
$\ln CS$	0.130	1.410				
$\ln EX$	1.859					0.637
$\ln TAS$				0.540	0.492	
$\ln TS$			-1.765	-0.394	-0.081	-0.155
$\ln TSS$				5.069		0.921
$DV1$	-0.258		-0.265	-0.420	-0.179	-0.022
$DV2$	-0.619					
$DV3$	-0.061	-0.264	-0.052			
TREND				0.056	-0.111	

Source: Martin and Witt (1988).

country – in either case such motivations would tend to cause these visits to be necessities rather than luxuries. The price elasticities vary considerably. In terms of tourists' living costs, tourism demand is price elastic for travel from the USA to France and West Germany, but price inelastic for travel to Canada and the UK. In terms of transport costs, demand is price inelastic.

In the models explaining UK outward tourism, not only do the costs of competing holidays play a more important role than for the USA, but also the exchange rate now enters into some models. The 1974 oil crisis appears to have had a marked impact on international tourism demand by UK residents, featuring in five out of six models, and the currency restrictions appear to have affected those destinations with relatively high tourists' living costs (as expected). All income elasticities exceed unity with the exception of Greece, which has a surprisingly low coefficient value. The coefficients estimated for tourists' living costs suggest that demand is price elastic for travel from the UK to Greece and Italy, but price inelastic for travel to Austria, France and West Germany. Air travel costs do not feature in the models, but the estimated surface travel cost elasticities show that demand is price elastic for West Germany and price inelastic for Greece, Italy and Spain.

Long-term influences on tourism demand
Major demographic changes are taking place in the main tourism generating countries, and this is likely to affect both the volume and types of holidays undertaken. For example, in general an increasing

proportion of the population will consist of retired people and couples with young children, and a declining proportion will consist of young singles. Also, changes in consumer preferences – say, away from sun/sea/sand holidays on account of the skin cancer link, and towards activity holidays such as rambling – may have a profound impact on tourism demand over the long term. Clearly, substantial changes in the amount of holiday entitlement will also influence the level of demand.

Tourism forecasting

It is widely recognized that one of the most important functions of the manager at all levels in an organization is planning, and planning creates a substantial need for forecasts. Reliable forecasts of tourism demand are essential for efficient planning by airlines, shipping companies, railways, coach operators, hoteliers, tour operators, food and catering establishments, providers of entertainment facilities, manufacturers producing goods primarily for sale to tourists, and other industries connected with the tourism market. Such forecasts are also of great interest to governments in origin and destination countries, and to national tourist organizations.

Both the *need* for forecasts and the importance of *reliable* forecasts have been stressed by several authors working in the tourism field. For example, Wandner and Van Erden (1980, p. 381) point out that:

> Since governments and private industry must plan for expected tourism demand and provide tourism investment goods and infrastructure, the availability of accurate estimates of international tourism demand has important economic consequences.

Also, Archer (1987, p. 77) states that:

> No manager can avoid the need for some form of forecasting: a manager must plan for the future in order to minimize the risk of failure or, more optimistically, to maximize the possibilities of success. In order to plan, he must use forecasts. Forecasts will always be made, whether by guesswork, teamwork or the use of complex models, and the accuracy of the forecasts will affect the quality of the management decision.

He goes on to point out that:

> In the tourism industry, in common with most other service sectors, the need to forecast accurately is especially acute because

of the perishable nature of the product. Unfilled airline seats and unused hotel rooms cannot be stockpiled and demand must be anticipated and even manipulated.

Considerable benefits derive from an accurate forecasting system. If forecasts of tourism demand are too high, then firms in related industries will suffer; for example, there may be empty seats on aeroplanes and coaches, empty rooms in hotels, unoccupied apartments, unused hire cars, and so on. It is likely that in general capital investment will be excessive, the labour force will be too big and excess stocks will be held of goods normally sold directly to or used by tourists. If, on the other hand, forecasts of demand are too low, then firms will lose opportunities: for example, there may be insufficient hotel accommodation or too few flights to cater for all those wishing to visit a certain area at a given time. Even if supply can be expanded to a limited extent at short notice, this is likely to impose additional costs on firms as, say, less efficient aircraft are used, and excessive overtime is worked.

A broad range of techniques is available for demand forecasting in tourism and the main quantitative methods are now reviewed (for more detailed discussion and a review of qualitative forecasting methods in tourism, see Witt and Martin, 1989).

Univariate time series methods

Univariate time series methods are non-causal quantitative techniques, i.e. they assume that a variable may be forecast without reference to the factors that determine the level of the variable – past history on the forecast variable is simply extrapolated. Univariate time series methods determine future values for a single variable through a process of identifying a relationship for past values of the variable. Thus, a great problem with forecasting by extrapolation is that it presupposes that the factors that were the main cause of growth in the past will continue to be the main cause in the future, which may not be the case. In an industry as highly volatile as international tourism, and one that is influenced by so many factors, trend extrapolation is a technique that should be used with extreme caution.

It is rarely possible to justify time series models on the basis of theory. The reasons for their use are essentially pragmatic: they often generate acceptable forecasts at low cost. Furthermore, univariate time series methods may be used where causal models are inappropriate on account of lack of data or incomplete knowledge regarding the causal structure.

Although time series extrapolation models are 'naïve' in the sense that the impacts of the forces that determine the behaviour of the time series are not taken into account, they often predict relatively well. Several of these methods are considered below:

1 MOVING AVERAGE (ARITHMETIC)

The arithmetic moving average forecast is very easy and cheap to compute; the data for previous periods are added together and divided by the number of observations to give an average figure, and then as a new data point becomes available this is included in the set, the oldest observation is removed, and a new average is calculated. For seasonal data with seasonality of s periods (for example, quarterly data has four-period seasonality), a moving average s periods long is free of seasonal effects. The moving average forecast for periods $t + 1, t + 2$, etc., is given by:

$$F_{t+2} = F_{t+1} = [x_t + x_{t-1} + \ldots + x_{t-s+1}]/s \qquad (3.5)$$

where

x_t is the value of a time series in period t
F_{t+j} is the moving average forecast of x_{t+j} (i.e. the forecast for j periods ahead), and
s is the length of the seasonal cycle.

The moving average model (3.5) attempts to estimate the non-seasonal portion of a time series. It is not applicable to series containing steps or trends (as is often the case with tourism data), as these would cause the moving average to lag behind the movement of the data. Thus, for example, if tourism demand were increasing the method would underforecast.

2 EXPONENTIAL SMOOTHING

Exponential smoothing models provide a relatively simple set of forecasting methods that tend to perform well in practice. The single exponential smoothing model in effect attempts to reduce forecast error by correcting last period's forecast by a proportion of last period's error:

$$F_{t+1} = F_t + k(x_t - F_t) \qquad (3.6)$$

where

x_t is the value of a time series in period t
F_{t+1} is the single exponential smoothing forecast of x_{t+1} (i.e. the forecast for one period ahead), and

k   is a constant, such that $0 < k < 1$.

Equation (3.6) states that the forecast for period $t + 1$ is given by the forecast for period t plus a proportion (k) of the forecast error for period t. This equation may be rewritten to give:

$$F_{t+1} = kx_t + (1 - k)F_t \qquad (3.7)$$

Single exponential smoothing methods are only applicable to stationary series, i.e. to data without steps, trend or seasonality components, and with constant variance. For non-stationary series other exponential smoothing models can be used. Adaptive smoothing models can accommodate sudden upward or downward steps in a series; Brown's double exponential smoothing model can be used for time series containing a trend, and the Holt-Winters' double exponential smoothing method is specifically designed for time series exhibiting seasonality (in addition to a trend).

3   TREND CURVE ANALYSIS

Trend curve analysis is widely used in tourism forecasting situations. In general, regression analysis is used to find a curve of best fit through time series data, which is then projected forward into the future. Trend curve analysis is relatively quick and easy to use and, using transformations, can be employed to produce forecasts from data showing a range of patterns, for example, straight line progressions, exponential growth, or patterns that display a gradual approach to a saturation level. A variety of trend expressions is shown below:

Linear	$Y = a + bT$	(3.8)
Constrained hyperbola	$Y = T/(a + bT)$	(3.9)
Exponential	$Y = ae^{bT}$	(3.10)
Log–Log	$Y = aT^b$	(3.11)
Semi-log	$Y = a + b \log T$	(3.12)
Modified exponential	$Y = ae^{b/T}$	(3.13)
Hyperbola	$Y = a + b/T$	(3.14)
Modified hyperbola	$Y = 1/(a + bT)$	(3.15)
Quadratic	$Y = a + bT + cT^2$	(3.16)
Log quadratic	$Y = e^{(a + bT + CT^2)}$	(3.17)

where

Y is the forecast variable
T is the time period

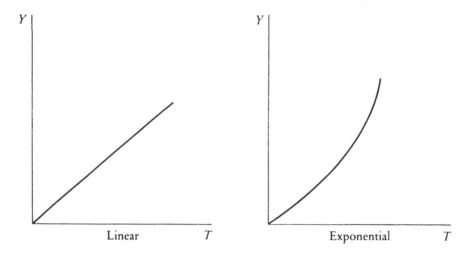

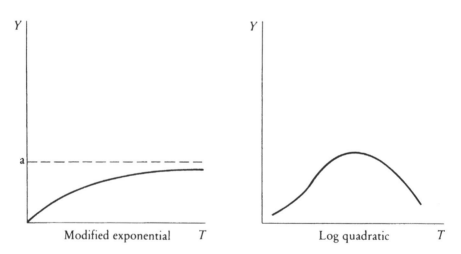

Figure 3.1   Examples of trend curve shapes.

$e = 2.718$, and
a, b, c are coefficients to be estimated using regression analysis.

Some of the above curve shapes are illustrated in Figure 3.1.

4   DECOMPOSITION METHODS

The observed values of a time series are usually the result of several influences, and here we are concerned with isolating and measuring those parts of the time series that are attributable to each of the components. Customarily, time series variations are considered to be the result of three or four basic influences: secular trend, seasonal variations, irregular or random changes, and possibly cyclical fluctuations.

The *classical* decomposition approach assumes that the observation of the time series at period t, x_t, can be represented as:

$$x_t = T_t \times S_t \times I_t \qquad (3.18)$$

where

T represents the trend value
S represents the seasonal component
I represents the irregular (unpredictable) component, and
t represents the time period.

Sometimes an additional longer-term cycle component is added to the classical decomposition model, but often this factor is ignored. This can be justified if there are insufficient data to detect it, which may well be the case with tourism series. Classical decomposition is best suited where trend or seasonality, and preferably both, are marked.

An alternative (though considerably more complex) approach to decomposition is provided by the *Census XII* model originally devised for the US Bureau of Census. This extends the basic decomposition model of equation (3.18) by allowing the trend term T_t to be non-linear.

5   BOX–JENKINS UNIVARIATE METHOD

The Box–Jenkins univariate forecasting method is a highly sophisticated technique and is rather more difficult to apply than the other univariate time series methods considered. The models usually incorporate autoregressive and moving average terms; the autoregressive component implies that the forecast variable depends on its own past values, and the moving average component implies that the forecast variable depends on previous values of the error term. These autoregressive integrated moving average (ARIMA) models are very flexible – they can represent many types of stationary and non-stationary time series. Furthermore, the models contain few parameters. The Box–Jenkins model-building approach can provide relatively accurate forecasts, but it involves complex mathematical and statistical algorithms, and subjective judgements on the part of the modeller. Experience is an essential prerequisite for improving the final models in the analysis of a time series and thus for successful application of the technique.

Causal quantitative techniques

1   MULTIPLE REGRESSION METHODS

The econometric approach to forecasting international tourism demand involves the use of regression analysis to estimate the tourism demand function (3.4) – or, more generally model (3.1) – and then combining the estimated relationship with forecasts of the explanatory variables to generate tourism demand forecasts.

A major advantage of econometric forecasting is that it explicitly takes into account the impact on demand of changes in the causal variables. Furthermore, econometric models may be used for active ('what if') forecasting, that is, to assess the consequences of possible changes in the causal factors. An additional advantage is that econometric forecasting provides several statistical measures of the accuracy and significance of the forecasting equations.

Econometric models, however, may be inappropriate in certain cases and are generally more expensive than non-causal models. Econometric forecasting also requires considerable user-understanding in order to develop the correct relationships. A major problem in attempting to generate accurate forecasts of tourism demand with econometric models is the difficulty of obtaining accurate forecasts of the variables that influence demand: income, inflation, exchange rates, and so on.

2   BOX–JENKINS MULTIVARIATE METHOD

The Box–Jenkins multivariate (or transfer function) approach to forecasting is considerably more complicated than the Box–Jenkins univariate method. It is a causal forecasting method in that other variables are allowed to influence the forecast variable. As with the Box–Jenkins univariate method, the model incorporates auto-regressive and moving average terms, and complex mathematical and statistical algorithms are involved. However, the existence of more than one time series results in additional modelling problems. Again, experience is essential in order to apply the technique successfully.

Box–Jenkins multivariate models may be viewed as extensions of the multiple linear regression model. For example, if there are just two explanatory variables, then the linear regression model

$$Y = b_1 X_1 + b_2 X_2 + U \qquad (3.19)$$

where

Y is the dependent variable
X_1, X_2 are independent variables

U is an error term, and

b_1, b_2 are parameters

may be modified as follows:

1   The terms $b_i X_i$, $i = 1,2$, can be replaced by transfer function models which permit present and past values of X_i to influence Y;
2   The error term can be allowed to follow an ARIMA model.

The multivariate Box–Jenkins model corresponding to the regression model (3.19) is thus

$$Y = Y_1 + Y_2 + Y_n \qquad (3.20)$$

where

Y_1, Y_2 are the input components of Y, such that $Y_i = TF_i(X_i)$, $i = 1,2$ (TF denotes transfer function) and

Y_n is the noise component, such that $Y_n = \text{ARIMA}(U)$.

Y is therefore the sum of components that are not directly observed, but are determined in the process of fitting the model.

Concluding remarks

There are many methods that can be used to forecast tourism demand, and selection of an appropriate technique will depend upon the requirements of the forecaster. For example, a company in the international tourism industry can use an econometric forecasting system to explore the consequences of alternative future policies on tourism demand ('what if' forecasting), which is not possible with non-causal models.

A small-scale questionnaire survey of tourism practitioners (including those working in tourist offices, consultancy companies and hotel chains/associations) was carried out by Martin and Witt (1988b), and the results suggest that the main forecasting techniques used in the tourism business are moving average, exponential smoothing and multiple regression. Moving average is the most popular technique for short-term forecasting (less than one year ahead), and multiple regression for long-term forecasting (more than two years ahead); these methods are both highly popular for medium-term forecasting (one to two years ahead). The only other quantitative forecasting method in general use among tourism practitioners appears to be trend curve analysis.

To date, attempts at forecasting international tourist flows using quantitative techniques have not proved particularly successful in terms of the accuracy achieved (Martin and Witt, 1989).

Further reading

Allcock, J. B. (1989), 'Seasonality', in Witt, S. F. and Moutinho, L. (eds), *Tourism Marketing and Management Handbook*, Hemel Hempstead: Prentice-Hall, pp. 387–92.

Archer, B. H. (1989), 'Trends in international tourism', in Witt, S. F. and Moutinho, L., op. cit., pp. 593–7.

Martin, C. A. and Witt, S. F. (1987), 'Tourism demand forecasting models: Choice of appropriate variable to represent tourists' cost of living', *Tourism Management*, vol. 8, no. 3, pp. 233–46.

Martin, C. A. and Witt, S. F. (1988), 'Substitute prices in models of tourism demand', *Annals of Tourism Research*, vol. 15, no. 2, pp. 255–68.

Witt, S. F. and Martin, C. A. (1989), 'Demand forecasting in tourism and recreation', *Progress in Tourism, Recreation and Hospitality Management*, vol. 1, pp. 4–32.

4

Methods of operation

Introduction

This chapter examines methods of operation in the international tourism industry. We first examine the general approach to international methods of operating, covering the conventional analysis of exporting, licensing and foreign direct investment. This analysis is then applied more closely to the tourism industry. Finally, we analyse each method of operation in detail. concentrating on direct investment, joint ventures, franchising, management contracts and turnkey operations.

Methods of international operation – the general case

At the crudest and broadest level, firms can operate in foreign markets in three generic ways: exporting (X), licensing (L) and direct investment (I) (see Buckley, 1989). Many peculiarities of the tourism industry result from the fact that tourism is an 'experience good' whose value cannot be established by inspection (as opposed to a 'search good'). This means that the bulk of the tourism product has to be consumed in the host country (McQueen, 1989). Exporting in tourism is applicable only where the services (and occasionally goods) are transmitted or transported as an essential part of the tourist product or package.

Exporting covers the indirect export of goods and services (through agents, distributors, merchant houses, trading companies and a variety of other intermediaries) and the direct export of goods and services. Its essential feature is that production activities are carried out in the home country, although marketing may well be carried out in the host country, separated by a transport cost barrier. Exporting is often regarded as merely the first step into a foreign market, but its persistence as a viable strategy mode even in the largest multinationals suggests that it still has a role to play. The sequentialist school has made much of the observed pattern of entering and servicing a foreign market over time, which goes $X \rightarrow L \rightarrow I$ or $X \rightarrow I$ (Buckley, 1982). This represents a means of increasing involvement in the foreign market while minimizing the risk of over-exposure to risk.

Licensing covers a variety of non-direct investment production operations, involving arms length co-operation with an external agency (or agencies). Some element of market transfer is included in this packaged sale of asset services. A spectrum of relationships is possible, ranging from (the rare) simple sale of embodied knowledge or assets (brand name, patent) through franchising, turnkey operations, contract manufacturing, management contracts, etc.

Foreign direct investment also covers a range of operations. The normal image of a foreign direct investment is a production facility involving a huge capital outlay. This is not necessarily so. A foreign direct investment can be the creation of a sales subsidiary – one man with stock working from his basement with a car! The key feature of the foreign direct investment is not scale but control from the parent. This control, exercised most usually through equity ownership, enables direct management of a foreign facility rather than control through a contract. These issues are widely debated in the internalization literature (Buckley and Casson, 1976, 1985; Hennart, 1982; Dunning, 1988, among many others). Direct investment thus covers marketing operations and production operations: both sales subsidiaries and production subsidiaries ranging from assembly to full production. Direct investment is regarded as the most risky form of entry in terms of capital committed, but is regarded as the most effective in securing market share and strategic competitive advantage.

At its most simple, X can be differentiated from the other two methods of foreign market entry and foreign market servicing by the location effect, as with exports the bulk of value adding activity takes place in the home country, while the other two methods transfer much of value adding activity to the host country. Similarly, L can be differentiated from X and I by the externalization effect. L represents a market sale of intermediate goods or corporate assets by the firm. In licensing, the firm sells rights and the use of assets to a licensee. In X and I such activities are internalized (Buckley and Casson, 1976, 1985). Broadly then, the internalization and location effects separate the three generic forms of market servicing.

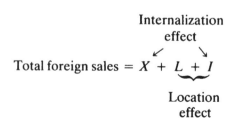

These simple differentiations are in practice highly complex. First, comparative costs are not easily calculable or obvious. In multi-product, multi-process and multi-functional firms, the internal division of labour and the costs associated with each activity are difficult to assess accurately. Further, there are many complex interactions between the activities involved. Location abroad of some activities will have knock-on effects on home costs and those of third countries within the firm's international network. Secondly, the costs and benefits of internalization are nebulous and difficult to measure. Both sets of complication are entirely contingent on circumstances. The difficulties of these calculations are that the situation is dynamic and the determinants of choice of optimal market servicing strategies are continually shifting.

Thirdly, a major complicating factor in the analysis of foreign market servicing policies is that the forms are often complements, not substitutes. This fact means that a careful analysis of the relationship between modes is essential. For instance, Hood and Young (1979) point to the existence of 'anticipatory exports' (goods exported from the source country in anticipation of building the foreign plant), 'associated exports' (complementary products exported by the parent after establishment of the subsidiary) and 'balancing exports' (which result when the first plant built abroad is operating at capacity). Foreign direct investment also has a dynamic effect in maintaining the world-wide competitive position of the investment firm (Hood and Young, 1979).

This crude threefold differentiation needs careful modification at the operational level. Table 4.1 shows that the variety of forms of doing business abroad is not a single spectrum of deepening involvement, but has a number of key dimensions which enable careful classification. These dimensions include: whether the venture is equity or non equity, whether it is limited in time and economic space (e.g. restricted to 10 years or to one defined territory), whether a complete transfer of resources and rights occurs and whether that transfer is internal, through the firm, or external by the market.

Constraints

It is essential to remember that an 'ideal' market servicing strategy only exists when proper regard is paid to the constraints on forms of market servicing. Exporting is not feasible for many firms in tourism because of the need to perform the service *in situ*. It is similarly ruled out for bulky or perishable products or where the key activity is location specific, e.g. natural attractions, sunshine. Licensing is often not feasible because of the difficulties of finding a licensee or

Table 4.1 A typology of international co-operation modes.

Form of co-operation	Equity or non equity	Time limited or unlimited	Space limited	Transfer of resources and rights	Mode of transfer
1 Wholly owned foreign subsidiaries	Equity	Unlimited	At discretion of MNE	Whole range	Internal
2 Joint venture	Equity	Unlimited	Agreed	Whole range?	Internal
3 Foreign minority holdings	Equity	Unlimited	Limited	Whole range	Internal
4 'Fade out' agreements	Equity	Limited	Nature of agreement	Whole range for limited period	Internal, changing to Market
5 Licensing	Non equity	Limited by contract	May include limitation in contract	Limited range	Market
6 (Franchising)	Non equity	Limited by contract	Yes	Limited + support	Market
7 Management Contracts	Non equity	Limited by contract	May be specified	Limited	Market
8 'Turnkey Ventures'	Non equity	Limited	Not usually	Limited in time	Market
9 'Contractual Joint Ventures'	Non equity	Limited	May be agreed	Specified by contract	Mixed
10 International Sub-contracting	Non equity	Limited	Yes	Small	Market

Source: Buckley (1985).

franchisee with all the right qualities, notably with the ability to exploit the transferred information to the full. Firms are also loath to lose their key proprietary advantages by market transfer. Direct foreign investment faces severe constraints in terms of capital availability and management skills. It is also regarded as high risk. This is particularly true for small firms and first-time foreign investors (Buckley, Newbould and Thurwell, 1988). Market servicing strategies, therefore, must be related to the firm's available resources. It is relatively easy for firms to become over-extended if they attempt to penetrate too many foreign markets in too short a time-span.

Consequently, we often observe an incremental or step-by-step approach to foreign market entry. This strategy can be based on the identification of markets that are 'close' to home in terms of business practices and conditions, language, lifestyle and historical background, in order to avoid problems of more 'distant' markets, which can be tackled as the firm's international experience grows. It is, of course, possible to exaggerate the similarity of foreign markets: 'two countries divided by the same language' has more than a germ of truth. Market servicing strategy is perforce sequential and dynamic. It must be constantly adjusted to the changing environment, not just economic but also political, social and technological. It must also reflect the changing requirements and resources of the firm in the industry, paying careful attention to competitive moves. This theme is taken up in chapter 9.

Application to international tourism

As mentioned above, tourism as a package of 'experience goods' is largely dominated by operations in the host country, involving combinations of investment and licensing. Both equity and non equity routes are used. The three key sectors operating internationally are hotels, airlines and tour operators.

Hotels

The UNCTC Report (UNCTC, 1982) identified four main groups of international corporations in the hotel sector: (1) hotel chains associated with airlines; (2) international hotel chains; (3) management advisory companies; (4) tour operators or travel agents.

The major form of international operation is not through direct investment where control rests with the foreign corporation, but through minority equity participation combined with the widespread use of franchising. Hotel chains associated with airlines have various

Table 4.2 Owners of travel firms and hotel chains.

Travel firms	*Parent company*
Thomas Cook	Midland Bank
A. T. Mays	Bank of Scotland
Pickford Travel	National Freight Consortium
Thomson Holidays ⎱ Lunn Poly ⎰	International Thomson Organisation
Hotel chain	*Parent company*
Hilton Hotels	Ladbroke
Holiday Inn	Bass

Source: Malcolm Martin (1989) and press notices.

arrangements, but most usually these are through a minority equity stake loosely tying the hotel to the airline and enabling cross marketing to take place and packages to be bought with 'associated hotels'. Specialized international hotel chains are a key component of international operations. Such chains frequently franchise operations that are often ultimately owned by a conglomerate parent company. Specialist international hotel development and management companies appear to be in decline. Their business has largely been in the developing countries, but with the desire for local participation the franchise has become more popular. Finally, tour operators and travel agents are involved in the international hotel business.

This enables the operator and/or agent to control the accommodation needs of the clients and to package operations. It is to be noted that the ultimate owners of travel firms (like hotel chains) are often conglomerates, whose other interests lie outside the tourism field. Examples are given in Table 4.2.

Airlines

The airline business has an essential international dimension. International airlines have benefited from the rapid growth in real disposable income in developed countries and in the lengthening of vacation periods. They have contributed to the decline in the real costs of international travel, particularly through their charter traffic.

As Dunning and McQueen (UNCTC, 1982) point out, there are considerable links between airlines and other groups in the tourism industry and among airlines themselves. The latter associations largely consist of technical assistance and co-operation agreements. Joint purchasing agreements for aircraft, joint maintenance and overhaul facilities and joint training schemes are ways of reducing the large costs of operating internationally, including overhead costs. These are ways of gaining economies of scale while avoiding full merger (Buckley and Casson, 1988).

Outside the immediate bounds of the airline industry, widespread involvement occurs in catering, insurance, computer services, technical services and shipping. Many airlines have diversified into tour operations with 'captive' tour companies. This has developed into airlines becoming major wholesalers and sometimes retailers of inclusive tour holidays. Links with hotels were discussed above; they tend to be minority holdings.

The methods of operation of international airlines tend to be wholly owned core business, combined with a network of joint ventures, minority owned operations and co-operative technical agreements in business areas bounding the core. The exception to this rule is the increasing diversification down the marketing chain into tour operation and the wholesaling and retailing of inclusive tour holidays and travel packages.

International tour operations

The wholesaling operation carried out by tour operators means that they combine the elements of a travel package – typically, accommodation, transport and other amenities (see also Chapter 5 and Buckley, 1987). As Dunning and McQueen (UNCTC, 1982) point out, these wholesalers are largely based in the tourist-generating countries because (1) they have the knowledge of the tastes and needs of the customers; (2) they can generate economies of scale and scope in serving many destinations, markets and market segments; (3) they have connections, often ownership connections, with airlines and hotels from the same country. The large, vertically integrated tour operator is in a strong position. The use of monopsony power enables prices to the operator to be reduced to a minimum – a fact that causes considerable resentment in many host countries. The integrated nature of operations means that strict control of quality can be maintained over all elements in the package. Diversification across many markets, destinations and market segments means that risks can be spread – particularly important in a cyclical and highly seasonal business. Internal prices can be managed to best effect, to reduce tax liabilities. There may also be the possibility of using differential pricing in various separable sub-markets in order to maximize profits. The scale and scope of large operators also enables them to ride out depressions that may bring down more specialized operators. On the other hand, the higher profit rates of niche operators may provide greater fat for survival in downturns.

Specific methods of international operation

This section covers the key means of operating in international tourism across industry divisions. The key methods covered are: direct investment, joint ventures, minority holdings, licensing and franchising, management contracts and turnkey ventures. First, we examine the choice of setting up an operation in a foreign country via a greenfield venture (building up the unit from scratch on a 'greenfield' site) or take-over, and then we discuss issues of ownership strategy – wholly-owned subsidiaries or joint ventures. The following sections then examine licensing and franchising, management contracts and turnkey ventures.

Greenfield ventures versus take-overs

A priori, there are strong arguments either to build a new foreign facility from scratch on a greenfield site or to acquire an existing firm or part of a firm. The proponents of greenfield entry support their case by reference to the following arguments. First, greenfield ventures can be a cheaper form of entry because the scale of involvement can be precisely controlled and the facility can be expanded exactly in line with achieved market penetration. This argument is likely to be particularly strong for smaller firms, who face difficulty in raising the capital necessary for a take-over. Secondly, building a new foreign facility means that there is no risk of inheriting problems. However, in the tourism sector there are many problems of externalities, e.g. the image of a country may affect even the best facilities. A health scare, for instance, will jeopardize even the best run hotel in the vicinity.

Thirdly, the most modern techniques of production, service provision and management can be installed. Fourthly, there is likely to be a welcome by the host government for greenfield ventures, which are seen as increasing activity, employment and competition. Positively, this may entail financial assistance and negatively, there is less risk of anti-trust action. Fifthly, the choice of location is open to the entrant and a least cost site, including possible regional grants, can be chosen. Finally, where no suitable take-over victim can be found, greenfield entry can be a second-best solution.

There are counter agreements in favour of entry by take-over. First, take-overs permit rapid market entry and allow a quicker return on capital and learning procedures. In cases of strong competition, the pre-emption of a rival firm's move may dictate take-over entry. Secondly, cultural, legal and management problems, particularly in the difficult start-up period, can be avoided by assimilating a going concern. Thirdly, the major advantage of a take-over is often the purchase of crucial assets. Such assets in different circumstances can be products, skills, management, brand names, technology and distribution networks. Fourthly, take-overs do not disturb the competitive framework in the host country and avoid competitive retaliation.

There are, however, several potential drawbacks to the take-over mode of entry. The entrant is faced with the task of evaluating the worth of the assets to be acquired. This involves a costly and difficult assessment of the synergy between these new assets and the firm's existing operations. Secondly, there may be severe problems of integrating a previously independent unit into a larger entity and, thirdly, the search for the ideal victim often involves heavy costs.

Almost every entry decision involves giving a different weighting to the above factors. Of particular importance in determining the outcome are the specific skills of the entrant and the environmental circumstances in the host country.

Ownership strategy

The arguments for 100 per cent equity ownership of a foreign subsidiary rely heavily on the fact that control by the parent is total and that there can be no conflict over potentially contentious issues of company policy such as dividend payments, exports, the distribution of new investment and internal transfer prices. In cases where the parent firm can supply all the necessary inputs for a subsidiary, these costs of interference need not be borne. Further information, both technical and competitive, is not leaked to outsiders who may not fully share the goals of the parent firm. Finally, some types of strategy are incompatible with the joint venture, notably those based on rapid and sustained innovation, on rationalization and on control of key inputs.

The arguments for joint ventures are more circumstantial and depend on finding a joint venture partner with complementary resources. The argument that unique resources are contributed by the local partner is usually the most important reason for joint ventures. These resources may be local knowledge, contacts or marketing expertise. Secondly, the entrant company's outlay is reduced and the risk of loss correspondingly diminished. This reduction of risk is an important reason why joint ventures may be a good way of effecting initial entry. Finally, in many countries, some element of local shareholding is made a condition of entry.

The success of the decision to enter a joint venture will, of course, depend on the choice of partner. There are many cases on record where a good agent or distributor has become a poor joint venture partner. It is, of course, difficult to appraise a prospective partner in advance, but on such an appraisal may depend the success of the foreign venture.

Licensing and franchising

A franchise is a specialized type of licence and it is worth examining foreign licensing in general before turning to the special case of franchising.

Licensing agreements represent the market alternative to the internalized transfer of resources (including information) and rights (Davies, 1977). Licensing is a generic term which encompasses a wide variety of contractual agreements between a foreign firm and a local firm for effecting transfers of rights and resources. Balasubramanyam (1973) uses the term 'technical collaboration agreements' to cover the sale and purchase of technical information. Typically, licensing will also include certain rights to market the product or service, which embodies the transferred information (a wider term than knowledge), and many ancillary transfers of resources and rights are included.

The transfer process in licensing is complex and time-consuming. Hall and Johnson (1970) say:

> Technology can be transferred into two basic forms. One form embraces physical items such as drawings, tools, machinery, process information, specifications and patents. The other form is personal contact. Put simply, knowledge is always embodied in something or somebody, the form being important for determining the transfer process and cost.

Telesio (1979) states that 'Licensing of manufacturing technology can be defined as the sale of "intangible property rights, such as patents, secret processes or technical information" '. To this transfer of technology must be added other forms of information transfer, including marketing and managerial aspects. The widest, and most terse, definition of a license is 'a covenant not to sue' (Prasad, 1981, quoting Finnegan, 1976), although the writer goes on to list the positive aspects of licensing.

In general, licensing as a mode of operation appears to combine the best of both worlds, the specialized advantages and skills of the foreign multinational entrant and the local knowledge of the licensee. However, there are several major barriers that stand in the way of a successful international licensing agreement. First, the special skills and advantages may not be easily or freely transferred. Where these are embodied in a brand name then transfer can take place. If however, specialized management or operation practices are involved, transfer may be much more difficult. Secondly, licences require policing, that is, the licensor must endeavour to ensure that the transferred knowledge is not used 'in ways which have not been paid for'. This may involve high monitoring costs by the licenser. Thirdly, the licensor runs the risk of creating a competitor. Fourthly, transferring knowledge between firms will have high costs in terms of training and other ways of ensuring that the key skills and knowledge are absorbed. Fifthly, licensing is subject to 'buyer uncertainty' (Buckley and Casson, 1976), i.e. the licensor must extract a return from the licencee without revealing in advance just what the knowledge or information is in advance of payment, otherwise the licencee could appropriate the knowledge at zero cost. This also poses problems for the potential licencee in knowing what to pay in advance of receiving the licence. Insurance and contingent contracts can be designed to obviate this difficulty, but these are not always desirable or acceptable. In many cases the worth of a licence depends on exclusivity, and a secrecy element is essential – unfortunately, this can inhibit market transfer of information. Finally, there may simply be no local firm that can profitably absorb and utilise the licence. This will be particularly true when international tourism companies are expanding into less developed countries or regions.

However, licensing will be a useful tool in certain circumstances. First, it can be used to enter markets that are restricted by government policy. In some countries the ownership of parts of the tourism industry is restricted to locals only. Examples are airlines, airports, hotels, game reserves, etc. Access to and a return from such facilities can be gained by licensing in its various guises (management contracts, franchising, etc.). Secondly, some tourism firms will be constrained by a lack of management skills or capital, and licensing will economise on the use of these resources while enabling effective market penetration. It should not be forgotten that licensing is a management-intensive process, particularly in the negotiation and start-up periods, and firms ignore this at their peril. Thirdly, licensing enables the life cycle of a project to be expanded and may be a way into markets in which it is simply not worth while to invest. Licensing can thus be used to extend the life of residual technology and information and to reach peripheral markets. Fourthly, it is argued that licensing reduces risk. In fact, it has a different risk profile from investment. Licensors are less likely to take a capital loss than investors, but they may lose something far more valuable – proprietary technology. Finally, licensing may be a useful competitive weapon, avoiding head-to-head competition (and thus lessening the risk of a post-entry price war, for example). It may further be used to reduce competition, by the use of cross-licensing, for instance, whereby one company licenses its key product or service in another's home market in return for the second company's key product in its own home market.

FRANCHISING

One specialized but important type of licence agreement is franchising. Franchising is 'a form of marketing or distribution in which a parent company customarily grants an individual or a relatively small company the right, or privilege, to do business in a prescribed manner over a certain period of time in a specified place' (Vaughn, 1979, pp. 1–2). The franchise contract usually has several elements:

1 Specification of the duration of the commercial relationship.
2 Grant of a set of rights to the 'franchisee' to offer, sell and distribute goods and services manufactured, processed, distributed or organized and directed by the 'franchiser'.
3 The franchisee as an independent business constitutes a component of the franchiser's distribution network.
4 The franchisee's business is substantially associated with advertising or other commercial symbol designating the franchiser.
5 The franchisee's operations are substantially reliant on the franchiser for the continued supply of goods and/or services.
6 The franchisee will be geographically limited (Vaughn, 1979; Izreali, 1972).

A large element of the franchise thus involves the carefully controlled transfer of managerial and marketing skills. Usually, the franchisee will be an individual or a small independent business. Franchise systems may be of the manufacturer-retailer type (car distributorship, petrol dealerships), manufacturer-wholesaler (soft drinks bottlers), wholesaler-retailer or trademark licenser-retailer types. The most salient franchise relationships occur in 'fast-food' chains and in hotels (see Dunning and McQueen, 1981, 1982). A key element of franchisees is segmentation of the market spatially into exclusive territories in order to prevent competition between individual franchisees. Grants of exclusive rights to these territories can then assure full market coverage without internal competition. Services are thus ideal for franchising.

The benefits to the host country from franchising are frequently adduced to be high, because training and development of management skills are frequently integral to the franchising 'package' (Wright et al., 1981). Management and technical training, assistance in locating, equipping (even decorating) and financial and advertising back-up are valuable imported components added to the franchisee's motivation to 'be his own boss' and to make franchising attractive to small businesses. For the franchiser, effective market penetration is often combined with minimal capital outlay. However indigenous alternative products (soft drinks, restaurants, hotels, for instance) are often unable to compete with internationally known alternatives and charges of cultural imperialism are frequently aimed at franchisers.

Management contracts

An option that has become more widely used in recent years is the *management contract*. This is employed in a variety of sectors – agricultural, extractive, manufacturing and service – but is widely found among hotels and transport undertakings. International hotel chains, such as Holiday Inns and Intercontinental, operate through direct investment, management contracts or franchising according to the local circumstances.

The distinctive feature of the management contract is that a contractor company enters into a contract with a client to manage a third company, the contract venture. This triangular relationship, illustrated in Figure 4.1, is the basic form on which many variations exist. Either the contractor or the client can be a group of companies, or the contract venture may be the same as the client, but the concept

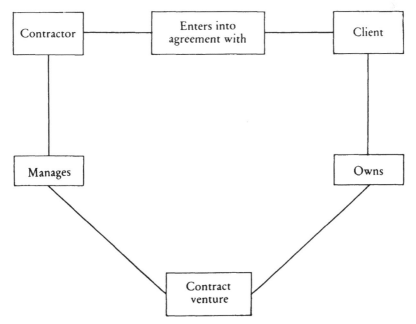

Figure 4.1 The management contract.

remains triangular. An entrepreneur in, for instance, Greece may want to invest in a hotel, but may lack the expertise to run it. He looks for an experienced hotel company, perhaps in France. As a result an agreement is drafted, whereby the French contractor undertakes to manage the hotel for five years with an option to renew the contract if both parties wish.

In drafting a contract, nine issues have to be addressed.

1 REMUNERATION

There are numerous ways by which the contractor company is paid for its services and the choice will partly depend on the bargaining strengths of the parties, partly on their perceptions of the future of the project and partly on external factors such as the tax systems in their two countries.

In one review (reported in Brooke, 1985, p. 156), twenty-four service sector projects used the following fee bases:

percentage of sales:	13
percentage of profits:	8
annual fixed fee:	3
fixed fee plus costs:	1
purchasing commissions:	1
marketing commissions:	0

An important consideration under this heading is the holding of equity. Although the client is, on principle, the owner of the venture, the contractor frequently takes some equity. From the client's point of view, this ensures extra commitment; for the contractor, there is an additional source of income, with the advantage that it provides a share in the success of the venture.

2 DURATION AND EXTENT

Five years has just been mentioned as an example of a time-limit to a contract; in fact, in the hotel industry, a longer period is usual, whereas a shorter duration of contract is common for transport undertakings, such as airlines. The extent also varies. For a railway system, the contractor may undertake the total management or that of the permanent way or maintenance facilities only. In the case of airlines, also, the contract may cover total operations or just maintenance.

Although there are such exceptions, the client normally argues for the maximum involvement of the contractor, at least when the contract is a new one. The contractor, on the other hand, may wish to stipulate that the various services – operations, marketing, accounting and training, for example – are contracted separately. This can enable a tighter control of costs and income.

3   REVIEW AND RENEWAL

Usually there will be clauses that provide for regular review during the period of the contract and renewal at the end. The client will wish the review clauses to include a performance assessment. The review usually covers the commercial success of the venture under the contractor's management, but is also likely to include issues that are particularly important to the client, such as the quality and image of the hotel. If the client is a developing country government, as happens in many transport undertakings, the review will probably extend to the contractor's success at recruiting and training local staff. The contract will stipulate arrangements for termination if the review demonstrates failures on the part of the contractor company, perhaps subject to a period (usually 30 to 90 days) for remedying the failures.

4   ARBITRATION

An essential clause is the one that provides for arbitration in the event of an irreconcilable dispute between the parties. It used to be fashionable to insist that licensing and franchising disputes should be regulated by the law of the licensor's country; and this became also the conventional wisdom for management contracts. Like much conventional wisdom, this is anachronistic, it goes back to colonial times. Nowadays it may not only be unenforceable, it may also be a positive disadvantage to the contractor. One example in which the law of the client country proved a positive advantage to a contractor was that of a transport undertaking in an African country. A court in the country awarded damages to the contractor for breach of contract on the part of the client – a public authority.

It is doubtful whether the damages would ever have been paid had they been awarded by a foreign court. Sometimes there is provision for an international arbitrator in the contract. The International Centre for the Settlement of Investment Disputes, in Geneva, and the International Chamber of Commerce, in Paris, provide facilities for this; but other arrangements may be possible, such as an individual or institution with a reputation that is acceptable to both parties.

A high proportion of the disputes brought before the International Chamber of Commerce's court have come from the hotel industry. Five main issues have emerged from these disputes:

(i)   poor drafting of the contract;
(ii)   inadequate performance on the part of the contractor;
(iii)   the client company misunderstanding its role and taking over some of the duties of the contractor, to the confusion of the contract venture;

(iv)   delays caused by third parties, such as when planning consents are required;

(v)   failure to prepare adequate accounts sufficiently regularly.

5   THE ROLES OF THE CONTRACTOR AND THE CLIENT

The essential feature of a management contract – as of other arrangements detailed in this chapter – is the business relationship. If this is satisfactory, the contract will remain unread in a filing cabinet. Drafting the contract is an opportunity to thrash out the kind of relationship that is desired. This includes broad issues, such as the extent of the powers of the contractor, and narrower questions such as the appointment of a representative of the contractor to the board of the contract venture or even of the client.

   In this connection, it must be remembered that there is an almost inevitable conflict of interest between the parties. The contractor will see the arrangement as part of a global strategy in which a commercial expertise is being sold where this method is more viable than that of establishing a subsidiary. The client will see the benefit in terms of the development of a specific business. In spite of this conflict, much evidence shows that a clear understanding of the respective roles can ensure a harmonious and profitable relationship. Spelling out the rival objectives can ensure this, although overemphasis can also produce unnecessary disputes. Skilful negotiations are required to ensure that the objectives of both sides can be achieved without introducing elements that make the roles incompatible.

6   LIABILITY AND INSURANCE

One reason for drafting a lengthy contract at all, especially when equity is at stake, is to clarify the liabilities that both parties are incurring. Suppose, for instance, a hotel burns down. The client company as the owner is liable to the local national laws. Naturally, it has recourse to the contractor if there has been a breach of an undertaking, but the contractor is not an insurance company and cannot be expected to undertake the role of one. In drafting the contract, the client will wish to ensure that the contractor does not limit his responsibilities unduly, while the latter will be concerned to avoid international liability for local problems. Insurance provision is an essential part of the contract.

7   SUPPLIES AND FACILITIES

In the case of tourist facilities or hotels, the contractor may also be a construction company or consultant. The provision of supplies and facilities may be a major source of remuneration, sometimes more important to the contractor than the fees for the management contract itself. This often leads to a conflict of interest when the client wants to limit its dependence on one source of supply. The demand for competition in purchasing may be included in the original bargaining, or may be incorporated when a review takes place.

8 ORGANIZATION

The management system is the most significant element in the expertise that the contractor is selling, and it will wish to incorporate its expertise in organization and control into the contract venture. If the venture is in a developing country, there may also be a problem with company law. Where this is not fully developed, it is often necessary to spell out the constitution of the board, the voting rights and the allocation of responsibilities among directors and managers.

9 STAFFING AND TRAINING

The transfer of management skills is a personal matter. It takes place through people rather than through systems. Both parties will wish that a proportion of expatriate managers are employed to effect the transfer; but there may well be disagreement about the qualifications and quality of the staff to be transferred and how quickly they can train local nationals. Management development policies are one of the most frequent causes of dispute, and clients are well advised to incorporate training targets into the agreement.

In sum, the management contract should be regarded as one option in the strategy of a tour operator, hotel chain or transport company. It enables extra revenue to be generated from expensively acquired expertise and, for the client, a rapid route to a viable business.

Turnkey ventures

Turnkey projects are arrangements where the process of constructing, making operative and usually initially running a facility are contracted to an outside enterprise (or enterprises) in return for a fee. The facility is then handed over to local interests. Most usually, the construction period is followed by a period covered by a management contract (and possibly a licensing arrangement) whereby continuing relationships with the outsiders provide for extended training and 'debugging'. The customers are usually governments who have decreed that a given product or service must be produced locally and under local control (Wright *et al.*, 1981).

Turnkey contracts, which end when the physical plant and equipment have been set up by the supplier in the host country, are referred to as 'light' turnkey contracts; those with clauses providing for the extensive training of local personnel are 'heavy' contracts.

Contracts referred to as 'product-in-hand' operations mean that the suppliers' responsibility is not fulfilled until the installation is completely operational with local personnel. Extension of contracts to 'market-in-hand' calls for the supplier to give assistance in, or in some cases to take responsibility for, the sale of at least part of the operation's output. Under some circumstances, 'buy-back', 'counter-purchase' or 'compensation' agreements call for the supplier to take payment direct in the form of physical output (Salem and Sansom, 1979; Weigand, 1980; Oman, 1980).

Conclusion

Firms in the international tourism industry face an array of methods of doing business. The choice of method will be contingent on circumstances. These circumstances may be restrictive, e.g. it may not be possible to enter a particular market via a wholly owned facility; it may be essential to have some element of local ownership. In this case, choice between a joint venture, a franchising agreement or a management contract will depend on the availability of skills in the entrant firm and in the host country, on the objectives of the entrant and on the forecast of market penetration likely to be achieved by each method – and on the likely return to the entrant. Alternatively, the determining factors may be permissive – which method represents the best way to enter a rapidly growing market when facing the threat of competitive entry by rivals? Is it necessary to build a complete network coverage of the market (e.g. for a hotel chain) or is entry only envisaged in a particular market segment? The internal constraints on international operation must not be forgotten – shortages of capital and management skills are the most obvious, but risk aversion may also be significant.

It is clear, however, that the choice of an appropriate set of methods of international operation is crucial to success in the industry. It is vital that firms pay attention to their market servicing strategy and adjust it to reflect changing circumstances. An appropriate market servicing strategy is not fixed, it is flexible and, given the dynamics of competition in tourism, it is necessary to give constant attention to the market servicing stance internationally.

Further reading

1 For an analysis of foreign market operations and the theory of the multinational firm, see Peter J. Buckley and Mark Casson (1976) *The Future of the Multinational Enterprise*, London: Macmillan, and the

same authors' *(1985) The Economic Theory of the Multinational Enterprise*, London: Macmillan. For a similar approach based on the 'eclectic theory', see John H. Dunning (1988) *Explaining International Production*, London: Unwin Hyman.

2   The role of multinational firms in tourism is most extensively examined by John H. Dunning and Matthew McQueen in the United Nations Centre on Transnational Corporations (UNCTC) 1982 publication *Transnational Corporations in International Tourism*. For a brief, concise summary, see Matthew McQueen (1989) 'Multinationals in tourism', in Stephen F. Witt and Luiz Moutinho (eds) *Tourism Marketing and Management Handbook*, Hemel Hempstead: Prentice-Hall.

3   The application of the 'eclectic theory' of international production to the international hotel industry is explained in John H. Dunning and Matthew McQueen (1981) 'The eclectic theory of the multinational enterprise and the international hotel industry', *Managerial and Decision Economics*, vol. 2, no. 4, and John H. Dunning and Matthew McQueen (1982) 'The eclectic theory of the multinational enterprise and the international hotel industry', in Alan M. Rugman (ed.), *New Theories of the Multinational Enterprise*, London: Croom Helm. The 1981 article presents a survey of the size, distribution and forms of international market servicing in the hotel industry.

4   For a detailed discussion of management contracts, including examples from the hotel and transport sectors, see M. Z. Brooke (1985), *Selling Management Services Contracts in International Business*, Eastbourne: Holt, Rinehart and Winston.

5

The international marketing of tourism

This chapter examines the international marketing of tourism from a number of viewpoints. First, we set the tourism market in context by examining the tourism transactions chain. This approach enables a framework of analysis of marketing decisions to be constructed. The main actors are considered and the relationships between them are delineated, thus enabling a more focused approach to targeting decisions. Secondly, we examine the marketing planning process from the viewpoint of a particular destination. This includes an examination of appropriate segmentation policies and the construction of a tourism marketing audit. It gives some tentative thoughts on the implementation of the tourism marketing plan. It should be borne in mind that a detailed knowledge of particular local tourism conditions may well modify the analysis given. Finally, we discuss the marketing of attractions, accommodation and transport and examine buyer behaviour.

It is important to differentiate between country-of-origin marketing, which is largely private sector, tour operator led, and destination country marketing, which is often public sector, national tourism organization driven. Marketing strategies must be conducted within a given institutional framework. Promotion strategies demonstrate that there is a fundamental difference in approach between tour operator led marketing, which is highly specific and segmented, and national tourism organization marketing strategy which is more general. National tourism organizations usually have no role in pricing decisions, because this major role is taken by an intermediary.

Tourism – the transactions chain

A great deal of time and effort is spent on the analysis of the tourism 'product'. Attempts to define the tourism market are also fraught with difficulty. The one element that can easily be defined is the tourist, although definitions differ (see Burkhart and Medlik, 1984, Appendix D, or P. E. Murphy, 1985, chapter 1). An analysis of transactions thus proceeds from the main actor – the tourist – and examines all the actor's transactions.

An individual transaction is carried out between two agents. One or both of these agents may then go on to carry out a further transaction, until the primary supplier or final consumer is reached. In this way, it is possible to build transactions chains of the types shown in Figure 5.1. Various typical forms of transactions chain may link the tourist with the primary suppliers of goods and services. The tourist product is then defined as all the goods and services for which the tourist transacts and the tourism market as the sum of these transactions.

Figure 5.1 shows four typical transaction chains. Transactions are shown classified by their spatial location: origin (the tourist's home), transit and transport, which may be within the origin country or transnational, and destination, which may be local or international. Tourist transactions are here listed as transport, accommodation, entertainment and amenities, and direct spend on (extra) food and accommodation.

Transaction chain *a* is the unpackaged chain, where the tourist

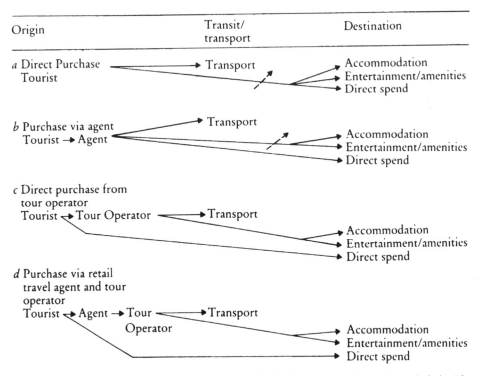

Origin	Transit/ transport	Destination

a Direct Purchase Tourist → Transport → Accommodation / Entertainment/amenities / Direct spend

b Purchase via agent Tourist → Agent → Transport → Accommodation / Entertainment/amenities / Direct spend

c Direct purchase from tour operator Tourist ⇌ Tour Operator → Transport → Accommodation / Entertainment/amenities / Direct spend

d Purchase via retail travel agent and tour operator Tourist ⇌ Agent → Tour Operator → Transport → Accommodation / Entertainment/amenities / Direct spend

Notes: The broken arrow indicates opportunity for brokerage. Food may be included with accommodation or be in 'direct spend'.

Figure 5.1 Transactional chains in tourism.

purchases all the transactions included in the tourist venture directly from the service providers. Type *b* shows a tourist purchase via a travel agent, who assembles some or all of the transactional elements, typically transport and accommodation, with some of the attendant entertainment and amenities. Type *c* shows the tourist purchasing a 'package' direct from the tour operator. Such direct selling of an 'inclusive tour' will normally cover transport and accommodation ready assembled and will possibly include certain other services, amenities and entertainment. Type *d* is the purchase of a package tour via a travel agent. Thus, a retail sale from agent to tourist is followed by a principal/agent relationship between the travel agent and tour operator, who provides ready assembled services.

There are opportunities for transactional brokers to interpose themselves at various points along the transactions chain. Such brokers will earn a commission by providing services to the transactional partners, involving specialist information (including local knowledge), opportunities to reduce costs by consolidating purchases or merely being more efficient transactors. The main brokerage opportunities are indicated by a broken arrow.

Organizational forces in tourism transactions

The organization of firms in the tourism transactions chain reflects the forces outlined above. In many cases, retail travel agents are able to offer services to tourists superior to those available by direct purchase. The agents' success depends on their superior access to information and specialist knowledge of markets and conditions. This enables agents to offer a service of advice and guidance to the individual tourist. Agents are also able to act on behalf of the principal, be it hotel, airline, tour operator or shipping company, in a personalized manner. The retail travel agent also offers a one-stop facility, allowing choice and enabling the customer to purchase the whole range of tourism products, thereby reducing the tourist's transactional search costs.

The tour operator consolidates the transactions that an independent tourist would make separately, and sells a single package to the customer. This not only gives the customer the convenience of purchasing a single composite product in one transaction, it also enables economies to be obtained on the supply side. The tour operator is able to enter into long-term contracts for accommodation and transport (often leading to internalization of this relationship, that is, the two functions are often combined in a single firm). Consequently, this permits high load factors for aircraft (ships and trains) and high occupancy rates for accommodation. Economies of scale and exercise of monopsony power can also reduce the operator's costs. This packaging enables mass marketing and standardization to take place. Branding by the tour operators across destinations results in increased consumer loyalty to the operator (and transference of loyalty from destination to operator). The operator can give explicit or implicit quality guarantees to the tourist and thus reduce the perceived risks of default, poor service and other transactional uncertainties. Tour operators can market their products via brochures, providing an initial screening of the myriad tourist products potentially available. For the tourist, uncertainty is reduced and quality guarantees are provided (see Burkart, 1975). M. F. Murphy (1985) shows that individual tour operators are perceived very differently with respect to their competition by travel agents.

The above analysis leads us to believe that the relationship between travel agents and tour operators is likely to be unstable.

IMPLICATIONS

The marketing implications of transactions analysis can be derived by reversing the transactions flow and looking back over the transactions chain. It is a peculiarity of the tourism market that final service providers must aim their marketing at quite different targets, as illustrated by the different types of transactions chain (Figure 5.1). The direct purchase, self-assembly package implied by chain *a* requires final service providers to reach the individual tourist directly. In the other types of transactions chain, intermediaries occur and marketing needs to be directed at them. These intermediaries may be tour operators and/or travel agencies. (A parallel analysis can be conducted for the strategies of National Tourism Promotional Agencies.) Similarly, tour operators must target marketing efforts at potential groups of tourists and travel agencies. In the rest of this chapter we shall examine, first, the marketing of destinations, secondly the marketing of attractions, acommodation and transport, and finally the marketing of tourist packages.

The analysis of linkages and the flow of intermediate products has implications not only for the packaging of tourism services but also for the nature of tourism enterprises in general. The above analysis shows that the nature of the transport function is crucial. The transport function is an important point in the exchange of rights in the tourism transaction chain. If this function is subcontracted to an independent operator this delicate and central function can go out of control: hence, the close integration of transport with other facilities in the integrated multinational. There are important cost implications also. Efficient utilization of capacity is crucial in keeping costs down in transport as well as in accommodation. Complete control of a fleet of aircraft or ships (one ship or aircraft for smaller companies) will impose severe cost penalties if these facilities are not fully utilized. Consequently, there is considerable instability arising from the necessity to balance control of transport with cost-efficient utilization.

The transport function is also important because it, uniquely, involves the transnational transfer of rights (and tourists). Its management, therefore, requires great skill and sensitivity. Further, it affords opportunities for international arbitrage and utilization of transfer-pricing techniques, which may have a significant impact on profitability.

Finally, the theory has important implications for quality management in tourism. Control of the transactions flow enables the integrated multinational to monitor and control the quality of services (Casson, 1985). This is often difficult to achieve through external contracts, because of the intangible nature of services and the difficulties of exercising day-to-day control other than by direct line management.

SUMMARY

The analysis of transactions and transaction costs provides a framework for the unification of concepts and analysis in tourism research. It provides a core theory that allows the analysis of tourism demand through the transactions chain and the organization of supply by its distinctive view of the forces driving organizational developments. The changing pattern of industry analysis and the scope of firms can be explained and predicted by internalization pressures. The approach has implications for marketing and for the future organization of the tourism industry, which we now examine.

The marketing planning process for a destination

This section concentrates on the marketing strategy of a destination country or region. The formulation of a tourism plan at various levels is essential, especially when the tourist sector has top priority in a country's overall development choices (Wahab, 1973). Further, the overriding aim of a systematic planning process is, as Argenti (1974) suggests, to focus attention on the relevant strengths, weaknesses, threats and opportunities. Consequently, the development of such a 'tourism-marketing planning process' identifies the main variables affecting international marketing operations of a national or regional tourism organization. The marketing of a destination by largely public sector bodies provides a framework within which private sector organizations can work. Figure 5.2 shows that the focus is on three areas:

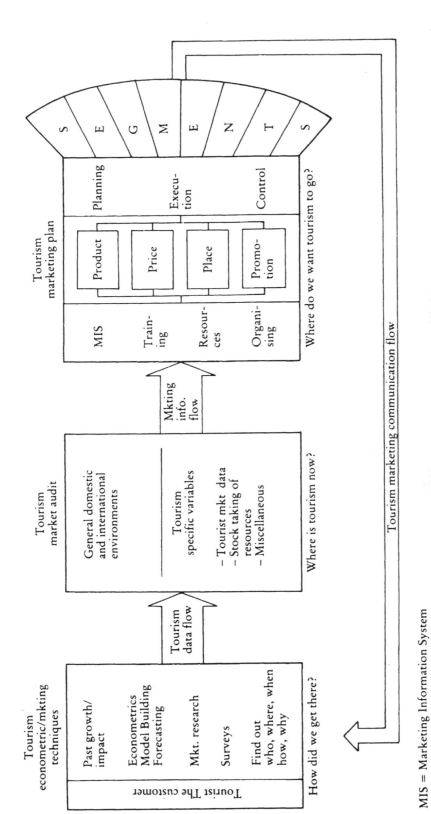

MIS = Marketing Information System

Figure 5.2 Tourism marketing planning process.

1   Where is tourism now?
2   How did we get there?
3   Where do we want tourism to go?

The main emphasis, therefore, is on a dynamic and continuous process with interrelated and interacting variables. It begins with the client (tour operator or tourist) and ends with the client. The overriding aim is to gather, process and utilize data when planning, executing and controlling marketing strategies and tactics in both the short term and the long term (see also Gilbert, 1990).

Visitor survey

Information on the current tourist market is essential. The large-scale survey of the United States pleasure travel market reported by Taylor (1989) is a model indication of this key fact. It is important to know:

* who the foreign tourist is;
* where (s)he comes from;
* when (s)he visits
* how (s)he travels; and
* why (s)he chooses the destination

A random sample of the foreign tourist population can be taken at the place of exit. Even a small sample can give a clear indication of the above vital issues (for the case of Greece, see Buckley and Papadopoulos, 1986). However, the weaknesses of asking about choice of destination after it has been made should be noted. This is sometimes inevitable on cost grounds, but it should be supplemented, where possible, by motivational studies elsewhere than at the place of visit. Reasons for travel to a destination may include: (1) 'cultural' tourism, (2) 'sun and sea' tourism, (3) winter sports, (4) 'lakes and mountains' type tourism and rural tourism. Although cultural tourism is a year-round activity, the other forms of tourism will exhibit seasonality. Luckily, winter sports counterbalance 'sun and sea' tourism to give some destinations all-year-round possibilities. New segments of the market can be investigated including:

1   Health resorts (including spas?)
2   Marine projects
3   Water ski resorts
4   Two-centre packages
5   Short-break holidays (off season?)
6   Conference tourism

Expenditure estimates for different categories of tourism are important. Expenditure varies by type of tourism (e.g. in general, business travellers are by far the biggest spenders) and by nationality.

Mode of travel is also important. Air facilities are crucial for international tourism. Good access by road and rail can provide a major boost for tourism. Cruise passengers may provide a further new and expanding segment, as a high proportion on cruise packages go ashore. The marketing challenge here is to increase spend per visit.

Seasonal fluctuations in demand are a considerable problem in planning tourism. Seasonality results in problems of employment, social and developmental difficulties and deterioration in the quality of services offered (Baron, 1975). These stem from the fact that tourist facilities, in particular in hotels and catering, are used to full capacity (or often overstretched) during the summer, but during the winter they are often under-used. The literature on tourism recommends efficient and effective promotional campaigns as a means to offset an uneven seasonal demand pattern. However, such actions have, on the one hand, to reflect existing and potential winter demand trends in the tourist generating countries and, on the other, to improve standards of winter tourist facilities in the host country. Apart from such promotional campaigns, there are other ways to reduce seasonality including lower fares and accommodation charges during the off-peak season, as well as special package deals for the winter months, conferences, festivals and sporting events. Unfortunately, control of these is not always in the hands of national or regional authorities and seasonality can be mitigated but not eliminated.

Target marketing

Policy makers and developers of tourism in destinations need to pay attention to visitor characteristics when developing a rational tourism marketing strategy. Clear market segments must be identified and an investigation made of the buying decision factors that predominate in that segment. The tourist product must then be aligned with the client profile. The tourist product is a composite product and there is more than one type of client. In particular, a careful distinction must be made between the tourist and the intermediary (tour operator and travel agent) in deciding on the marketing mix, with particular attention being paid to promotional elements and pricing policies. In addition, the products and services offered by the industry must match prevailing market demand.

Although the above tourist profile may suffice when formulating strategies and policies at a general-purpose level – for example, planning basic tourist infrastructure and amenities – such a tourist profile will do little in terms of developing an advertising campaign policy in a specific country or market segment. Hence, the need exists for a tourist profile for each market segment (major country of origin), which in turn can be interpreted in terms of an 'advertising brief' for individual promotional campaigns. As Kaynak and Yavas (1981) suggested in their study 'A profile analysis of visitors to Halifax, Canada', once purpose-oriented segments are identified they can be mapped, and forecasts can be made of their future importance based on projections of trends, thus helping policy makers to target their strategies more precisely.

A visitor survey can establish a visitor profile for each major country supplying tourists. Research findings of such studies can be incorporated in the 'tourism-marketing planning process', as presented in this chapter, to explain foreign tourist arrivals and assess the impact of promotional expenditure by the tourist organizations in major foreign tourist market segments.

TOURISM-MARKETING AUDIT

As far as 'where is tourism now?' is concerned, Table 5.1 shows that the main elements of a tourism-marketing audit consist of the general domestic and international environments and tourism-specific variables. The tourism-marketing audit begins with an examination of data on the general (domestic) economy, and then proceeds to the outlook for the growth of the market segments served by tourism. The international competitive environment is also included as part of the audit of the main tourist-generating markets served by the tourist industry. The main purpose of the 'external environment' audit is to assess the extent to which sociocultural and economic factors affect the likely course of the action the marketing executive might take in promoting tourism in various markets. This is because world tourist-generating countries exhibit considerable variation in industry structure and national income, both of which critically influence the tourist goods and services they are likely to need, and their ability to buy.

When the general domestic and international environment has been examined, the next step is to identify the tourism-specific variables that affect tourism, and study their relative importance when considering international marketing strategies. As regards tourist market data, it is essential to maintain periodic surveys to identify the type of tourist who travels to the destination and to pinpoint the factors that determine his preferences and purchasing behaviour.

In considering the stocktaking of resources, the main objective is to develop a comprehensive list of the tourist sector's 'supply elements', such as tourist infrastructure, tourist accommodation

Table 5.1   Tourism market audit.

DOMESTIC AND INTERNATIONAL COMPETITIVE ENVIRONMENT (Past, Present, Future)		
Economic		
Political		
Fiscal		
Sociocultural		
Business		
Legal		
Technical		
Environmental		
Ecological		
Relevant products		
Cost structure		
Marketing skills		
Key success and failure factors		
Consumerism		

TOURISM SPECIFIC VARIABLES (Past, Present, Future)		
Tourist market data	*Miscellaneous*	*Stock-taking of resources*
– Number of visitors, nationality and origination points	– Image abroad and reputation	– Tourist resources: cultural/historical environmental/ ecological
– Destination points	– Distance from points of origin	– Climate and other natural resources
– Purpose and reasons for visit	– Time from points of origin	– Recreational/dining/ entertainment/ shopping
– Attractions visited	– Costs from points of origin and within destination	– Conference/business/ exhibition facilities
– Services used in the destination and stopover area	– Propensity to travel	– Transportation
– Seasonality pattern	– Determinants and motivators	– Tourist accommodation
– Group or individual travel	– Sociocultural ties	– Tourist and other infrastructure
– First time or repeat visit incidence	– Educational ties	– Support industries
– Length of stay and expenditure	– Business links	– Land
– Sex and age group	– Safety and security	– Labour
– Occupation and income level	– Governmental attitudes	– Capital
– Means of transport and place of entry		– Public and private resources
– Satisfaction and complaints level		– Communications and scenery
		– National tourist offices

and a host of other facilities and services necessary to sustain a growing number of foreign tourists. This is because failure of the tourist sector to meet future tourist demand at the right time, right place and at the right price could lead to social and environmental problems, as well as the loss of much needed foreign tourist receipts. For a marketing audit to be successful, however, it needs to be carried out on a regular basis; audit programmes should be clearly defined and executives should be trained to use them effectively.

Supply of facilities and attractions

Some of the 'supply' aspects of tourism are listed above: cultural sites, sea, climate, winter resorts, mountains and countryside. Tourism based on such attractions is precarious unless the region can provide the various elements of the 'tourist supply', such as accommodation, infrastructure and the host of other services necessary to sustain a growing number of foreign tourists. In many destinations these elements represent a supply side constraint on tourism. There is clearly a need to develop the supply side in parallel with demand (for example, hotels). Segments, such as conference tourism, cannot be exploited until further large investment has taken place.

Implementation of the tourism marketing plan

Once the market study and resource analysis are carried out the planned application of available resources to achieve tourism objectives should begin. Successful tourism-marketing planning should include eight procedural steps, which are expressed in a flow chart in Figure 5.3. The chart identifies objective and comprehensive procedures, which the tourist authorities can take in translating goals into reality. Thus, the overall policy and major functional plans must be linked to, and exercise influence upon, the current operational decision-making process of all parts of the tourist organization. This can be done by bringing longer-term plans together with annual tactical planning activity for compatibility purposes. In this way, the resultant tourism strategy can be as Glueck (1976, p. 3) said, 'a unified, comprehensive and integrated plan designed to assure that the basic objectives of the enterprise are achieved'. The important distinction to be made between the tourism-marketing planning process and the tourism-marketing plan is that the former is a continuous function, whereas the latter is an expression of the output of the planning process at a particular moment and for a specified period. As Figure 5.3 shows, the tourism-marketing plan is part of the overall planning process and it represents the application of available resources to achieve tourism-marketing objectives.

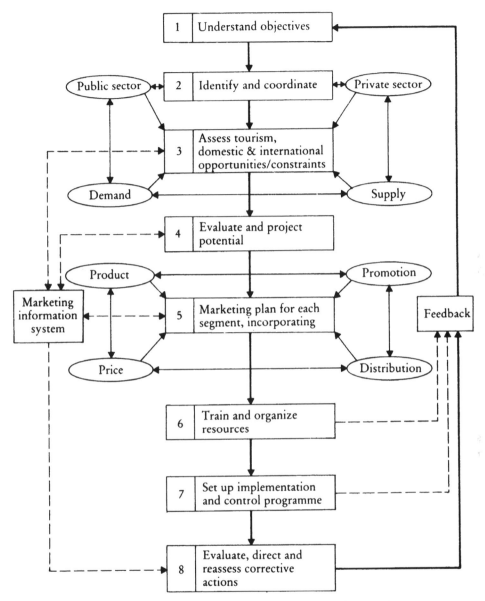

Figure 5.3 Tourism marketing plan – prerequisites and procedures.

After the analysis of strengths and opportunities, under the auspices of the marketing audit, setting tourism objectives should be relatively easy. Objectives should be realistic statements (qualitative or quantitative) of what the tourist authorities desire to achieve as a result of market-centred examination of each tourist segment. In addition, these objectives must be reassessed on a regular basis, having received feedback once plans are implemented.

The main purpose of step two in the planning process is to identify and co-ordinate the public and private sectors so that common marketing strategies can be formulated. Related to this is step three, which is to assess opportunities and constraints at the domestic and international levels. The overriding aim of these two steps is to examine the existence and efficiency of the various supply elements (for example, tourist accommodation, infrastructure, labour and other tourist amenities), in order to assess whether the tourist sector can meet future tourist demand.

After the main demand and supply aspects of tourism have been examined, step four proceeds to evaluate and project the potential for each major tourist-generating market by means of specially commissioned market research studies and forecasts. In addition, market intelligence information can be gathered, processed and utilized through a formalized marketing information system.

The heart of the marketing plan is step five, where the emphasis is placed upon the manner and extent to which each controllable marketing-mix variable is used and the way such factors are combined into a single strategy for each segment. The construction of individual programmes for product, price, distribution and promotion is a direct consequence of the overall tourism-marketing objectives, which in turn are influenced by internal and external constraints.

After the marketing-mix variables have been decided, the next step is to assign specific responsibility for carrying out individual tasks of the plan to various people, to instruct these people what to do and how to carry out their tasks, and to integrate time schedules so that allocation and sequencing of marketing effort are run efficiently. As soon as specific procedures are agreed upon and implementation begins, a control programme must be established, which should provide the tourist authorities with the necessary information to monitor progress towards predetermined objectives. Once the plan is implemented and performance monitored, implementation and objectives should be re-examined and revised in accordance with newly emerging market facts, and the whole cycle should start again.

The conclusion to be drawn from the above remarks is that the use of such a customer-oriented process has the advantage of being a simple and effective tool for analysis and implementation of strategies. However, it is essential for the tourist authorities to make sure that future prospects of inward tourism are adequately assessed by volume growth, tourism revenue and relative market share in each tourist-generating country before decisions on the desirable target market are taken and the allocation of strategic marketing funds among the various segments is made. The ability of national tourism organizations to have a major impact on the market is limited in many cases because the relative resources available are much less than those of carriers, operators and other actors in the market.

SUMMARY

A tourism-marketing planning process has been developed, in which the main variables affecting the international marketing operations of the regional and/or national tourist organization have been identified. The main emphasis is on customer rather than product orientation and on a dynamic and continuous process with inter-related and interacting variables. The importance of a market-driven rather than a product-driven approach cannot be overemphasized. The planning process begins with the client (tour operator/tourist) and ends with the client. The overriding aim is to gather, process and utilize data when planning, executing and controlling marketing strategies and tactics for both short-term and long-term dimensions.

The purpose of the above process, expressed in its simplest form, is to answer three central questions:

1 Where is tourism now, that is, what is the current state of the tourist industry?
2 Where is tourism heading?
3 How should the regional tourist authorities organize their resources to get there?

This marketing planning process can be used as a marketing tool to identify the problems, in order to avoid treating the wrong symptoms, and to take advantage of opportunities. In short, this is a structured approach to the collection and analysis of information in a complex tourism environment, which is an essential prerequisite to problem-solving. It is a conceptual framework that can be useful to all tourism-marketing planners when formulating target-marketing strategies.

Tourism-marketing planning, therefore, is multifaceted and requires an interdisciplinary and integrated approach. In addition, the applicability of the above marketing planning process in a dynamic market place depends on its flexibility and adaptability to market changes. Marketing decision-making activities, however original and exciting they may be, must be compatible with the organization's own resources, constraints and objectives (Majaro, 1980).

The market for tourist services is not static and it requires constant adjustment on the part of destination marketers. The ability of the destination's organizations to influence other key actors is often limited. One of the key roles that a national tourism organization can play is to increase the bargaining power of domestic actors (such as local hotels) versus tour operators. Co-operative behaviour in the destination country across the public–private sector divide is likely to be important in increasing the local value added from marketing efforts. Studies of marketing destination regions can be found in Goodall and Ashworth (1988), Ashworth and Goodall (1990) and Pearce (1989).

The marketing of attractions, accommodation and transport

Elements of marketing

Classic analyses of marketing examine the four Ps: product, pricing, promotion and 'place' (distribution). These elements are crucial in the analysis of marketing elements of the tourism package. The following section examines the problems of product formulation in tourism. Then pricing is considered, followed by an analysis of promotion and targeting strategies. Distribution systems and their organization follow. The use of SWOT analysis (Strengths – Weaknesses–Opportunities–Threats) is presented in order to unify the approach to these disparate elements of the tourism package.

Product formulation

One of the basic difficulties in marketing attractions in particular (historic buildings, parks and gardens, wildlife, museums, art galleries, amusement and leisure parks, natural scenery, monuments, etc.) is product formulation, that is, deciding what the product actually is and how it should be sold. As many aspects as possible should be encapsulated, but the product should not become so diffuse as to be unmanageable. This has a physical aspect – delineating and protecting the boundaries of the attraction (and preventing free entry) – and a conceptual aspect – selling the quintessential elements of the product and appropriating all the returns from this. Consequently, a holistic approach should be taken to packaging, selling, advertising and distributing the attraction: the experience needs to be 'all of one piece' to create distinctiveness. A great danger with high-profile unique attractions (for example, Stonehenge, the Alhambra in Granada) is the feeling that the product does not need to be marketed. This is a misconception. Benefits to the locality, region and country will be lost if a marketing approach is not taken – for instance, excursionists only will be attracted, spending only the admission fee in the locality, or high-spending segments (such as business travellers) will be missed altogether.

Similar problems occur with transport facilities and accommodation. Operators are selling a service, and this has to be marketed in a comprehensive fashion. Transport users demand ease of access, promptness, friendly and courteous treatment during the (often harrowing) experience of travel, information, comfort and secure delivery. All too often one aspect is promoted (for example, airline food) – often the most trivial element – on the grounds that the operators take for granted more crucial elements, which may lead consumers to discriminate in favour of rival suppliers and substitute means of transport.

Accommodation providers also need to consider the key elements that lead a consumer to choose their product rather than a competitor or substitute. As in all other cases, price will be a factor, but so too will quality, ease of access, location – including proximity to other attractions and facilities – services provided and promotion.

Pricing policies

Pricing policies in the tourism services industries are dictated by a number of key structural characteristics. These include:

1   Perishability of the product.
2   Volatility and seasonality of demand.
3   Capacity constraints.
4   Competitor strategies and the existence of close substitutes.

The perishability of the product requires that instantaneous decisions are necessary, and continuous reappraisals of strategy and tactics, in the pricing area as elsewhere, are the norm. The volatility and changing nature of demand, both seasonally and secularly (changes of taste), also require attention to information collection, understanding and response. Capacity constraints mean that price can be used to ration scarce capacity or as a weapon to fill spare capacity in order to at least cover fixed costs.

In any discussion of pricing policy it is necessary to say that changes in price are not necessarily the best response to changes in the external environment or to strategy changes. However, price is a flexible tool and one that takes instant effect, given that demand is not completely inelastic. Pricing does not take place in a vacuum. As well as the customer response or demand side constraint, it will usually be the case that pricing policy will be constrained by the reaction of competition. In markets dominated by a few producers (oligopolies), it is virtually certain that pricing moves will be matched and possibly anticipated by competitors, leading (in the extreme case) to a price war.

The crucial strength of pricing policy is the ability to discriminate on prices. Ideally, different prices should be charged to each group or individual, with a different price elasticity of demand. In an ideal world, this infinite price discrimination would maximize profits. In practice, this can be achieved only imperfectly. To achieve good practice in price discrimination, the operator needs to have a clear view of segmentation possibilities. Price discrimination can be practised spatially, temporally, by price–income elasticity and by tying in the product to other purchases, including bulk or repeat buying. Success in price discrimination depends on the ability to prevent arbitrage (or reselling) in the market. Spatial price discrimination can be practised where it is difficult to transport the service (as in most cases of tourism services) or where it is difficult or prohibitively expensive for the consumers to travel to purchase the service in a different location. Temporal price discrimination means selling the same service at different prices at different times. This practice can exist only in the absence of adequate future markets, which is generally the case in tourism markets. Discrimination by income categories depends on a targeting approach. Tied purchases of services are largely involved in package deals and repeat buying in deals offered by chains of hotels. The potential for all these forms of price discrimination exists in tourism services.

We should not, therefore, be surprised by the multiplicity of prices that exist in tourism services or by the complicated price structures that companies offer. In general, the service will have a published price – a long-term benchmark price with a number of effective prices, fixed only in the short term. The effective price will vary in space, time, segment and according to what else is purchased.

Pricing, like any other policy weapon, will be used to achieve the goals of the company: profitability, growth, market share, return on investment. The goals will vary according to prevailing demand, competitor reaction and the strategic situation of the company (including the need to cover costs).

Promotion

The marketing of tourism-related services is a complex issue because of the different means needed to reach the end-user. If we examine Figure 5.1, providers of accommodation, transport and entertainment services need to aim their promotional activities at a different target audience according to the type of transactions chain that they face. The independent traveller in the 'unpackaged' chain is an end-user and, as an individual or family purchaser, he will be difficult to reach other than by mass advertising techniques. The purchase of services through a travel agent requires travel agents to be informed of the services that suppliers can provide, requires point of sale terms to be available to the agent and may require incentives to agents to encourage them to push the services in competition with alternative service providers. The tour operator, who provides an inclusive tour (commonly known as a package tour) will have considerable bargaining power when confronting a single service provider (for example, a hotel) or destination. It will be necessary to present a more subtle type of promotion to the tour operator to gain favourable terms or to achieve a contract! Once an end-service provider is included in an inclusive tour, then the responsibility for promotion rests largely with the tour operator. Having contracted for a given number of beds in a hotel for a season, for example, the tour operator will wish to fill those beds by adequate promotion. In a sense the ultimate supplier of tourist services is even more removed from the end-user by the full transactions chain – purchase of an inclusive tour via a travel agent. Independent travel agents will be dealing with a number of competing tour operators, who will be aiming promotional activities at them and through them to the purchaser. Competition for the agent's space and time can lead to a transfer of returns from tour operators to travel agents. This has given a major incentive to direct selling operations by tour operators and to 'captive' travel agencies, related to selling holidays of one operator or to preferential selling of the co-owned operator's holidays.

Promotion strategy is thus closely linked to the make up of the market facing the service providers and the institutional setting of the tourism market. Co-ordination between the efforts of the largely public-sector destination marketing and the more specialized targeted private-sector firms is an essential element in successful marketing and planning.

Distribution

The basic aim of a distribution channel is to bring the product to its market. However, as we have seen, it is difficult to define product and market with exactitude in tourism services. The first part of this chapter illustrated the different distribution chains, and each chain has its own imperatives. For travel agents, like any retailer, the choice of location is vital in order to encourage entrance to purchasing the goods and services on offer.

DISTRIBUTION: THE INTEGRATION AND CONTROL OF ACTIVITIES

The forces making for the internal organization, control and co-ordination of separate activities within one firm have been the subject of analysis for a considerable time (Coase, 1937; Buckley and Casson, 1976; Williamson, 1975). Indeed the internalization of

previously unrelated activities within a single organization determines the scope of the firm. Internal markets, particularly those for
labour services, enable co-ordination and planning of sets of
transactions. Such internal arrangements are frequently more
satisfactory than long-term contracts. This may be because of
increased efficiency, largely through the reduction of transactions
costs, or it may enable the entrepreneur to appropriate more of the
gains from contracting. The boundary of the firm is governed by the
margin where the costs of organizing an extra transaction within the
firm are equal to costs involved in carrying out that transaction on
the open market. Changes that enable the entrepreneur to carry out
direction more effectively (for example, the development of systems
of communication, computerization, improved management
techniques) will thus tend to increase the size and scope of the firm.

The task of the entrepreneur is thus to carry out the direction of
resources at lower cost than the market. He may be aided in this by
exogenous factors, such as the tax system. Transfers of intermediate
goods and services within the firm are governed by internal transfer
prices, largely set at the discretion of management, rather than by
market prices. Such transfer prices may be manipulated in order to
reduce the firm's tax bill. This benefit of internalization is particularly
important in cross-national transactions where transfer prices can be
used to move funds and engineer profit increases in low tax regimes.

In markets, like tourism, that are information intensive, there are
additional advantages arising from internalization of certain
activities. The market for information is subject to uncertainties
arising from the possibility that the buyer cannot use or understand
the information that he is purchasing. Organizing insurance for
buyer uncertainty is costly and difficult. When buyer and seller are
the same firm, mutual insurance can be arranged and a satisfactory
price can be fixed. Discriminatory pricing of information can also be
exercised in an internal market. When resale is possible, price
discrimination cannot be practised in an external market. In
addition, internalization avoids difficulties arising from bilateral
concentration of market power, for example, a hotelier in a favoured
location transacting with a tour operator. If the tour operator owns
the hotel, uncertainty is reduced, although this, of course, is not
insurance against unpredictable externalities such as terrorist
activities or political crises.

The application of these principles applies in three directions:
horizontal integration, vertical integration and conglomerate
diversification. Horizontal integration applies to integration of
similar activities. A hotel chain is an example of the integration of
similar facilities in order to gain economies of scale and market
power. Economies of scale are gained in central booking facilities,

staff training, bulk purchasing, etc. Market power is gained in increasing the chain's share of the total market and facilitating practices such as branding (across essentially separate facilities), joint advertising and promotion, and cross-group pricing policies.

Vertical integration occurs where facilities in different positions in the value chain, or marketing channel, are combined under one ownership: for example, the integration of an airline within a tour operator's facilities. The superiority of internalization over con-tracting out of these facilities is generally that internalization gives complete control and allows quality of service to be carefully monitored. The integration of ownership of travel agents and tour operators is a further illustration. Such vertical integration choices are strategic moves by key actors to secure control over facilities upstream or downstream, in order to improve efficiency (and quality of service) or to deny the facilities to rival operators.

Conglomerate diversification is the integration of essentially dissimilar activities within a firm: for example, a book retailer owning a travel agency. Often the motive here is risk-reduction. The firm spreads risk across a number of disparate activities and is able to sustain troughs in business activity is one area while remaining able to siphon off profits during peaks. The naturally cyclical nature of the travel and tourism industry means that many of its constituent parts – hotel chains, travel operators and agencies – are ultimately owned by large, diversified, conglomerate firms.

At a less elevated level, there is often a case for hotels, attractions and leisure facilities to come together on a voluntary basis in order to conduct large-scale activities such as central booking or advertising. This quasi-internalization is an attempt to retain the independence and entrepreneurial flair of the smaller unit while reaping economies of scale in other areas.

Marketing analysis – the SWOT framework

In order to deal with the problems listed above, it is useful to have a fixed framework in which to organize the essential foundations of a marketing exercise. Such a framework is provided by organizing these elements into strengths, weaknesses, opportunities and threats. The best way to illustrate is to give an analysis of one attraction as an example. Here, we take the National Museum of Photography, Film and Television in Bradford, England. Figure 5.4 provides a suggestion of how a SWOT analysis might look.

The cruciform chart (Figure 5.4) is a means of organizing a considerable amount of information. The upper two quadrants (strengths and weaknesses) are the outcome of an internal appraisal. This is an attempt to identify key competitive competences and

Strengths	Weakness
National Museum	Image of Bradford
Extensive exhibits	Lack of support facilities
Unique niche – clear target markets	(hotels, infrastructure, transport)
Locational centrality in UK	Lack of awareness of Museum
Large regional catchment	
Population/travel time to Bradford	

Opportunities	Threats
Urban leisure market	Cost of travel increasing
Packaging with other attractions	Overcrowding of facilities
(e.g. Victoria and Albert in Bradford)	Switch in taste
Regional tourist node	Potential substitute developing
Cheap site – development of local area	
Lack of regional competition	
Expanded awareness through	
promotions	

Figure 5.4   The National Museum of Film, Photography and Television: SWOT Analysis, Cruciform Chart.

significant deficiencies in the operating organization. The lower two quadrants show the outcome of an environmental analysis, focusing on likely changes in the environment, both positive (opportunities) and negative (threats). The SWOT analysis is therefore a distillation of a great amount of (it is hoped) reliable information. The conduct of internal appraisal and external analysis should be a continuous and constantly updated process (Ansoff, 1965; Argenti, 1974).

Buyer behaviour

The analysis throughout this chapter has emphasized the necessity to pay attention to demand. Purchasers and their needs are not homogeneous. It is necessary, therefore, to collect and to update information on purchasers and their behaviour. It is dangerous to define buyers and their purchasing behaviour too closely. The alternative purchase for a package holiday may be a new bathroom, kitchen or down-payment on a car. 'Do-it-yourself' purchases and leisure expenditure are close substitutes for the disposable incomes of many families. Factors that reduce disposable income will have a prior impact on spending, reducing all forms of consumer expenditure – examples are taxation levels, and interest rates, which make the burden of debt greater.

Analyses of consumer behaviour have moved away from reliance on price as the sole indicator of purchasing patterns. There is a necessity to investigate and influence wherever possible the motivations underlying the purchase of tourism products by firms hoping to sell them. See, for example, the motivational study on Saudi Arabian travellers by Yavas (1987).

It is essential that tourism firms and operators identify and monitor the key variables that determine consumer behaviour. These include income levels, factors that influence disposable income (such as taxation), changes in the distribution of income (by age, region, occupational groupings), patterns in consumer spending. A variety of models is available to do this (see Mazenec, 1989, and Chapter 3 above).

The understanding and prediction of consumer behaviour is a vital competitive skill for firms in the industry. Social, political and technological change will all affect buyer behaviour. In addition, the promotion and advertising strategies of tourism companies can affect purchasing patterns. Promotion strategies introduce the product offering, attempt to confirm and reinforce positive attitudes to the product, extend and deepen consumer awareness of the product, and attempt to change attitudes and behaviour toward purchasing the firm's product. Promotion does not end with purchase. Customer services and aftercare are vital elements of promotion essential to ensuring repeat purchasing.

Conclusion

The key issue in examining marketing in tourism-related industries is marketing 'by whom, to whom?'. The crucial operational question for marketing professionals is 'what is the target market(s)?'. It follows from that operational question that product formulation, pricing, promotion and distribution must be predicated on a clear strategy of targeting. This can only be achieved by an extensive and ongoing policy of information-gathering and analysis. An understanding of organizational forces is a key element in a coherent market strategy.

Information is the lifeblood of tourism planning. It is essential for destination marketers to have information on the type of visitor attracted. This also applies to operators of hotels and attractions, whose customer lists are vital sources of excellent marketing information. Marketing efforts must be targeted at those segments most likely to respond and to the desired client profile.

Key marketing issues include product formulation, pricing, promotion and effective distribution. It is essential to place these elements in a coherent and consistent framework, such as the SWOT (Strengths, Weaknesses, Opportunities, Threats) analysis presented in outline above. The marketing strategy must be compatible with the overall corporate planning policies detailed in Chapter 9.

The marketing of tourism does not and should not exist in a vacuum. It must be responsive to economic, social, political and technological changes. It behoves tourism firms, destinations and operators to monitor movements in these underlying factors. The use of free and cheap information is a vital input to this – marketing information systems need not be expensive. Much useful information is under-used: for instance, information on past buyers (and non buyers) is held by many firms. A great deal of marketing competitiveness depends on awareness and responsiveness.

Further reading

1   For a theoretical analysis of the tourism industry see: Peter J. Buckley (1987) 'Tourism an economic transactions analysis', *Tourism Management*, vol. 8, no. 3, September 1987, pp. 190–5.
2   An example of marketing mainly at the national tourism organization level is given in P. J. Buckley and S. I. Papadopoulos (1986) 'Marketing Greek tourism – the planning process', *Tourism Management*, vol. 7, no. 2, June 1986, pp. 86–100. See also P. J. Buckley and S. I. Papadopoulos 'Foreign direct investment in the tourism sector of the Greek economy', *The Services Industries Journal*, vol. 8, no. 3, July 1988, pp. 370–88.
3   A comprehensive text on marketing in tourism is: V. T. C. Middleton (1988) *Marketing in Travel and Tourism*, London: Heinemann. See also A. Jefferson and L. Lickorish (1988) *Marketing Tourism: A practical guide*, London: Longman.
4   An extensive analysis of marketing is given in S. F. Witt and L. Moutinho (1989) *Tourism Marketing and Management Handbook*, Hemel Hempstead: Prentice-Hall.

6

Finance and control

Introduction

Although the tourism industry comprises a variety of organizations – hotels, tour operators, airlines, and so on – financial considerations are important to all of them. Firms create wealth by making successful investment decisions, which generate positive net cash flows. They make money, satisfying consumer wants by matching the resources of the organization to the needs of the market place. *Investment* decisions are crucial in that they decide the level of future cash flows, generated from successful trading, but *financing* decisions also have an impact on profitability (Dobbins and Witt, 1988). In particular, foreign exchange management can be very important for firms in the international tourism industry.

Tourism managers need to plan in order to ensure that the activities of the organization are financially feasible. The control function consists of making sure that these plans are carried out, taking into account the need to modify the plans where necessary in order to meet changing circumstances (Chisman, 1989).

Investment appraisal

The value of money is time-dependent – $1 now is worth more than $1 at some future date – and this needs to be taken into account in assessing investment opportunities. The appropriate technique is known as discounting; thus, a future sum of money may be transformed into an equivalent present sum of money by applying a discount rate. Selection of an appropriate discount rate allows the present values of all the project's forecast cash flows at various future dates to be obtained. As the cash flows are valued on a consistent basis, they may now be compared. Therefore, the forecast cash flow profiles attaching to investment opportunities may be evaluated in terms of their present values in order to determine the profitability of the projects. The discount rate chosen depends upon the riskiness of the forecast cash flows; those that are subject to considerable variability (risk) need to be discounted at a higher rate than less risky cash flows.

Financial management is concerned with how much the firm should invest and in which projects. Although it is clearly important for firms in the tourism industry to evaluate investment opportunities correctly, successful investment programmes are more dependent on the ability of the firm to *create* profitable investment opportunities than on its investment *appraisal* ability.

Net present value

An investment is only wealth-creating if the present value of all forecast cash inflows (from customers) associated with the project exceeds the present value of all forecast cash outflows (to suppliers of labour, goods, etc.) relating to the project. Investment decisions usually involve an initial capital expenditure, followed by a stream of cash receipts and disbursements in subsequent periods. The following net present value (NPV) formula may be used to evaluate the desirability of investment opportunities:

$$NPV = \sum_{t=1}^{n} \frac{X_t}{(1 + k)^t} - I \qquad (6.1)$$

where

NPV = the net present value of the project

$\sum_{t=1}^{n}$ = summation over years, 1,2, . . ., n

X_t = the forecast net cash flow arising at the end of year t, that is, the difference between operational cash receipts and operational cash expenditures (including additional investment)

k = the required rate of return (or discount rate)

n = the life of the project in years

I = the initial cost of the investment

Thus, the net present value of a project is obtained by summing the forecast net cash flows over the project's life, discounted at a rate which reflects the cost of a loan of equivalent risk on the capital market, and deducting the initial investment outlay. Hence, an investment is profitable if its NPV is positive, so *all projects that offer a positive net present value when discounted at the required rate of return for the investment should be accepted* in order to maximize wealth.

For example, suppose that a particular tourism project requires an initial investment of $1,000 and that the forecast net cash inflows are $620 receivable after one year and $580 receivable after two years. The firm divides its various projects into three categories: class A where the risk is below average and the required rate of return is 10 per cent; class B where the risk is average for the particular sector of the tourism industry and the required rate of return is 13 per cent; class C where the risk is above average and the required rate of return is 16 per cent. The project may be evaluated from the NPV viewpoint by substituting into equation (6.1) as follows:

If the project falls in class A

$$NPV = \frac{620}{1 + 0.1} + \frac{580}{(1 + 0.1)^2} - 1,000$$

$$= \$40$$

If the project falls in class B

$$NPV = \frac{620}{1 + 0.13} + \frac{580}{(1 + 0.13)^2} - 1,000$$

$$= \$0$$

If the project falls in class C

$$NPV = \frac{620}{1 + 0.16} + \frac{580}{(1 + 0.16)^2} - 1,000$$

$$= -\$30$$

Thus, if the project is classified as below average risk, then it has a net present value of $40; as the NPV is positive the project should be accepted – given the forecast cash flows, the profitability of the tourism firm should rise by $40 as a result. If the project is classified as average risk, it has a net present value of $0; the project is barely acceptable in this case. If the project is regarded as being of above average risk, then the NPV is −$30; as the NPV is negative the project is unacceptable and should be rejected.

Investors do not like risk, and the greater the riskiness of returns on an investment, the greater will be the return expected by investors. Accordingly, there is a trade-off between risk and expected return, which must be reflected in the required rates of return on investment opportunities.

Figure 6.1 shows the risk–return relationships of seven projects. Investors can diversify shareholdings across companies, so they only

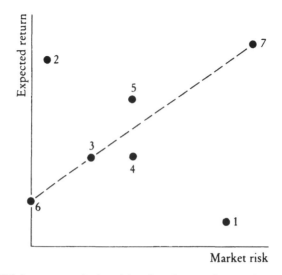

Figure 6.1   Risk-return relationships for alternative projects.

need compensation for the risk that cannot be diversified away, that is, that part of the riskiness of cash flows that is associated with general movements in the economy (the market risk). That part of the total riskiness of cash flows that is unique to the individual company (the specific risk) is of no concern to the investor with a well-diversified portfolio. Note that the dotted line in Figure 6.1 indicates the trade-off between expected return and market risk for *securities*. Projects 3, 6 and 7 fall on the line and thus their expected returns just compensate for their riskiness, that is, they have net present values of zero. Projects 2 and 5 lie above the line and thus their expected returns are higher than those required for the corresponding risk levels, that is, they have positive net present values. Projects 1 and 4, which lie below the line, have negative net present values. The efficient market hypothesis (which states that, at any point in time, share prices fully reflect all information available to stock exchange participants) implies that the risk–return combinations of all quoted securities fall on the line. Product markets, however, are not perfectly efficient, and it is a tourism manager's task to locate projects (such as 2 and 5) that lie above the line. These projects have positive net present values and, therefore, offer profitable opportunities.

The precise form of the relationship between risk and return for a quoted security is given by the capital-asset pricing model:

$$E(R_i) = R_F + \beta_i [E(R_M) - R_F] \qquad (6.2)$$

where

$E(R_i)$ is the expected rate of return on any individual security (or portfolio of securities)

R_F is the risk-free rate of interest,

$E(R_M)$ is the expected rate of return on the market portfolio, and

β_i is the market sensitivity index of the individual security (or portfolio of securities).

The market portfolio contains all risky securities in proportions reflecting the total equity values of the companies they represent. Equation (6.2) states that there is a linear relationship between the expected return on a security and its market risk as measured by its β (beta) factor. When $\beta = 0$, the expected rate of return is equal to the risk-free rate of interest, but for risky investments ($\beta > 0$), the expected rate of return exceeds the risk-free rate of interest by an amount proportional to the market sensitivity (β) of the investment. A β value of unity implies that the market risk of the security is equal to that of the market portfolio, a β value greater than unity implies that if the market rises (falls) by one per cent the return on the security is expected to rise (fall) by more than one per cent, and a β value less than unity implies that the security is less sensitive to market fluctuations than the market portfolio.

The capital-asset pricing model (6.2) shows the minimum rate of return acceptable on *all investments* for a given level of market risk; it represents the *opportunity cost of investment*. Substituting this minimum acceptable rate of return for the required rate of return (k) in the net present value formula (6.1) gives:

$$NPV = \sum_{t=1}^{n} \frac{X_t}{\{1 + R_c + \beta_i [E(R_M) - R_F]\}^t} - I \qquad (6.3)$$

In order to calculate the net present value of project i it is necessary to substitute its market value, β_i, into equation (6.3).

A firm's beta can be calculated by regressing its periodic returns on the periodic returns of the market index using least squares estimation. Alternatively, the beta value of a quoted company may be located in one of several *risk measurement services*, and the beta value of an unquoted company (or each division of a divisionalized quoted company) can be approximated by the average beta of independent quoted companies in the same tourism sector or risk class.

The firm's beta identifies the average required rate of return from the capital-asset pricing model (6.2), but this average cost of capital cannot be used for individual projects. Figure 6.2 shows the errors

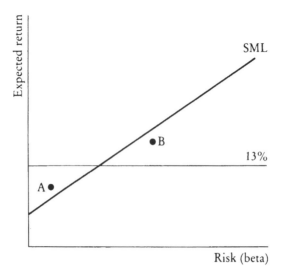

Figure 6.2 Trade-off between risk and return.

that can be made if the risk on individual projects is ignored. Suppose that the tourism company has two projects – a low risk investment and a high risk investment – and we know that the average required rate of return is 13 per cent. The security market line (SML) depicts the linear trade-off between risk and return embodied in the capital-asset pricing model (6.2). Now if the financial manager ignores individual project risk and discounts the anticipated cash flows on all projects at 13 percent, then project A would be rejected because it earns less than 13 per cent. However, the SML illustrates that project A should be accepted because it earns a higher rate of return than the required rate of return. It has a positive net present value. Project B earns more than 13 per cent. The financial manager might accept it. However, it is expected to earn a lower rate of return than the required rate of return for a project with its individual level of risk. It should be rejected. If we ignore risk in the capital budgeting process, then there will be a tendency to reject low risk profitable projects such as project A, and a tendency to accept high risk unprofitable projects such as project B. It is, therefore, essential to discount anticipated cash flows on individual projects at different discount rates. The discount rate or required rate of return depends upon individual project risk.

Theoretically, a beta coefficient should be estimated for each individual project within the firm, but this would prove extremely difficult, and for practical purposes all that is necessary is to classify projects into, say, three risk categories as illustrated in Figure 6.3. In our example, we have a firm operating in a sector of the tourism industry where average risk projects (group B) have a required rate of return (k) of 13 per cent, below average risk projects (group A) have a required rate of return of 10 per cent and above average risk projects (group C) have a discount rate of 16 per cent. These rates are calculated from the capital-asset pricing model as follows. Suppose that the risk-free rate of interest is 9 per cent and the expected rate of return on the market portfolio is 16 per cent (that is, the risk premium for investment in the market portfolio is 16 − 9 = 7 per cent). The β value for the firm is 0.57. Substituting into equation (6.2) gives

$$k = R_F + \beta_i [E(R_M) - R_F]$$

$$= 0.09 + 0.57 \times 0.07$$

$$= 13 \text{ per cent}$$

which is the required rate of return on average risk projects.

The discount rates for below average and above average risk projects are calculated as follows. The categorization of projects into low risk, average risk and high risk depends upon the extent to which the cash flows anticipated on the project are expected to move with the average for the firm. Now the risk premium for investment in the market portfolio is 7 per cent, and suppose that the risk premiums for investment in low risk and high risk projects are 2 per cent and 12 per cent respectively. By substituting into equation (6.2), the required rate of return on low risk investments is

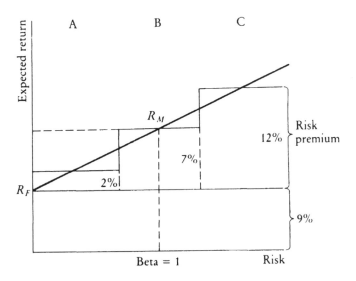

Figure 6.3   Assessing individual project risk.

$$k = 0.09 + 0.57 \times 0.02$$

$$= 10 \text{ per cent.}$$

Similarly, the required rate of return on high risk investments is

$$k = 0.09 + 0.57 \times 0.12$$

$$= 16 \text{ per cent.}$$

The procedure is obviously crude, but it is an improvement on net present value using the estimated overall cost of capital regardless of the riskiness of individual projects.

A firm's beta is influenced by economic risk and financial risk. Financial risk arises on the introduction of debt into a firm's capital structure. Projects should offer returns commensurate with their *economic* risk, and it is, therefore, necessary to reduce the reported or calculated corporate beta to an unlevered corporate beta for the purposes of capital expenditure analysis. A published beta can be reduced to an ungeared beta as follows:

$$\beta_u = \frac{\beta_l}{1 + (1 - t)\,(D/E)} \tag{6.4}$$

where β_u is the ungeared beta,
  β_l is the published leveraged beta,
  t is the tax rate,
  D is the market value of debt, and
  E is the market value of equity.

For example, suppose that an airline's published or levered beta is 1.5, its debt-equity ratio is 0.4, and the tax rate is 52 per cent. The unlevered beta is given by substituting into equation (6.4):

$$\frac{1.5}{1 + (0.48)\,(0.4)} = 1.26$$

The net present value rule offers a theoretically correct answer on whether an investment opportunity should be accepted or rejected, but in practice many other techniques are used in investment appraisal. Some alternatives to NPV are now considered.

Internal rate of return

The internal rate of return (IRR), or yield, on a project is the rate of return which equates the present value of anticipated net cash flows with the initial outlay. To calculate the internal rate of return it is necessary to solve the following formula for r:

$$0 = \sum_{t=1}^{n} \frac{X_t}{(1 + r)^t} - I \qquad (6.5)$$

where

X_t = the net cash flow arising at the end of year t
n = the life of the project in years
I = the initial cost of the investment.

r is thus the rate of return, which gives a zero NPV. A project is acceptable if its yield or internal rate of return is greater than the required rate of return on the project (k). This method of project appraisal usually gives the same accept/reject decision as NPV. Projects with positive NPVs will have values of r greater than k. In the case of the example used to illustrate the NPV rule, the internal rate of return on the project is 13 per cent, that is:

$$0 = \frac{620}{1 + 0.13} + \frac{580}{(1 + 0.13)^2} - 1000$$

Hence, in our previous example, if the tourism project is in class A then it is acceptable, because the yield of 13 per cent is greater than the required rate of return of 10 per cent. If the project is classified as B, it is just about acceptable, but it would be rejected as a class C project.

Tourism managers are recommended to use the NPV method to assess capital projects because it is easier to handle than IRR. In addition, there are several problems associated with internal rate of return. For example, the size of a project needs to be borne in mind. Suppose there are two mutually exclusive investment opportunities, project (i) involving a $20,000 initial outlay and offering an internal rate of return of 30 per cent, and project (ii) involving a $10,000 initial outlay and offering an internal rate of return of 40 per cent. In this case project (i) may well have a higher NPV than project (ii). Thus, the smaller project has a higher IRR and the larger project a higher NPV. If an investor has $20,000 to invest, then he can either select project (i), or alternatively invest $10,000 in project (ii) and $10,000 elsewhere. The NPVs of the two $20,000 investment schedules may then be compared and that with the higher NPV selected. NPV is a direct measure of wealth creation and, therefore, is the relevant criterion upon which project acceptance or rejection should be based.

A second problem associated with internal rate of return is that multiple solutions may exist to the IRR equation (6.5). Multiple solutions occur when the net cash flow changes sign: for example, a negative initial outlay may be followed by a positive net cash flow at the end of the first year, a negative flow at the end of the second year, and a positive flow at the end of the third year. When several internal rates of return satisfy equation (6.5), it is difficult to use this method to assess projects, whereas the NPV rule presents no such problems.

Other complications occur with the IRR rule when it is necessary to make decisions between mutually exclusive projects with different lives or with different patterns of cash flows.

Profitability index (cost–benefit ratio)

The profitability index (PI), or cost–benefit ratio, on a project is the present value of the forecast net cash flows divided by the initial outlay. The only difference between the NPV and PI methods is that when using the NPV technique the initial outlay is deducted from the present value of anticipated cash flows, whereas with the PI approach the initial outlay is used as a divisor.

$$ PI = \sum_{t=1}^{n} \frac{X_t}{(1 + k)^t} \bigg/ I \qquad (6.6) $$

where X_t, k, n and I are as defined in equation (6.1). A project is acceptable if the profitability index exceeds unity. Clearly, if the NPV > 0, then the PI > 1.

If we return to our previous example, where the NPV of the tourism project was $40 as a class A project, $0 as a class B project, and −$30 as a class C project, we can see that the corresponding PI values are 1.04 for class A, 1.00 for class B, and 0.97 for class C.

The PI method gives exactly the same accept/reject indication as that offered by NPV. As with internal rate of return, however, complications occur with the PI rule when it is necessary to make decisions between mutually exclusive projects.

Payback period

The payback period is the length of time required to recover the initial investment. It is generally assumed that the shorter the payback period, the better is the investment. In our example, the payback period is two years if the cash flows are received at the end of the first year and the end of the second year. By the end of the second year the sum of $1,200 is expected to be received, which more than recovers the initial outlay of $1,000. If the cash flows are receivable on a monthly basis, the payback period is approximately one and two-thirds years. Given the estimated payback period, it is necessary to decide whether the project is acceptable. Clearly, however, we do not have enough information to make a decision, because we do not know whether or not the project is wealth-creating. The payback method involves the subjective establishment of an acceptable payback period (frequently cited as two and a half years), and ignores possible big returns beyond the payback point. Most managers, however, are eminently sensible people, who in practice do not ignore big payoffs beyond the cut-off point. The main advantage with the payback period criterion is its simplicity. Payback period is used to test a manager's gut-reaction to a project; it gives him/her a feel regarding the length of time cash is at risk. However, it does not indicate whether a project is wealth-creating.

Discounted payback period

The discounted payback period differs from the payback period in that the payback period is calculated after discounting the cash flows, so in general it is longer than the payback period. In our example, the NPV for a class A project is $40 over two years on an initial outlay of $1,000. The discounted payback period is, therefore, just under two years. For a class B project the NPV is $0 over two years, so the discounted payback period is two years. For an above-average risk project (class C) payback is never achieved.

Discounted payback period represents a considerable improvement over payback period in that it allows for the riskiness of the project to be taken into account. As with payback period, we cannot decide on an appropriate given period for discounted payback that would show whether a project is wealth-creating, but once discounted payback is achieved any further discounted net cash flows would result in the creation of wealth. This method of investment appraisal does not give an indication of the magnitude of wealth-creation, however.

Return on capital employed

Return on capital employed (ROCE), or accounting rate of return, is widely used as an indicator of performance. It is generally assumed that the greater the ROCE, the better is the investment. ROCE is simply accounting profit measured as a percentage of capital employed, but this ratio ignores the size of cash flows, the timing of cash flows and risk.

In the tourism example we are considering, the cash flows are $620 at the end of year 1 and $580 at the end of year 2. If the initial investment is written off on a straight-line basis, then depreciation would be $500 in year 1 and $500 in year 2. Accounting profit is therefore $120 in year 1 and $80 in year 2. The capital employed of $1,000 falls to $500 at the end of year 1 and zero at the end of year 2. The average capital employed is therefore $750 in year 1 and $250 in year 2. Hence, the tourism project offers a return on capital employed of 16 per cent in the first year and 32 per cent in the second year. We now have to decide if the project is acceptable, but we cannot make a decision on the basis of this information. ROCE does not indicate whether the project is wealth-creating. It is also clear that ROCE depends to some extent on the firm's depreciation policy.

Effect on earnings per share

Earnings per share (EPS) is calculated by dividing acounting profit by the number of shares issued. It is generally assumed that the higher the EPS, the better. The ratio ignores the size and timing of cash flows, and risk, and thus is inappropriate. It is, however, another widely used indicator of performance, showing the amount of accounting profit a company has earned in one year for each share issued by the company.

In our example, suppose that the company issues 100 shares of $10 each to finance the project. In year 1 accounting profit is $120, and thus EPS amount to $1.20. In year 2 accounting profit is $80, and so EPS amount to $0.80. We now have to decide if the project is acceptable, but cannot do so on the basis of this information. EPS does not show whether the present value of the forecast net cash flows generated by the project exceeds the initial cost of the investment.

Summary

The objective of the firm is to maximize the wealth of its shareholders. An investment is wealth-creating if its net present value is positive, so *all projects that offer a positive net present value when discounted at the required rate of return for the investment should be accepted*. Uncertainty surrounds the future returns from any capital investment, and the discount rate must reflect the riskiness of the project.

Although NPV is the theoretically correct approach to project appraisal, in practice simple models such as payback period are still popular, and have the merit of being easy to understand and calculate. One reason given for the use of payback analysis is that its strong emphasis on the early years of a project's life is appropriate to recent economic conditions under which medium and long-term tourism forecasting have been extremely difficult and hazardous.

Furthermore, when tourism investment in 'risky' countries is under consideration the payback period may well be very important.

The major problem with the NPV approach is the difficulty associated with forecasting cash flows. On balance, then, the *NPV rule is a practical and rational approach to project evaluation.* Notwithstanding its intrinsic faults, however, *payback analysis is the most popular technique used by managers.* Perhaps, then, *both techniques should be used*; NPV because it gives a guide to the amount of wealth being created, and payback because it tests a manager's instinctive reaction to cash at risk and because it is very easy to calculate. It is up to managers in the tourism industry to decide whether the calculated payback periods are acceptable.

Profit planning and control

Contribution

Sales minus total costs equals profit:

$$S - TC = P \qquad (6.7)$$

where

$$
\begin{aligned}
S &= \text{sales} \\
TC &= \text{total costs, and} \\
P &= \text{profit}
\end{aligned}
$$

Total costs can be split into those costs that vary with the level of output and those costs that do not. Those costs that do vary with the level of output or sales are cailed *variable* costs (for example, the cost of aviation fuel for an airline). Those costs that do not vary with the level of output are called *fixed* costs (for example, office rent and straight-line depreciation).

$$VC + FC = TC \qquad (6.8)$$

where

$$
\begin{aligned}
VC &= \text{variablc costs, and} \\
FC &= \text{fixed costs}
\end{aligned}
$$

The theory of profit planning suggests that we should first deduct the variable costs from sales to identify the contribution towards fixed costs and profit.

$$S - VC = C \qquad (6.9)$$

where

$$C = \text{contribution towards fixed costs and profit.}$$

Having identified the contribution, we can deduct the fixed costs to give the profit.

$$C - FC = P \qquad (6.10)$$

For break-even:

$$S - TC = 0 \qquad (6.11)$$

$$C - FC = 0 \qquad (6.12)$$

Once we have identified the fixed and variable costs, it is possible to plan for profit. For any target level of sales we can estimate the resulting profit, and for any profit target we can estimate the required level of sales or units sold. Furthermore, on the launch of a new product (say, a new inclusive tour by a tour operator), a manager will usually want to know the level of sales required for break-even, where the venture makes no profit but at least does not result in a loss. From the above, we can identify two definitions of break-even. First, when sales and total costs are equal, the profit is zero. Secondly, when the contribution (sales less variable costs) is just enough to cover the fixed costs ($C - FC = 0$), the venture shows neither profit nor loss.

The two alternative definitions of break-even embodied in equations (6.11) and (6.12) are illustrated in Figure 6.4, the break-even chart. Part A corresponds to equation (6.11); here the break-even level of sales arises when sales are equal to total costs. Part B corresponds to equation (6.12); here break-even arises when the contribution is equal to fixed costs.

Absorption (total) costing versus marginal costing

Marginal costing is the system whereby the contribution towards fixed costs and profit is identified. However, many companies use total or absorption costing for reporting periodic profit and loss. Under this system the fixed costs are allocated on some rational basis between the different products and divisions of a company – for example, between the holiday travel and business travel sections of a travel agency. However, fixed costs can be allocated on several

A

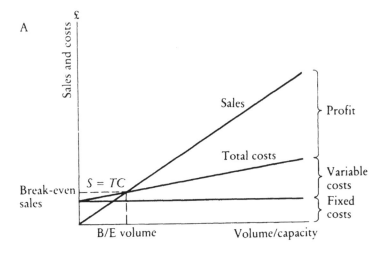

B

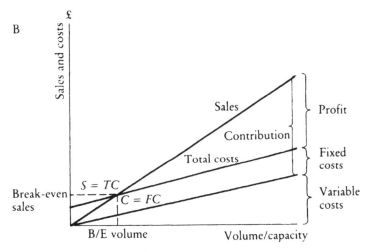

Figure 6.4 The break-even chart.

different bases – for example, as a percentage of wages, sales, number of employees or floor space. Different bases of allocation will lead to different accounting profit/loss figures. Hence, marginal costing rather than absorption costing should be used for profit planning; the success of tourism products and divisions of a tourism company should be assessed in terms of their contribution rather than their reported profit after the discretionary allocation of fixed costs.

Accounting policies

The theory of financial management suggests that financial decisions should be based on the assessment of cash flow and risk. On the other hand, financial accounting is concerned with the measurement of accounting profit in the profit and loss account and with a list of a company's assets and sources of finance in the balance sheet. Practical financial management often involves the making of decisions based on accounting profit and balance sheet effect. Because a good deal of importance has traditionally been attached to a company's published financial statements, several principles, postulates, conventions or concepts have been developed over the centuries to provide a framework for financial reporting, and these are now considered.

1   *Going concern*
    expected continuance of operations
    distinction between capital and revenue
2   *Accruals*
    matching of earned revenue and incurred costs, including accrued expenses
    recognition of liabilities when arising, rather than when paid
3   *Realization*
    income recognized when value transferred; i.e. invoiced, not paid
4   *Consistency*
    similar accounting treatment of like items in each accounting period
5   *Conservatism (prudency)*
    profits recognized when realized, liabilities provided for when anticipated
    understatement rather than overstatement of assets and profit
6   *Money measurement*
    omission of balance sheet and profit and loss account items that cannot be measured in monetary terms
7   *Business entity*
    business affairs dealt with separately from owners' affairs
8   *Duality*
    capital + liabilities = assets
9   *Cost*
    assets and expenses usually recorded at historic cost
10   *Accounting period*
    assumption that life of enterprise can be conveniently divided into a series of periods
11   *Materiality*
    omission of insignificant items
12   *Objectivity*
    accounting information based as far as possible on fact

13 *Informative disclosure*
　　　financial statements should include all information necessary
　　　to make the statements not misleading to users.

It is clear that different accountants preparing the accounts of the same tourism company are very likely to arrive at different figures for reported profit. In recent years attempts have been made by the publication of accounting standards to develop techniques for measuring profit across different companies on a consistent basis, but reported profits are still to some extent a function of accounting policies. Nevertheless, in practice, firms often judge their performance and set targets in terms of accounting profit, and spend a good deal of time analysing and making decisions on the basis of accounting profit. Measures of performance and targets are often expressed in terms of return on capital employed and earnings per share. Neither cash flow nor risk are ingredients in return on capital employed and earnings per share calculations. One of the major problems with the *use* of accounting profit is that it is subject to some extent to the methods chosen for *measuring* profit, and the major difficulties in this respect are now discussed.

1 *Stock valuation* Although the majority of retailers and wholesalers in the tourism industry carry only little stock or none at all, in certain sectors (for example, outlets selling tourist goods) stock can be an important item. Stock can be valued in various ways. We may assume that the last goods to enter the shop/warehouse are the first ones to leave (LIFO), that the highest cost items are the first ones to leave (HIFO), that the first goods to arrive are the first to go out (FIFO), or that we should use the cost of our next purchase to charge goods to production (NIFO). Alternatively, we could use average cost, we could develop a unit or standard cost, we could use adjusted selling price, or the net realizable value. In valuing stock we may choose to add on an amount to cover overhead expenses. The general rule in accounting is that we value stock at the lower of cost or net realizable value.

2 *Depreciation* Several methods have been devised for estimating depreciation, including the straight line method, reducing balance method, machine hour rate, labour hour rate, the sum of the digits method, and numerous complicated annuity systems.

3 *Inflation* A great deal of time and effort has been spent in trying to determine a reasonable method for adjusting accounting numbers for inflation. No universally accepted method has been developed, and we emphasize that the method adopted will affect the level of reported profit, but it will not affect cash flow.

4   *Research and development*   This may be written off in one period, or spread over a number of years.

5   *Long-term contracts*   The profit on a long-term contract may be apportioned over the life of the contract, or perhaps only recognized on completion of the contract.

6   *Expenditure provisions*   Accounting profit is invoiced sales less invoiced cost of sales and depreciation. We can take an optimistic or pessimistic view of after-sales service, and other expenditures likely to arise in the future.

7   *Deferred taxation*   We may or may not include a charge in the accounts for the taxation that would be payable if we disposed of our fixed assets.

8   *Hire purchase charges*   The profit and interest may be spread over the life of the agreement by different methods.

9   *Rental income*   Sometimes a substantial premium is received at the commencement of a rental agreement. The total amount of the premium may be included in this year's profit and loss account or perhaps spread over the life of the agreement.

10   *Reserve accounting*   We may choose to charge rationalization and other non-recurring costs not against this year's profit and loss account, but against balances on profit and loss account and general reserves brought forward from previous years. This will increase the amount of reported profit for the current period.

Ratio analysis

Although we have seen that accounting policies can have a marked impact on reported profit, one measure of corporate success or failure used by most companies is return on capital employed (ROCE), where accounting profit is traditionally used as the measure of return and total capital used in the business is often taken to be the measure of capital employed. ROCE compares accounting profit measured against total capital, with interest earned on a bank deposit. If a bank deposit of $100 earns $10 in interest, then the return on invested capital is 10 per cent. Similarly, if a company earns $10m on a total capital investment of $100m, then the return on capital employed is 10 per cent.

Ratio analysis is largely based on the following equation:

$$\frac{P}{S} \times \frac{S}{CE} = \frac{P}{CE} \qquad (6.13)$$

where

$$
\begin{aligned}
P &= \text{accounting profit (net)} \\
S &= \text{invoiced sales, and} \\
CE &= \text{capital employed}
\end{aligned}
$$

Return on capital employed is thus determined by two other ingredients. First, one important measure of operational success or failure is the accounting profit as a percentage of sales. This is a measure of the firm's ability to buy and sell or produce and sell goods and services at a profit. The sales figure in the accountant's profit and loss account is the quantity of invoiced sales. Accounting profit is invoiced sales less the cost of sales (although *gross* profit is calculated by deducting the cost of goods sold from invoiced sales, *net* profit involves the further deduction of depreciation, wages, rates, insurance, and so on). In general, a high profit ratio is preferred to a lower one.

The second determinant of return on capital employed is the number of times the capital employed in the business (total capital) is turned over in terms of invoiced sales, the capital–turnover ratio. This statistic is calculated by dividing invoiced sales for the period by the total capital employed, and it is generally assumed that a high value is preferred to a low one, as this indicates greater efficiency or profitability.

Return on capital employed can be improved by either increasing the profit as a percentage of sales or by increasing the number of times we turn over our capital employed in terms of sales. Profitability can be improved by either increasing selling prices or reducing costs. However, selling prices are largely market determined, and we may have exhausted the possibilities for cost reduction. We can still achieve an improvement in return on capital employed by using our assets more efficiently. For a given level of turnover and profit, we need the minimum investment in fixed assets. We require careful control of stocks where relevant – raw materials, work-in-progress, and finished goods. We also need to control the level of debtors, and negotiate the best possible credit terms from our suppliers. We can often improve the return on capital employed by concentrating on the reduction in capital employed, rather than attempting to reduce costs and increase selling prices.

Various other ratios in common use are now considered.

$$\text{Current ratio} = \frac{\text{current assets}}{\text{current liabilities}}$$

This statistic gives an indication of whether the company can pay its creditors in the short-term. Current assets include cash, the amount that debtors are expected to pay in the near future and stock that it is hoped to sell to debtors. Current liabilities are the amount owed to trade creditors for goods and services supplied, plus other amounts payable in the near future, including taxation and accrued expenses such as telephone and heating bills. A high current ratio is good in that it shows a high ability on the part of the company to pay its way in the short term.

A more stringent assessment of the ability of a company to meet its current obligations is given by the liquidity ratio, which ignores the stock figure (although, for those tourism companies that do not carry stock, the current and liquidity ratios are equivalent).

$$\text{Liquidity ratio} = \text{cash} + \frac{\text{amount expected from debtors}}{\text{current liabilities}}$$

The liquidity ratio is also known as the acid test, quick ratio, or solvency ratio.

A widely used measure of corporate performance is earnings per share (EPS).

$$\text{EPS} = \frac{\text{net profit available for shareholders}}{\text{number of shares}}$$

Other things being equal, a higher EPS value is preferred to a lower EPS value.

The price–earnings (P–E) ratio is also widely used.

$$\text{P–E ratio} = \frac{\text{price per share}}{\text{earnings per share}}$$

The P–E ratio should be used with extreme caution. It is a sort of payback indicator, in that it gives the number of years it would take for the company to earn the current share price if earnings remain at their historic level. However, the current share price depends upon expectations regarding the future, whereas earnings per share relate to the past, so the P–E ratio is a rather strange concept. If the company achieves break even, then the P–E ratio is infinite; if the company makes a loss then the P–E ratio is negative. In general terms, a relatively high P–E ratio suggests that the firm's future is judged to be brighter than its past, and a relatively low P–E ratio suggests that recent profits are not expected to be maintained.

Equation (6.13) embodies the three key ratios used by financial managers – profit as a percentage of sales, the number of times capital employed is turned over, and ROCE – but many other financial ratios related to these concepts have been developed. For example, turnover can be divided by fixed assets, current assets, number of employees, etc.; material costs, labour costs, etc., can be calculated as a percentage of sales; fixed assets, current assets, etc., can be divided by the number of employees; and so on.

In our discussion of ratio analysis, no mention has been made of either cash flow or risk, the two key variables in the modern theory of financial management, but business ratios are widely used in practice. Operations managers use ratios to analyse and control costs and revenues. Financial managers, working alongside production/ operations and marketing managers, use ratios to analyse and control the rates at which fixed and current assets are 'turned over' in terms of invoiced sales.

Ratio analysis can be particularly useful in four areas of tourism management:

1 *Trend analysis* The historic ratios of a company can be plotted to show historic trends and variability. These may provide signals that stimulate thought for greater efficiency.
2 *Inter-firm comparison (IFC)* The performance of a company in terms of ratios can be compared with the performances of similar companies in that sector of the tourism industry. Different ratio values may indicate different corporate strategies. The objective of IFC is to isolate those indicators which suggest that the company is out of step with the industry averages, and hence focus on problem areas.
3 *Performance appraisal* Ratio analysis can be used to compare actual performance with targets set.
4 *Forecasting* Established financial ratios can be used for financial statement forecasting, that is, to forecast next year's profit and loss account and balance sheet. However, managers in the tourism industry should bear in mind that selling prices and costs will change, new fixed assets may be acquired, and so on.

While managers may be eager to find ratios that give the key to corporate success, we must recommend a great deal of caution in making decisions on the basis of a few ratios. The theory of finance suggests that decisions should be based on cash flow and risk. Ratios are all-other-things-being-equal numbers. There may be good reason why stock, amount owing by debtors, amount owing to creditors and cash balances are high or low at the year-end. In ratio analysis we usually use year-end numbers because these are readily available. A company going into liquidation will tend to have a low stock figure, giving the company an excellent stock turnover ratio for the year. Another company has difficulty collecting cash at the year-end from two of its largest customers. Using year-end balance sheet numbers, this will give a much longer debt collection period than has existed during the year. Balance sheet numbers and profit and loss account numbers are affected by accounting policies relating to stock valuation, depreciation, inflation, research and development, profit on long-term contracts, etc. These policies, and changes in these policies, will have some considerable influence on accounting numbers. Overall, we conclude that ratios help to give managers a feel for the company's performance in relation to its targets and its competitors. Financial managers in the tourism industry should not seize upon two or three ratios as offering the key to corporate success or failure.

Cash management

The objective of the firm is to generate positive cash flows from successful trading. Firms that do generate lots of cash from successful trading can finance new investment, and are usually able to raise additional finance as required. They generate their own cash surpluses, which can be invested. Even companies that trade successfully may experience occasional cash deficits when projects generate occasional negative cash flows. These cash deficits must be financed. Cash shortages can result in the making of sub-optimal investment and financing decisions. Sub-optimal investment decisions would include the disposal of profitable lines or divisions, inability to undertake profitable investment projects, and failure to maintain an adequate level of working capital. Sub-optimal financing decisions would include the taking out of very expensive loans, and being granted overdraft facilities subject to restrictive covenants, which could include personal guarantees from directors, restrictions on investment, restrictions on additional finance, restrictions on directors' remuneration, and restrictions on dividend payments.

All companies use cash and bank balances. Cash is used to pay creditors for various inputs, and to pay wages and salaries. This cash expenditure results in the creation of finished products (that is, goods or services or combinations of goods and services), which are sold to customers who pay in cash. Therefore, cash is essential to finance the working capital cycle. Cash is also used to acquire fixed assets, which are written off over their estimated useful lives, and to pay interest on loans, taxation, and dividends to shareholders.

Cash balances

There are several reasons for holding cash balances.

1 *Transactions* Firms use cash to finance working capital and fixed assets.
2 *Interest earnings* On a short-term basis cash balances can be placed on bank deposits or invested in government securities to earn interest. Loans can be made to subsidiaries, associated companies, and other companies.
3 *Precaution* Some firms hold a safety stock of cash to provide against unanticipated fluctuations in their ability to generate cash. We would expect this to be less likely to occur in those firms that have easy access to additional finance.
4 *Speculation* Some firms hold very high cash balances with a view to taking advantage of speculative investment opportunities. Such cash balances are often justified in terms of their ability to finance mergers. On the other hand, many companies have been acquired because they have large cash balances.
5 *Investment* Firms with cash surpluses can give more credit to customers, thereby generating additional sales. They can undertake promotional exercises to increase sales to utilize unabsorbed capacity. Cash balances can be used to provide loans to customers, and make available lease finance to increase sales. Firms with surplus cash balances can undertake additional investment in fixed assets and working capital, and even acquire other companies for cash.

Cash forecasting

We emphasize that all firms in the tourism industry should generate cash flow forecasts for one month, three months, six months, one year, and five years. These cash flow forecasts should be continuously updated, and action taken to invest surpluses and finance deficits. A target should be set for a minimum or safety stock of cash.

Cash flow must be carefully planned for and monitored. Many firms have survived for long periods without making much profit, but they have successfully managed cash. Firms that have run out of cash have not survived. When you stop paying wages, employees stop working for your company. When you stop paying bills, suppliers stop supplying or demand cash with order. When your bank manager decides to call in the overdraft, this heralds the start of liquidation proceedings for companies. Firms can survive without making a profit by disposing of fixed assets, sale and lease-back of property, sale of the fleet of cars and then leasing, mortgaging property, cutting back on investment in stock and debtors, extending supplier credit, borrowing, issuing more shares, disposing of subsidiaries, and cutting back on plant replacement and research and development. We *encourage* firms to make *profits*, but for survival *cash management* is *essential*. In general, for the small and new business, cash flow is far more important than profit flow.

Foreign exchange management

International tourism is very much concerned with people buying goods and services priced in a foreign currency. It is, therefore, crucial for companies in the international tourism industry to identify and manage exchange rate exposures (Lockwood, 1989). International tourism involves risks for operators on account of the uncertainties about future rates of exchange between currencies: for example, inclusive tour operators in the USA selling packages to the UK receive most of their revenue in dollars, but incur a substantial part of their costs in pounds sterling, and therefore pricing the holiday involves forecasting the $/£ exchange rate; airlines buy aviation fuel priced in US dollars, and thus non-USA based airlines need to forecast exchange rates in order to set air fares.

It is extremely difficult to forecast exchange rate movements over the short/medium term. If any increase in costs resulting from exchange rate fluctuations can be passed on to the tourist with no adverse impact on the company, then exchange rate exposure does not exist, but generally this is not the case, as tourism markets tend to be highly competitive.

Lockwood (1989) identifies three types of foreign currency exposure: transaction, translation and economic. Transaction exposure occurs when a company has an amount to pay in foreign currency or expects to receive some foreign currency at a future date – the exposure arises when the commitment to buy or sell in a foreign currency is taken. Transaction exposure can be controlled in several ways. First, try to find an opposite exposure to the original one; a future commitment to buy and sell in the same currency at the same time would cover the exposure. Secondly, if the timing of inflows/ outflows of foreign currency is known with a high degree of certainty, then it is possible to take out forward cover in the foreign currency markets whereby the exchange rate to be applied to a future transaction is set now. (Today's exchange rate for 'immediate' delivery of currency (usually within two working days) is the *spot* rate. Exchange rates agreed for delivery of currency at some time in the future (usually 30, 90 or 180 days) are *forward* rates.) Clearly, if uncertainty is prevalent, then having a forward contract in place may create an exposure that would not otherwise exist. A third possibility for controlling transaction exposure is to take out a currency option; here the payment of an option premium guarantees a future exchange rate, but the contract does not have to be taken up – the option may be exercised or allowed to lapse. Hence, if the receipt/ payment does not occur, the option need not be taken up so no exposure is created. Similarly, if the exchange rate prevailing at the time when the receipt/payment occurs is better than that specified in the option contract, the option would not be exercised.

The second type of foreign currency exposure is translation exposure. This arises when a company owns assets denoted in a foreign currency, such as an international hotel company. When the company prepares its (usually annual) balance sheet, all foreign-currency denoted assets are translated into domestic currency at the exchange rate prevailing on the date the balance sheet is prepared. Currency fluctuations alone can give rise to substantial gains or losses. The method that is generally used to control translation exposures is to borrow in the same foreign currency needed to finance assets. Hence, a change in asset value is offset by a corresponding change in the value of borrowings, and the earnings stream generated by the foreign-currency denoted assets can be used to make interest repayments. Although it is possible to avoid translation exposure in the short term by using forward contracts or options, these are generally considered to be inappropriate and expensive for this type of exposure.

The third type of foreign currency exposure is economic exposure. Here we are referring to the impact of exchange rates and hence prices on holiday selection. If the US dollar strengthens in relation to the Austrian schilling, this will encourage more US residents to travel to Austria. Similarly, if the US dollar weakens compared with the German mark, then some US tourists are likely to switch their intended destination from Germany to Austria. The US tour operator selling holidays to Austria thus has economic exposure to the Austrian schilling *and* the German mark; in fact, he/she has economic exposure to the currencies of all countries that may be considered to be competitive holiday destinations for Austria (see Martin and Witt, 1988a). The most appropriate strategy for covering economic exposure is diversification. Thus the tour operator can sell holidays to a variety of foreign destinations, in which case a downturn in demand (say, due to a price increase for one destination) would not be catastrophic; in fact, the company may well also pick up the increased demand for the relatively cheaper destination(s). In order to fully cover economic exposure, it should be borne in mind that if the domestic currency weakens, some people will substitute a domestic holiday for a foreign one; some involvement by the company with domestic tourism or inbound foreign tourism could offset losses resulting from a weakening exchange rate, as these forms of tourism are both likely to increase should the domestic currency weaken. Again, although it is possible to avoid economic exposure in the short term by using forward contracts or options, these methods are not considered to be particularly appropriate.

Exposures to third world currencies create additional risks, such as lack of convertibility and the inability to create two-way currency flows. In general, a very short payback period is required on any investment in order to minimize the exposure period.

Further reading

Chisman, N. R. (1989), 'Financial planning and control in tourism', in Witt, S. F. and Moutinho, L. (eds), *Tourism Marketing and Management Handbook*, Hemel Hempstead: Prentice-Hall, pp. 157–62.

Dobbins, R. and Witt, S. F. (1983), *Portfolio Theory and Investment Management*, Oxford: Blackwell.

Dobbins, R. and Witt, S. F. (1988), *Practical Financial Management*, Oxford: Blackwell.

Lockwood, R. D. (1989), 'Foreign exchange management', in Witt, S. F. and Moutinho, L., op. cit., pp. 175–8.

Sternquist, B., Davis, B. and Pysarchik, D. (1989), 'Financial analysis in tourism', in Witt, S. F. and Moutinho, L., op. cit., pp. 151–5.

7

Organization and staffing

The components of the tourism industry include travel companies (airlines), hospitality (hotels) and arrangers (tour operators). Each of those categories has features and requirements that determine organization and personnel policies. These are considered in the following pages, where we shall see that typical organizations derive from strategies which, in turn, relate to size, diversification and similar factors; but, above all, a service industry requires organizing, recruiting and training policies that support customer satisfaction while working on a 24-hour cycle. With retailing, travel and tourism provide classic examples of industry sectors in which the typical employee, rather than the specialist salesperson, is in constant contact with the public. A paradox is that this commonplace fact, all too well known in the industry, is only gradually permeating corporate cultures; several reports have pointed to the inadequacies of training. This chapter examines the industry in the context of established knowledge about international corporate policies, starting with organization.

Requirements of an international organization

An international company needs an organization framework that is capable of holding together far-reaching operations with long lines of communication across boundaries of nation and life style. Coping with the following essentials can be a severe test, but the organization must fulfil the need to:

(1) stimulate and support the correct *decisions* in the right place;
(2) ensure that *authority* is exercised competently where and when required;
(3) provide *reports* from subsidiary units that will enable senior managers to identify problems as soon as they arise and to notice excellence in performance as well;
(4) provide an effective channel for *other communications*;
(5) build a management development system and *career* structure;
(6) ensure that the *aims and objectives* of the company, including quality and service, are achieved in every unit.

Every international company has to take those issues on board, but with different priorities. In the case of most sectors of the tourism industry, the first four cannot be ignored but numbers five and six are critical. Let us examine each in turn.

The implications of the six elements for building an organization structure overlap and may be hard to distinguish, but the following are among the most significant issues that cause change. They must be taken together. Planning may revolve around communications, who reports to whom; if career expectations are overlooked, the organization may well fail to work.

1   Decisions

Some decisions have to be made at the centre – an airline is unlikely to allow a foreign station the discretion to buy a hotel chain without permission from head office – while many everyday decisions (like the purchasing of small items of equipment) will be at the discretion of the locals, albeit within an agreed budget. Between these two lie numerous decisions that are sometimes taken at head office, sometimes in the foreign unit and sometimes between the two. There is a *decision-making* process, which a company evolves, and which is itself controlled by two considerations – where is a decision allowed to be taken and how do managers around the world know the limits of their discretion? If only a limited number of key decisions – such as entry into new products or markets, major new investments and the appointment of chief executives of subsidiaries – are retained by the centre, the company is known as decentralized; if many other decisions such as smaller investments (smaller in proportion to the size of a particular company), recruitment and training policies, corporate image and promotion standards are taken at head office, then the company is centralized internationally.

Studies of centralization and decentralization have revealed centralizing tendencies in many, especially larger, international companies. Most elements of the tourism sector are more centralized and made up of smaller companies than is the case with manufacturing firms. This arises from the need to provide a standardized service: tours that happen, schedules that are international, hotels that guarantee a uniform standard.

The implications of centralization for the organization are fourfold:

Head office must carry a staff capable of processing the decisions fast enough to match the competition abroad. A problem of centralization is slow decision-making. A local unit is prevented from seizing an opportunity because of the need to refer back. When this is realized headquarters' staff is increased to promote the decision-making more rapidly. Centralization is then seen to have a cost that may be greater than the less obvious costs attached to incorrect decisions in the subsidiary.

The lines of communication must be clearly drawn and enable the rapid passage of information both ways. The ability to communicate rapidly and direct to a decision-maker increases the speed of communication, provided that the system and the decision-makers are not overloaded.

The management development programme has to be capable of providing international promotion, so that managers with restricted responsibilities can expect international promotion. A company is unlikely to retain effective international managers if the limit of promotion is their own national organization – and this is a subordinate position in a centralized system.

The arrangements and the regulations must be understood (see p. 134, 'Structures').

2 Authority

The central issue in organization is authority, a fact that writers on the subject are apt to overlook. An appointment carries the means of ensuring that its responsibilities can be implemented. The degree of authority vested in any particular position varies with the degree of centralization, but internationally there are certain complications. A foreign subsidiary has to be incorporated and managed in accordance with the laws of its own country. However many decisions are reserved to head office, local management will be prosecuted for breaches of the law and normally will not be allowed to plead instructions from abroad. A hotel burns down, and both criminal charges and civil pleas for damages will be made against the local managers, even though they may have acted under head office instructions. In that particular instance international corporate standards will presumably have been designed to ensure safety; but even climatic conditions or the availability of construction materials can make local discretion desirable. There are many issues on which discretion is required, but not always allowed in an attempt to ensure that commercial skills learned in one market are used in others. There is always tension between the hard-earned experience – in standards and operating methods – that has made it possible for a company to expand internationally, and the relevance of that experience in a particular market.

The complicating factor in the allocation of authority is that responsibilities are necessarily divided. This is true of domestic companies, but the international dimension adds an extra complication. A travel agent may have both wholesale and retail operations and provide financial services (such as travellers' cheques). Thomas Cook fits this description, and American Express is an example of a company that is even more diversified – partly in the tourism sector and partly in banking. The chief executive of a foreign subsidiary, in these circumstances, is likely to have multiple responsibilities. Authority will be needed to produce results for the national organization overall without neglecting the various components. The section on structure (see p. 134) considers how possible conflicts of authority are coped with.

3 Reports

Head office needs to know the results of the decisions – how each unit is performing at any given time. The financial control system has been outlined in chapter 6, and is the heart of a reporting system that includes marketing, safety, personnel and other statistics.

The reports serve other purposes besides identifying problems. They provide statistical information for corporate planners as well as standards of comparison to judge the success or viability of a particular operation; they also keep the attention of foreign executives fixed on corporate priorities and provide an educational process for those executives by doing so. Tourism companies are likely to find that the demand for information is even more easily inflated than it is for other sectors. Modern technology makes the collection and transmission of information easier, but also makes it even more liable to inflation. Head office can easily take the view that keying in a little more information is not a burden, forgetting the time spent in accumulating and recording the information if local managers do not see the need for it in their own businesses. Customer service can suffer if managers of small units devote too much of their time to completing forms reporting on their standards of service.

4 Other communications

The organization also has to facilitate a network of communication in many different directions at once. In the past, companies that only permitted *vertical* communication – that between subordinates and superiors, head office and foreign operations internationally – simplified their communications at the expense of effectiveness. In any case, a centralized system demands more communication. Questions, answers, comments, information and many other items have to be passed across frontiers, and the sheer volume of information is often self-frustrating.

There are two established means of improving communications. One is the use of comparisons, for which caution is needed: conditions vary in different markets and comparisons may be invalid or appear unjust, when vital elements are outside local control. Different forms of comparison suit different companies. Some use return on investment (income before tax divided by net amount of capital invested); some use productivity, and this itself may be measured in several ways: one is the number of employees required to perform a certain task, or the labour costs in a business. Comparisons can also be circulated on reliability (maintenance of schedules, for instance) or safety or any other measure that reflects major issues; the main limitation is the amount of control that the local unit has over its own performance, or how dependent it is on decisions outside. If the aircraft or cruise ships are chartered by head office, there may be no point in judging local operators on their punctuality. If used carefully, however, comparisons can stimulate a response from subsidiaries and help them to see the purpose of the control system. More significant is that a small amount of face-to-face communication is often more effective than a considerable use of mechanical means – post, telephone, telex, fax and on-line links (see chapter 8).

5 Careers

Questions like 'Why does our organization not work more efficiently?' may well call for a reply in the form of: 'Because it does not provide an adequate career structure.' In an industry sector in which many nationalities have to work closely together and in which authority resides at the centre, the logic of international management development is inescapable. A suitable organization structure provides for this; the implications will be examined later.

6 Aims and objectives

Another example of a normal requirement that has a special meaning for the tourism sector is the need for conformity to aims and objectives. The international traveller looks to a standard of service in the hotels visited; he or she has expectations about other tourism facilities in the various countries. The organization must ensure that these are met, and met within the constraints of local customs and cultures. Some hotel chains have even had to modify the rigours of international standardization in order not to offend domestic customers. A much-quoted example is that of Holiday Inns in

Germany. In this case an organization that had always stressed international standardization down to the smallest of details found itself compelled to relax the rules in the face of customer opposition in Germany. Internationalizing objectives is not a simple matter as many operators have found to their cost. However centralized a project is, local advice has to be given some weight. How much is a subject on which generalization is difficult. Segmenting the market helps. If a particular facility is aimed primarily at an international market, detailed international aims can be enforced. More caution is needed as the proportion of local customers grows. McDonald's is an example of a company that caters mainly for domestic customers in each country in which it operates; at the same time it asserts that the basic principles established in the United States of quality, service and reliability (QSC) are 'applied rigorously' everywhere.

Structures to meet the requirements

The possession of facilities abroad is the first question to be addressed in determining a suitable organization. A travel agent may be booking holidays in many parts of the world without possessing offices outside the home country. The foreign activities of such a company are confined to purchasing and to inspection, either of which may be operated through an intermediary. The operations abroad will require some extra expertise at head office, even a small specialist department, but will not influence the organization greatly. It is the possession of facilities, the ownership of property, in other countries that strains an existing organization. These strains will cause severe problems unless an organization is developed to cope with them.

The second question is the degree of diversification. Tourism is a fragmented industry, with few firms among the world's largest and many operating in only one business – travel agency, tour operation, transport, hotels or tourism facilities. Nevertheless, there are many diversified companies, some of them in sectors outside travel and tourism. One example is American Express, with a core business in banking, extensive travel agency interests and one product – travellers' cheques – that bridges both sectors. Many airlines have diversified, such as JAL (the Japanese airline), which owns tour operators and hotels and is diversifying into retailing. A German company, Touristik Union International, is also in tourism, hotels and retailing. It also manages joint ventures with the German railway system, an airline and a shipping line. The company operates many subsidiaries abroad.

There has been buying and selling of individual units during the 1980s. Sometimes a reduction in the range of activities appears necessary for survival, as when Pan Am sold its hotel chain; at other times it appears as a more effective use of resources. Among the options for organization structures, some are mainly relevant to a single core business company, while others are made necessary by diversification.

The two questions can be stated in the following terms:

Are there enough facilities abroad to make an international organization necessary?
Is the company diversified to an extent that rules out a single product organization worldwide?

Once the first question is answered in the affirmative, the structure inevitably becomes more complex. At this stage there are five options employed to cope with international requirements. These can be studied in detail in one of the many books on international company organization,[1] and are briefly outlined here. The following numbers 1, 2 and 3 correspond to those in Figure 7.1, where the organizations are outlined; under number 4 we discuss other options not shown in Figure 7.1.

1   International functional

Companies operating in one core business can maintain a relatively straightforward organization – although it may not appear quite so simple to the units abroad. The larger subsidiaries will have a direct link to the chief executive or a colleague designated to take responsibility for specific operations. Smaller subsidiaries, branches and franchisees will report to an international controller or similar officer. Meanwhile, other departments at head office will involve themselves directly in the affairs of the foreign unit, ensuring that customer service, staffing, training, safety, maintenance and other standards are maintained. Managers abroad report to their national chief executive or branch manager, but have a relatively closer link with their opposite numbers at head office than is common in other businesses. Figure 7.1 illustrates the position but, to simplify an already complicated picture, only major over-arching functions are included. Subordinate departments like business development, customer service and training will be directly involved abroad in this type of organization, but less directly in others.

This can operate abroad by method (1)
International Functional, thus:

Functional

A top management team representing *functional* specialists, such as:

OR by method (2) International or regional divisions

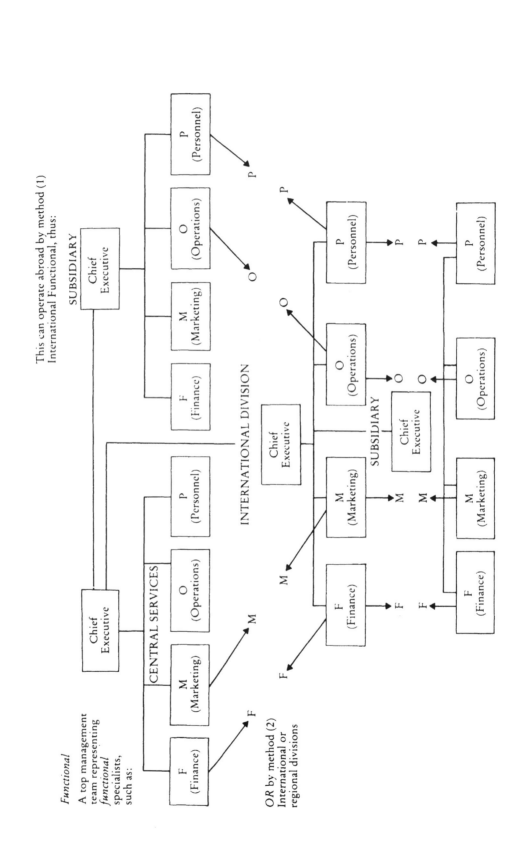

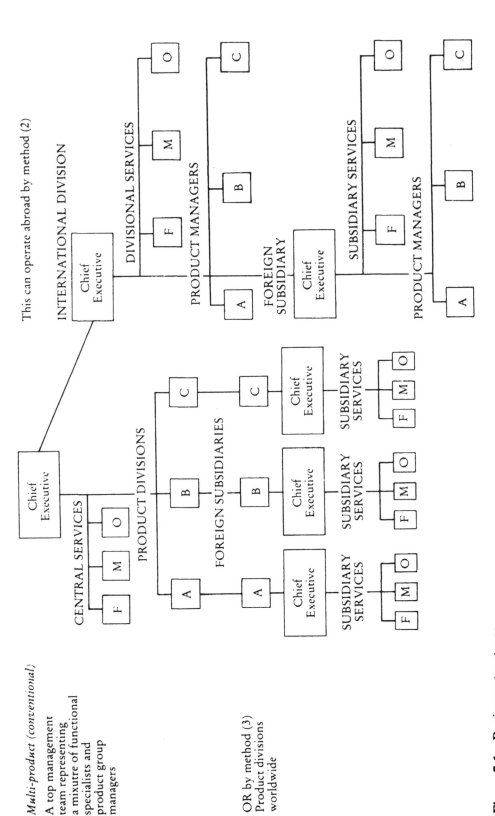

Figure 7.1 Business structures.

2   *International or regional management*

Either single product or diversified firms can operate abroad through an international division. Concentrating the management of foreign businesses in a department responsible for the world or a region outside the home country is common among international companies. This method is not so common among tourism companies – it is found more frequently in other service industries such as banks. One advantage of the international division is that it brings together the specialists in international business. For this reason, it is likely to be irrelevant to tour operators and hotel chains, all of whose senior staff are international specialists.

3   *Product or customer divisions worldwide*

This method treats each division as a world business in its own right, to be integrated at the highest level. Some tourism businesses are multi-product, some are in firms that have other divisions outside tourism; in either case, each division controls its own operations worldwide. This is a logical consequence of one way that diversification comes about – through the purchase of an existing company as a going concern rather than through the gradual growth of a particular product. This system favours the sale as well as the purchase of a division such as an hotel chain. Where the division bought or sold is organized into a separate division, there is likely to be less of an upheaval and less resistance.

The essence of the product division worldwide, as illustrated in Figure 7.1 (method 3), is that the foreign subsidiary reports to the divisional head office. One consequence is that there may be more than one subsidiary in a particular country. A problem then arises if one subsidiary is profitable and another is not. If they are independent units, it becomes impossible to offset the tax losses of the one against the profits of the other. As a result, it is common to set up a holding company in countries where this applies, to co-ordinate the finance, pay the taxes and pay a joint dividend to central funds.

Thomas Cook has followed another trend in fixing the boundaries between its divisions by the type of customer. The corporate sector deals with companies and financial services. The consumer sector includes retail shops, phone centres and retail foreign exchange. This is a formula that is likely to be more used in the future. The formation of customer divisions rather than product divisions has already come into existence in other consumer-oriented businesses, such as electrical and electronic appliances.

4   *Experimental organizations*

Two other options are available. A matrix organization brings together both the international and the product divisions; the foreign subsidiary reports both ways and the accounts are made up nationally, internationally and by product. The other experimental option is even more flexible and occurs when temporary project teams are set up to manage particular foreign operations. Both of these organization methods are used in service industries, but seldom if ever in tourism companies. This does not mean that they are unlikely to spread to tourism. On the contrary, the greater flexibility internationally would appear suitable in an industry that has to adapt rapidly to changing circumstances. The problem is to bring together management teams for international operations without damaging the rapid communications that are also needed.

Staffing

The tourism sector is following other service industries in emphasizing the importance of an international cadre of managers and key operators; but the arrangements seem more casual and unplanned than in the more detailed manpower planning developed by some banking and retailing organizations. Different traditions in different countries in individualistic businesses, such as hotels and tour operators, have built up different expectations on the part of both employees and customers. A result is that operators have difficulty in achieving the degree of international staffing that is expected to produce more equal standards of service. Airlines employ local and foreign nationals in many of their stations. Those that are operated under a management contract have a stiffening of nationals of the contractor company at all levels.

The rapid growth of tourism has caused stresses and strains in recruitment in many countries. The problems have increased because customer expectations have also grown. High standards of service and personal links with customers combine with unsociable hours to produce special pressures that are exaggerated on the international scene. One company (Falcon Leisure Group) expresses staff requirements in the following words:

Our overseas representatives are the company's ambassadors overseas and in many cases the only contacts our customers have with the company . . . Apart from having more energy than an atomic power station you must have a sincere interest in helping people and good organisational and accountancy skills. Aged at least 21 and educated to A-level standard, you'll also have a working knowledge of either Spanish, Greek, Portuguese, Turkish or Italian (quoted from *The Handbook of Tourism and Leisure 1989*). Hobson, 1989

Next Travel is an example of a company that recruits couriers from many European countries for service in sites in others. Their recruiting literature, like that of most tour companies, emphasizes personality traits rather than qualifications.

The two companies mentioned are sending operating staff abroad. For management staff, there are different considerations. The emphasis on local management has already been noted. Expatriates are expensive. Labour costs at the same level of salary can be three times as high for an expatriate as for a local colleague. Such costs will not, of course, discourage a company from transferring managers internationally where special skills are required or where knowledge of head office is vital. The costs and the other advantages of local managers should stimulate more international management development programmes, the subject of the next section.

Training

Two factors combine to make training[2] especially important to tourism. First, large numbers of employees have direct contact with customers: this is common to many service industries, but contrasts with manufacturing in which only sales and maintenance staff normally meet the public. The second factor is common to other industries: that management is becoming more complex as strategic issues come to play a more important role. These issues vary from major market innovations to more routine tactical considerations. All make demands on management education. The attention to add-on facilities or to market segmentation defined as type of traveller in hotels, for instance, means that the same rooms can be filled at different prices for business people, tour parties or weekenders. The same is true of seats in trains or planes; transport enterprises make a further segmentation into groups such as students or old age pensioners. There are also niche markets, such as special interest tours. The issues become more complex when operating across frontiers, and can be further complicated by specifically international considerations – for example, government regulations or those of international organizations such as the International Air Transport Association.

Another complication that affects both domestic and foreign operations is the move away from direct ownership. In France only

33 per cent of hotels belonging to chains are in subsidiaries. The remainder are managed either by franchisees or under a management contract.

The transferability of skills is a key factor in determining international developments, and training is the means by which much of the transfer has to be carried out. Additionally, training programmes themselves prove to be transferable. A recent report gave an example of a tourism management training programme developed by Cornell University being franchised elsewhere. In many programmes the international element is limited to the means of welcoming citizens from other countries. Much training is restricted to domestic horizons, although some can be readily applied in foreign countries as well. Doubts are often raised about the extent to which the required training is actually provided. In Britain a newspaper article quoted a Consumer Association report, which said that even the minimal training available in this country was being cut to save costs. Tourism courses have been developed over many years in countries such as Switzerland, France and Italy.

International aspects of such training as exists are identified in a number of examples from travel agents, tour operators, hotel and catering companies and airlines. The European Community's Social Fund subsidizes training for tourism in less-favoured regions and exchange programmes designed to improve the linguistic and cultural knowledge of young workers. The European Centre for Vocational Training evaluates the level of professional training needed for hotels and restaurants in Community countries; it is hoped that this will make it easier for workers in the industry to move between states. The European Treaties stipulate that those working in the industry can set themselves up or offer their services anywhere in the Community. A directive standardizes the recognition of qualifications.

Travel agents and tour operators

Competition has stimulated heavy investment in training by travel agents and tour operators. Thomas Cook, for instance, employs 6,500 people. It is based in the United Kingdom, but is federated with other travel agents, such as Wagon Lits in Belgium, and has affiliates in India, Egypt, Canada, the United States, Australia and New Zealand. Ten years ago there were 300 British expatriate managers in the company. The number is now between 20 and 30. In the United States all the key jobs are held by Americans.

The company is now setting out to gain an improved market share and presence in what it sees as a rapidly changing market. It is attempting to develop global operating procedures combined with an internationally uniform culture and common ethos. These developments demand international training. During the past decade the giants of the travel industry have changed travel from a branded service into a commodity, and this has eroded loyalty. Thomas Cook is developing an ability to predict changes, to consider long-term issues, and maintain a strong customer focus, based on judgement and skills. Such objectives demand specialized training. There is a central training department in the British headquarters. Tuition covers subjects that vary from the handling of foreign exchange, through customer care and ticketing, to sales and marketing as well as accountancy. There are arrangements to enable retail trainees to review their own performance in a selling situation. Distance-learning programmes are also arranged.

The training centre at Thomas Cook is also responsible for a method of job evaluation and performance appraisal known as 'Gemini'. There are six levels of staff and management in the organization, all of whom are subject to the Gemini scheme: office staff, travel consultants, junior managers, divisional managers, divisional directors, group board directors. Gemini has four main features:

1 The evaluation of the skills content in jobs.
2 The assessment of performance – by employees on a preparation form, which is confirmed on an output and quality report after appraisal interview by his or her boss.
3 Rewards and salaries based only on job performance; other features such as the cost of living are ignored.
4 After performance assessment, the employee is prescribed further training for performance improvement, under the following aspects of personal development: knowledge and experience, human relations, theory and resources, numeracy and information technology skills, personal qualities, physical skills.

Hotel and catering: public sector

In Britain one person in ten is employed in the hotel and catering business and the industry is growing at the rate of 40,000 jobs a year. To meet this demand, the Hotel and Catering Training Board, a government-sponsored organization, has launched its *Caterbase* scheme. This is providing courses that enable participants to operate in the world industry and is itself being marketed internationally – at present in Australia, Turkey and Cyprus. Caterbase awards are made through continuous assessment of performance in the work-place. The programme is modular in format and each module specifies performance criteria for the task it covers. To gain a Caterbase award for a module, the criteria must be met consistently, demonstrating the ability to perform to the required standards over extended periods and under normal work pressure. The scheme can be offered by employers and other organizations approved by the Hotel and Catering Training Board.

Entry to Caterbase is open to all individuals who carry out tasks covered by the modules. There are no pre-entry qualifications. Each candidate is registered with a Caterbase Approved Organization and is issued with a Passbook in which achievement will be recorded. Assessments are carried out in the workplace by the staff who have day-to-day responsibility for supervising candidates' work and who are technically proficient in the skills being assessed. The modules in Caterbase illustrate the range of skills required in the sector, which can then be deployed throughout the international hotel and catering sector. From basic courses in operations – such as food preparation and organizing accommodation – provided by Caterbase, there is a hierarchy of courses rising to an MBA that specializes in the hotel and catering industry.

The private sector

Hotel chains are noted for international in-house programmes.[3] This is especially the case with American chains, but also applies to some European such as Trusthouse Forte.

TRUSTHOUSE FORTE

The international division of Trusthouse Forte manages hotels in London, the Irish Republic, North and South Europe, and the Western Atlantic including Bermuda, Guyana and Jamaica. It also possesses an Academy for training international staff. The Academy, established in 1987, has a small permanent staff. Tutors are drawn from elsewhere in the division. The mission of the Academy is to obtain a common and high standard of management proficiency in a group of hotels in various countries, and to achieve this across cultural differences, including the low esteem in which catering is held in much of northern Europe.

The philosophy of the Academy is achievement through personal responsibility, and a three-day programme on developing management style covers: style analysis, personal development, team leadership, interviewing, counselling skills, financial systems, financial awareness, and an analysis of strengths and weaknesses. Apart from its direct tutorial role, the Academy is a centre for research into on-the-job training techniques. It conducts a quarterly meeting of training managers from the various units of the international division to review training being carried out, new methods being tried, the revision of methods that have proved unworkable and how the training can be made more interesting. Language training is likely to be added.

BRITISH AIRWAYS

Airlines are international by the nature of their business; they need to train staff in management and operations drawn from the different countries in which they maintain stations. There is also the additional need of developing communication skills between employees in different places and varying circumstances (air and ground staff). Out of the various types of training emerge skills that then become saleable. As a result, airlines frequently have occasion to manage other airlines and to train their staff, while being able to sell their training packages to yet other lines. British Airways is an example of an airline that undertakes all these activities.

Training is centred in its Academy of Travel Management, founded in London in 1986. The Academy has a full-time staff of twenty-two people, eleven of whom are themselves trainees, and six part-timers. The tutorial programmes are continuous, mainly at the college in Ealing but also in Glasgow, Manchester and Birmingham. Correspondence courses are also used. The programmes have been enfranchised internationally to colleges in Bahrain, Cyprus and Trinidad. The examiners and investigators are British Airways staff.

An objective of the Academy is to raise the standard of service to members of the public who are potential passengers of British Airways. Its teaching, therefore, is provided for the employees of travel agents and tour operators as well as by members of their own staff – yet another requirement of airlines. The courses cover the subjects listed below (some of the subject titles are self-explanatory):

- *The travel industry* (a basic introduction) covers world geography, world airlines, the major United Kingdom travel and tourism organizations.
- *Basic airlines* provides a broad overview of scheduled air transportation and grounding for a career in the travel industry. This course is designed to increase productivity among operators.
- *Fares and ticketing* is designed to cover the technicalities that retail staff have to master, whether they are employed by travel agents, tour operators or airlines.
- *Telephone techniques and selling* emphasizes the importance of the telephone in building and maintaining good client relations and in winning new clients.
- *Winning with people*
- *Counter sales techniques*

- *Advanced sales techniques*
- *People management skills*
- *Recruitment and interviewing skills* covers designing job and personal specifications, choosing media for advertising, screening initial applicants, preparing for interviews, getting the most from interviews and making a job offer.
- *Maketing awareness* covers the retail environment, planning retail marketing strategy, identifying marketing opportunities, and promotional activity.
- *Presentation skills* is designed to instil confidence about public speaking, selling and instructing.
- *Key account sales development*

NORTH SEA FERRIES

An Anglo-Dutch joint venture (50 per cent owned by Royal Nedlloyd Group and 50 per cent by P and O), North Sea Ferries operates training and refresher courses for all levels of staff. The hotel department emphasizes customer relations, and staff exchanges between the Netherlands and Britain are a feature of training programmes. The company also provides educational tours for travel agents.

Notes and further reading

1   Each book emphasizes different characteristics. The scheme outlined here is explained in the first publication listed, but note the differences for the tourism sector.

Brooke, M. Z. (1986), *International Management*, London: Hutchinson (chapter 11).
For greater detail, see: Brooke, M. Z. (1984), *Centralization and Autonomy*, Eastbourne: Holt, Rinehart and Winston.
For examples of other accounts, see:
Daniels, J. D. and Radebaugh, L. H. (1989), *International Business*, 5th edn, Reading, Mass.: Addison-Wesley (chapter 17).
Robock, S. H. and Simmons, K. (1983), *International Business and Multinational Enterprise*, 3rd edn, Homewood, Ill.: Irwin (chapter 16).
2   Material for this section has been collected by William R. Mills, to whom the authors are indebted. The report mentioned is the *Hotel and Catering Training Board, Strategic Plan 1987/88–1989/90*; the press reference is to *The Sunday Telegraph*, 7 May 1989.
3   This information has been supplied by Paul Moore, a travel industry consultant.

8

Research and innovation

Research in tourism is by nature interdisciplinary (or trans-disciplinary). However, academic and subject boundaries being as impermeable as they are, a considerable amount of work has been carried on within traditional subject boundaries. An attempt is made here to break down these barriers by using a task- or problem-oriented schema rather than a discipline-based one. However, it will be recognized that most 'impact' studies of tourism are made by economists just as most studies of the cultural changes wrought by tourism are the province of sociologists. The aim is to pinpoint areas of research of particular relevance to management of tourism.

A major feature of tourism research is that it is closely related to practice. Indeed, the borderline between research and innovation in the industry is blurred. This is a major strength of much of the work reviewed below. However, the weakness of some of the research is that it is imperfectly grounded in any theoretical perspective, which leads to descriptive work and the lack of real analytical bite. Attempts to remedy this defect are under way and there is a trend to tighter frameworks, more careful definitions and quantification of key dimensions.

Most research in tourism is multidimensional, that is to say it is rarely a pure type. Thus, 'impact studies' will also include elements of the tourism planning system, descriptive elements and management issues. This is a healthy sign in that the research area has not become too compartmentalized.

Tourism within the service industries

There has been a recent upsurge of interest in the service industries as a subject of research, particularly their internationalization. The founding of a journal, *The Service Industries Journal*, has been an important focus for dissemination of information. It is an indication of the perceived importance of the service industries internationally that a large part of the 1989 report of the United Nations Centre on Transnational Corporations (UNCTC), *Transnational Corporation in World Development: Trends and prospects*, was devoted to the internationalization of services.

Naturally, a considerable amount of time and effort has been given to attempts to define the nature and scope of 'services' and 'the service industries'. A composite view of what constitutes a service includes: intangibility, perishability, customization, simultaneity of production and consumption, consumer participation in production and use without ownership (Boddewyn, Halbrich and Perry, 1986). Every one of these *by itself* is insufficient to differentiate a service from a non-service, and the concept remains rather elusive except in a multi-faceted definition. Further, most companies producing physical goods also produce services, and many service companies such as airlines are heavily equipment based. Differentiation cannot proceed then, except very crudely, by counting firms.

Much has been made of the increasing proportion of services in the Gross Domestic Product of advanced countries, so much so that it has become commonplace. However, the interdependency between manufacturing and services must also be emphasized. Tourism ranges from highly equipment-intensive service businesses, such as airlines and hotels, to much more people-based companies, such as tour operators, and information-based operations, such as travel agents. Even within these sectors differentiation occurs. For instance, the centralized reservation system of international hotels and airlines is based on the collection, manipulation and transmission of large quantities of information. Research on advances in technology, particularly information technology, in the tourism sector thus goes hand-in-hand with advances in the use of this technology.

An increasing amount of research is being conducted on service industry multinational firms. The 1989 UNCTC study is an example of a rapidly growing research focus. Multinational firms in the tourism industry feature greatly in this work. A review of this research is made by John Dunning (1988). Largely, this strand of research has concentrated on the methods by which multinational firms in tourism service foreign markets and the study of particular modes of market servicing such as franchising (see Chapter 4). The relationship between this work and practical international corporate planning is strong.

Thus, tourism as a set of interrelated service industries is one of the leading research areas for the study of the uniqueness of the services sector. The peculiarities of service industries lead to particular management problems, which are also the focus of research.

Case studies in tourism

In order to delineate an area of academic research, it is necessary to describe the phenomena to be encompassed. Much of the work in tourism to date has been descriptive, at least in the early exploratory stages of new projects and prior to the development of concepts.

A great deal of work has been carried out of the case study type. This involves the examination of one destination or facility (accommodation, hotel or attraction) and less usually one origin (country, region or town exporting tourists). Subsets of descriptive studies include urban tourism, rural tourism, tourism in difficult areas, island tourism.

Urban tourism

Several case studies of urban tourism and a related concept, tourism in difficult areas, have illuminated the potential and problems in using tourism as (part of) a strategy to regenerate declining cities. These studies relate strongly to policy prescriptions, to methods of planning and to visitor motivations. They have played a most useful role in moving tourism research away from excessive concentration on 'sun and sea' tourist destinations. Studies such as that of Jansen-Verbeke (1986) present a model of city tourism relating the main product (inner city environment) to the tourist and promoters. The Jansen-Verbeke study also presents a profile of inner city visitors, including activity patterns, the importance of product characteristics and the role of promotion in attracting visitors to inner city areas. Thus, a descriptive study of historic Dutch cities moves rapidly into analytical work on the motivations for inner city tourism and to policy implications. Similarly, the case study approach of Buckley and Witt (1985, 1989) on 'difficult areas' examines the promotion and planning role of local government bodies. The degree of sophistication of the responsible bodies varies enormously, even in the restricted sample covered and there are policy lessons to be learned. The 1989 case study also examines the question of viability – what attractions, infrastructive and accommodation does a city or 'an area' need to be a discrete, viable destination? Where one town or city does not have the minimum critical mass, a policy of co-operation regionally is suggested. This approach is taken further by Vandermey (1984), who presents a preliminary conceptual model of an urban tourism system.

Urban tourism research has been a prime example of policy oriented research, beginning with a descriptive base but building on this to develop a conceptual system. Many examples of research that outline the tourism potential of 'outworn industrial areas' such as those above and Travis's study of the South Wales valleys (1984) have gone hand-in-hand with the implementation of innovative policies by local and national governments and tourist boards. Indeed, a guide for local authorities was produced by the English Tourist Board in 1980 (English Tourist Board, 1980). The example of US cities in this regard has been path-breaking, notably Baltimore's inner harbour and Lowell's historic textile mills (Falk, 1986). Urban tourism research has shown that, by innovating, regional and local bodies can use tourism as part of a regeneration strategy. They have also sounded a warning that tourism is not, and cannot be, a panacea for all economic ills.

Rural tourism

Research on rural tourism has illustrated an essential element of 'balance' in tourist development. Indeed, much of it has had an implicit cost-benefit calculus. Tourism in rural areas has played a positive role in raising rural incomes and introducing 'growth poles' into backward, low-income agricultural areas, thus preventing or slowing out-migration. However, it has had disruptive effects on the rural environment, on local cultures and life styles, on agricultural patterns and even productivity. Consequently, the litany of the rural tourism researcher is to call for planning. It is clear that infra-structural development is essential if tourists are to be transported to and accommodated and amused in the rural area. As this is usually the province of public bodies, then such bodies have a degree of control over access. The key concern is largely that the very thing that rural tourists require – a bucolic environment – is not destroyed by the sheer weight of tourists. Unique attractions, which exist in an essentially rural environment, such as the cave dwellings of Spain, France and Turkey, and Stonehenge in England, pose particularly difficult problems of balance, access and destruction of the environment.

However, it should be noted that not all the economic effects are positive. Often rising land values make it impossible for (young) local people to buy or maintain property, and the purchases of holiday homes by tourists can destroy local communities.

Several examples of case studies of rural tourism are contained in Bouquet and Winter (1987) including the Isles of Scilly, the Valle d'Aosta, Cornwall, Brittany, and the Great Barrier Reef in Queensland, Australia. The primary aim of this collection is to offset the economic (income-generating) aspects of rural tourism against the social and cultural costs. Environmental concerns, which loom large in rural tourism research, are examined in the section on environmental consequences of tourism (see p. 157).

Island tourism

A subset of case study research has examined island tourism. A feature of islands is that it is possible to spatially delineate effects on the community under study and to examine feedback effects. Leakages from the island economy can be more easily identified. A considerable amount of this work has been carried out in the Caribbean and is related to issues of the impact of tourism on development (Bryden, 1973; Archer, 1977).

The issues of development also impinge on the marketing of tourism in small island states, where tourism is often the major sector of the economy. Issues of dependence on tourists, on the perceived negative effects and of benefits largely flowing abroad need to be taken into account in development policies (Wing, 1989).

Summary studies

The importance and scope of the tourist industry is illustrated by OECD's study of the evolution of tourism in member countries, *Tourism Policy and International Tourism* (1988), which examines the labour market in the hotel industries, the international tourist flows and the economic importance of international tourism in member countries. The OECD, of course, represents all the major developed market economies of the world, and the statistical annex is a particularly useful presentation of data on international tourist flows.

The study by the Commission of the European Communities of *The Tourism Sector in the Community* (1985) complements the OECD study by examining the degree of concentration, competition and competitiveness of the industry, covering suppliers of hospitality, hotels (including hotel chains) and tour operators (airlines are neglected). Tourism in Asia and the Pacific is examined by Mak and White (1988), and Japan's international tourist flows, both inward and outward, are set in the context of Japan's international economic relations by Buckley, Mirza and Witt (1989).

Impact studies

Studies of the impact of tourist development on a particular destination or destinations have been the largest single element of tourism research. Much of this work is predominantly the work of economists and has concentrated on the effect on incomes and employment, possibly to the exclusion of social and environmental factors. This neglect is much less true of more recent work. The major concerns of impact studies are the estimation of the impact of tourism on income levels and on employment generation. To this end, tourism multiplier analysis has developed.

Tourism multipliers

The direct spending of a tourist on transport, accommodation, food, amenities and other services will have a direct effect on incomes in the destination (see also chapter 1). Part of this expenditure will be re-spent by its recipients on meeting their needs. Thus, a second round of spending is generated. This second round expenditure generates a third, fourth and fifth, and so on, until the final round becomes negligible. The ratio between the initial spending and the final accumulated total expenditure is termed the multiplier effect. In each round leakages occur on savings and on imports, which have no further expenditure generating effect. The size of these leakages, governed by the propensity to save and to import, determine the ultimate size of the multiplier effect. Tourist expenditure thus has a *direct* effect, an *indirect* effect through the increased expenditure of the tourist sector and an *induced* effect, arising from the increase in income levels resulting from the direct plus indirect effect. (For a detailed exposition, see Archer, 1977; for a cautionary tale on the misuse of multipliers, see Bryden and Faber, 1971.)

Multipliers have been calculated for national economies, regions, cities and towns, using a variety of methodologies. A summary is given in Fletcher and Snee (1989b), and individual examples are found in Pallard (1976) for Antigua in the Caribbean and Sadler, Archer and Owen (1973) for Anglesey, Wales. Naturally, the larger the area covered, the larger is the multiplier, because the import leakage is correspondingly smaller. National multipliers for large countries range between 1.2 and nearly 2, for small island states from 0.56 to just over 1 and for cities and towns from 0.15 to 0.3.

Calculation of multipliers has become a major element in policy analysis. If the ultimate economic benefit of tourism is the extra income generated for the destination, then it is essential to have a quantitative estimation of this benefit. The policy use goes further, however, because it is with employment multipliers that, in an age of less than full employment, policymakers are concerned.

The employment multiplier shows how many full-time jobs (or full-time-equivalent jobs) increased tourist expenditures generate. It requires additional detailed information on the precise amounts of spending and additional assumptions on the rate of conversion of spending to (new) jobs.

An important adjunct to multiplier effects is input–output analysis. Input–output analysis is a general equilibrium technique, which maps the structure of an economy by quantifying the inputs from different sectors into final demand. For a given increase in final demand, by tracing the impact through an input–output table, the effect on each subsector can be estimated. Thus, for a given projected increase in tourist demand, the effect on the construction industry, for example, can be estimated. This provides a flexible planning tool. The use of the technique in general is described by Archer (1977) and Fletcher and Snee (1989b). A study of Gibraltar using the technique has been conducted by Fletcher, Snee and MacLeod (1981).

The impact of day trips

The excursionist, as distinct from the tourist, is a visitor who stays less than a maximum of 24 hours in his/her destination. The effect of such visitors is often underestimated. The amount of international excursions is growing within Europe and in North America. Developments in international travel, including the Channel Tunnel, will rapidly expand this sector of the international tourism market. The impact (largely uninational but not exclusively so) of day trips in many countries is examined in AIEST (1988).

Cost-benefit studies

Cost-benefit analysis is a generic name for a set of techniques used to evaluate the viability or impact of new expenditures or developments. Its essential elements are: a complete inventory of all the effects, good and bad, of the development and a valuation of these effects. In practice, of course, it is difficult to capture and evaluate every effect.

Cost-benefit analysis can be used as a straightforward financial tool. All costs are listed and rated by market prices and all revenues are accounted for in the same way. If the net present value is greater than or equal to zero, then the project is viable; if not, it should not be undertaken. Thus, a commercial valuation of a project over a given time period with a given discount (interest) rate can be arrived at. Under normal circumstances, such as the establishment of a new hotel, estimates will have to be made of certain key parameters, such as the projected costs of fixtures and fittings, and forecasts of demand will have to be made. Under these circumstances, cost-benefit analysis provides a framework into which to fit all the known facts and assumptions and a decision rule on outcome (see Etzel and Swensen, 1981; Walsh, 1986).

However, it is in the area of social cost-benefit analysis that the technique can be most useful. Social cost-benefit analysis allows non-commercial factors to be built into project appraisal. This is achieved by weighting certain benefits and costs at values other than market prices. Such accounting or shadow prices are intended to reflect more accurately the opportunity costs in situations where market prices are distorted by monopoly, or government intervention, including taxes and subsidies, exchange controls or tariff and non-tariff barriers to trade. This may be a particularly acute problem in less developed countries, particularly those following an import substitution policy. In these cases, world prices of traded goods may be used and non-traded goods, such as electricity, can be valued by breaking them down into equivalent trade goods. Labour can be valued at the prevailing wage rate or at its opportunity cost, that is, the value it would provide if it were not employed in the tourism project. This is derived from the Little–Mirrlees method of project evaluation (Little and Mirrlees, 1968).

It is further possible to include the impact on saving and on income distribution by adding weighting factors to projects, which generate extra savings or lessen income maldistribution. Where foreign exchange is scarce, net earnings of foreign exchange can be given extra weight.

The use of cost-benefit analysis in planning tourism projects is widespread. It is a versatile technique which allows (government) objectives to be built directly into the calculations. It also allows decisions to be made where market prices would dictate otherwise. For this reason, all deviations from market prices (shadow prices) must be carefully justified. Several examples of its use are listed in Curry (1989). Again, research and implementation in international tourism are closely linked.

The development effects of tourism

A major area of controversy and of research interest is the question whether tourism contributes to development or hinders (distorts) development. This is an issue not only for less developed countries but also for advanced industrialized societies (Williams and Shaw, 1988).

Needless to say, conflicting results have emerged from research on this topic. Tourism has been described as 'a passport to development' (de Kadt, 1979) and has been attacked as distorting development into desirable outcomes (Turner and Ash, 1975). There is no doubt that the conclusion depends upon the nature of the destination, the type of tourism and the way tourism is managed (or not managed), but it remains true that at least sometimes the outcome depends on the predilections of the researcher. Even with the most sophisticated research techniques, judgements remain important.

The nature of the destination will influence the development impact through factors such as: the alternative income earning opportunities facing the indigenous population, the geographical spread or concentration of tourist modes, the demographic features of the host country (density, age structure, cultural background), ecological and environmental background, infrastructural provision and political structure. The type of tourism will also influence development: the level of spending of the tourists, the form of tourism (business, holiday), the national groups involved, the type of tourism ('sun and sea', cultural tourism) and seasonality factors. Neither of these two factors are given nor immutable. The host environment can be altered by investment, by planning and controls and by (government) incentives, subsidies or penalties differentially applied. The type of tourism can be altered by promotion, prohibition and planning.

The most important economic impact on development arises from tourist spending, which, through the multiplier, can play an important role in stimulating the host economy. This will have effects in increasing income and creating or preserving employment, particularly given the labour intensive nature of tourism.

Other effects have been noted. These include the 'demonstration effect' of tourism, which presents the local community with models of behaviour different to their traditional mode and, therefore, may distort behaviour. This may be both negative and positive. Negative effects have been adduced to include an increased desire for luxury goods, which also has a negative balance of payments effect in many developing countries because of the high import content. Other influences are changes in political structures, the impact on family life (because of the increased demand for female labour), on morals (particularly where sex tourism is a major element, an example being Thailand), on local culture and communities, and migration. A difficulty of such a research agenda is that many of the 'impacts' attributed to tourism are the result of *any* economic development.

A further element of impact is that upon income distribution within the host country. The rapid development of many tourist modes has induced spatial differences in income levels and, where divisions exist on ethnic lines within countries, it can produce benefits for one tribal or ethnic group when others remain stationary, thus inducing political tensions. The influence on the class structure has also been the subject of research.

There are many studies of the development impact of tourism

(see Allcock, 1989; Williams and Shaw, 1988) and, because of the importance of the subject, there will be many more. Future research needs to be more careful in specifying the precise area of benefit and costs. With rigorous and transparent cost-benefit analysis, where the value judgements and assumptions are all carefully specified, more progress will be made. We should beware of seemingly unbiased research, which is really a cloak either for increased state intervention or for laissez-faire policies. Either policy might be justified in certain circumstances, but consumers of research and policy-makers need to be crystal clear on what those circumstances are.

Transport studies

Transport plays an important role in the tourism industry. It is, of course, a major object of study in its own right. Despite this, or possibly because of it, the subset of transport studies that directly relates to tourism is relatively neglected. Research in transport studies covers transport policy and planning, traffic models, traffic control (including route choice and route guidance), assessment and planning issues, public transport (supply and demand uses), studies of regulatory and organizational change, and accident and safety studies. Many of the techniques developed in transport studies are of direct relevance to tourism research, notably information technology applications, survey design issues (including preference experiments) and the general use of quantitative models. The high level of development of mathematical models in transport studies is exemplified by *Transportation Science*, the quarterly journal of the Transportation Science Section of the Operations Research Society of America, which publishes mathematical models and heuristics of transportation systems, including strategic planning models. More policy oriented journals include the *Journal of Transport Economics and Policy*, the *International Journal of Transport Economics* and *Transportation Research A*. The field of transport economics is well developed and mature, and it would pay tourism researchers to integrate this work more closely with their own.

It is clear that tourism transport plays a major role in determining the effects of tourism on the origin and destination countries. An outline of this is given by Heraty (1989a, 1989b) in examining the local effects of tourism transport on less developed countries. Improvements in transport infrastructure are specified: airport–hotel transfer, sightseeing and ground tours, provision for individual travel, and transport for cruise ship passengers where this is important. Studies of major transport companies such as airlines are an important input into the tourist literature. An example is the comparative review of Singapore Airlines and British Airways by Sikorski (1990). It is a major task of research to bring together the work done in transport studies with that more specialized work on tourism. In fact, many of the relevant studies in transport are privately commissioned and often not widely disseminated.

Descriptive statistics on tourism

In order for quantitative estimates of the extent, impact and nature of tourism to be made and for effective forecasting, the body of data on tourism has to be improved. Essentially, this is the task of central government in each tourism generating and destination country. International tourist arrivals and receipts data for receiving countries and outbound tourism data for generating countries are collected and compiled by the World Tourism Organization (WTO), which enables a satisfactory and compatible data base to be generated. However, the WTO data are only as good as the basic information supplied by individual countries, and this varies wildly. Most information is provided by 'grossing-up' sample surveys, based on a very small sample in many cases. Consequently, subsets of data may be grossly misleading. The more micro the level of analysis, the more likely are errors to exist. There is a constant demand for improvements in national statistics, because intracountry tourism is less likely to be accurately measured than international tourism. Consequently, the size, shape and future development of the tourist industry may be greatly mis-specified. There is a continued need for improvement of information, particularly as the industry grows in importance. Much of the research conducted relies on published, secondary data and its accuracy must command constant attention. There are many countries in the world where the quality of data is actually decreasing because of lack of resources devoted to the statistical services. This trend calls into question the accuracy of some tourism research. A criticism of statistics on tourism is given by Withyman (1985) (see also Allard, 1989).

Tourism forecasting

Tourism development and planning takes place in an uncertain world. One of the key uncertainties, from the point of view of suppliers of tourism services, is the level and nature of future demand. For practitioners, this is a crucial variable.

Methods of tourism forecasting were reviewed in chapter 3, and this section merely reinforces the importance of the research carried out in that area. Both the econometric approach and non-causal quantitative techniques have been developed to enable tourist arrivals and a breakdown by types of tourism to be more accurately foreseen (Witt, 1989a, 1989b). In addition, models have been developed which enable major events to be factored into models. Techniques such as the Delphi method, which relies essentially on achieving a consensus of informed experts, are an important tool, particularly when the factors driving developments are imperfectly understood (Hawkins, 1989). With the demand for better forecasts and better calibrated predictions in the area of tourism (demand) forecasting, it is reasonable to expect further developments in the forecasting area.

Information studies in tourism

Given the difficulties of obtaining accurate data in many areas of tourism, the growth of research in information studies and in data bases is encouraging. Such research is beginning to provide the foundation for more accurate research and, therefore, policymaking and management practice.

Important data bases now exist covering:

1 General tourism resources, including bibliographic sources, search mechanisms, and abstracting services.
2 Statistical and quantitative databases, including air travel and other industry indicators.

The growth of information systems and the means of access through the spread of microcomputers gives an opportunity for important developments in research and immediacy of access to research. The expansion of computer software also enables the study of modelling, information networks and market information (Witt and Moutinho, 1989).

The environmental consequences of tourism

With the growing worldwide concern for environmental issues, it is not surprising that there is an increasing amount of research related to the tourism industry's environmental and ecological effects. Much of this research is policy driven and a large part of it is financed by bodies that are not neutral but committed to an environmentalist position.

As with many of the other research issues reviewed, the impact of tourism in the environmental area depends on the quantity and nature of the tourism in question. Again, much of the concern is with the effects of mass tourism, but, almost uniquely, the environmental impact of small numbers of tourists into virgin areas can have a disproportionately negative effect on the environment and wildlife.

The countervailing forces are important also. There are many occasions where environmental change has been prevented by the earnings (or possibility of earnings) that the tourism industry brings. In addition, it is necessary to distinguish between the environmental effects of tourism and other continuing pressures. Aesthetic and ecological degradation must be distinguished. There remains a great requirement for further case study work and for synthesizing efforts. Despite the shift to 'green' politics in recent years, environmental issues are often treated as a residual. There is a pressing need for environmental, ecological and even aesthetic factors to be built into comprehensive cost-benefit analyses of tourism projects.

Spatial issues in tourism

A great deal of fundamental research in tourism has been carried out by geographers, or analysts with a geographical background. The spatial issues of tourism are obvious and important, as tourism involves the spatial movement of large numbers of people. The movement of people also necessitates the movement of resources and results in a changed pattern of economic activity. The spatial impact of tourism has a concentrated aspect in and around the destination, and a ripple effect on nearby areas plus a further effect on the origin.

The development of concepts such as the *tourism system* and the *tourism environment* draw for much of their inspiration on spatial analysis (see Mill and Morrison, 1985; Travis, 1989). The locational aspects are emphasized in concepts of tourism destination zone, tourism destination area and areas of regional impact. These concepts have evolved into a system of spatial planning which is an essential aspect of tourism planning for destination regions. Much of this work is the province of consultants and specialist consultancy firms rather than of individual researchers, and so much of it has a proprietary (and competitive) element. The major virtue of research on tourism destination areas is that it enables an integrated, adaptive and action-oriented strategy to enable spatial planning of rapid tourist development (Travis, 1989). The seminal work has been carried out by Gunn, working in a North American context, but the theoretical base has been adapted to planning internationally. It allows the integration of physical planning and, through this, environmental elements into a holistic approach.

The development impact of tourism has also been enhanced by spatial work conducted by geographers, often in collaboration with specialists in other disciplines (see, for example, Williams and Shaw, 1988). The analogy of tourism with international migration, albeit an imperfect analogy because of the temporary nature of tourism, allows the adaptation of models of migration to tourist flows. In an age of 'mass' tourism, the impact of the constantly replenishing flow of tourists has a similar impact to a migratory inflow.

The social and cultural impact of tourism

All too often, the social and cultural impact of economic changes are treated as residuals. If there was a danger of this occurring in tourism research, it is no longer true. As many studies have found benefits in terms of income and employment generation, it has been left to sociologists to take up the mantle of 'the dismal science' and point out many of the dis-benefits in terms of social costs (Allcock, 1989a). As Allcock points out, much early work was conducted as an attack on tourism without a solid sociological base.

Several concepts have now been developed to begin to encompass the social effects of tourism. One important concept is the 'demonstration effect', which, it is suggested, often corrupts local people and presents models of lifestyles that they cannot hope to attain, thus breeding discontent and the possibility of corruption and crime. There can also be knock-on effects of local class and status structures and disruptions to traditional hierarchies. Political and spatial relationships will also be reorganized. Family structures, the role of women, the cohesion of the local community, moral problems and microeconomic structures have all been shown, in individual cases, to be affected by tourist development. However, few of these sociological studies have been conducted on a comparative basis and generalization of the results is difficult. Many of the studies see destination areas as passive recipients of external change imposed from without. Many elements attributed to tourism should more accurately be attributed to more general factors and to any kind of development. There is also concern that the sociology of tourism should not be theoretically isolated from the development of the discipline as a whole.

Leisure and recreation

Tourism, leisure and recreation are clearly interrelated concepts, and it is in the study of leisure that sociologists have made considerable research progress. Class differences in patterns of leisure, patterns of leisure change over time and the positioning of tourism within a wider social and cultural context have all been contributions (Allcock, 1989a). The distinction between work and leisure and the structuring of leisure time place tourism in a wider cultural context. The management of leisure services is well covered by Gratton and Taylor (1988).

Motivation of the tourist

The social psychology of the tourist is the fundamental factor in buyer behaviour and demand patterns in tourism, and it is fair to suggest that it has been studied more in the commercial context, by market researchers, than in the pure research sense. Terms such as the 'quest for excitement' and the 'quest for authenticity' are coined to explain some of the primary human motivations in undertaking tourism (MacCannel, 1976; Elias and Dunning, 1978). The process of privatization (that is, attempts to appropriate public goods as private ones) has also been seen as a key element (Habermas, 1976). It is fair to say that coherent and comprehensive social psychological models are not yet available. Despite this, each of the attempts above to encompass tourist motivations conceptually has a great deal to teach us in the fundamental restructuring of basic motivations, which needs to be a research priority. Otherwise, our understanding of consumer behaviour in tourism will remain superficial. There are encouraging signs that this is beginning to happen, as is shown in the analysis by Chon (1989), applied to the recreational traveller.

Consumer behaviour in tourism

Research on consumer behaviour in tourism has largely a market research focus. The main input is from analyses of tourist responses to standard pre-programmed questionnaires. It therefore qualifies rather more as innovation than research. In this framework tourists, or rather tourist motivations, are treated as a 'black box'. In goes the stimulus (perhaps an advertising campaign), and out comes the response (perhaps an increase in purchases of the heavily promoted product). The underlying elements in this result, the motivation for the behaviour observed, is unknown or assumed away (see

Middleton, 1988, chapter 5). The great amount of data collected by market research organizations represents a largely untapped resource for the testing of hypotheses on consumer response. The fault lies not in data availability but in the structuring of hypotheses to examine basic motivation. This leads back to the previous section, where a deficiency was noted in the understanding of the social psychology of tourism.

This is not to say that, at the level of understanding purchasing patterns in the short run, there are deficiencies. Clearly, the excellence of much consumer research in the tourism industry enables patterns to be predicted with a reasonable degree of accuracy. What is lacking is a longer-term understanding of fundamental motivation. Large-scale switches in demand over the medium term, such as the trend towards environmentally friendly purchases, can only be understood when fundamental concepts are developed and refined.

A major problem with consumer motivation research is that much of it is privately commissioned and is often not made available to the general enquirer.

The politics of tourism

There can be little doubt that the politics of tourism, in the sense of resolving conflicts that arise from tourist development and the process of reconciling (or failing to reconcile) opposing points of view, are crucial to the development of the industry and the phenomena of international tourism. Apart from the area of policy studies, this aspect has received relatively little attention. There is a great deal of scope for a political science analysis of the disparate scope of international tourism. Many aspects, touched on in other sections of this review, require careful study by political scientists. Conflicts within the destination country, the impact of foreigners both as tourists and developers, conflicts in the origin country (staying in the home country generates more domestic income) and between countries are all themes that surface again and again. At conferences on tourism, interested parties have axes to grind and viewpoints that are diametrically opposed – the developer and local residents, the foreign investor and environmental groups, trade unionists and entrepreneurs are some examples. The political process is crucial and is worthy of further analysis.

Policy analysis in tourism

Policy analysis and evaluation is a major element of tourism research. The consequences of tourist development *ex post* are an important indicator of likely *ex ante* benefits and costs of similar development. Much of tourism research can be seen as policy review work. This is likely to be influential for decision-makers and for future innovations in the industry. It will be seen from previous parts of this chapter that some elements of the outcome of tourist developments are likely to be more effectively evaluated than others. It is a frequent complaint that the more easily quantifiable elements, such as employment creation, are more likely to be given weight against elements less easy to quantify, such as environmental damage. The level of sophistication of policy analysis in international tourism is increasing, but it remains dependent on developments in the core disciplines and their successful integration.

Management research in tourism

Much of this book is concerned with developments in management technique, skills and outlook as they apply to the international tourism industry. It is in this area that great progress has been made. The application of state of the art management skills and techniques is, of course, differentially distributed throughout the industry. Access to research in this case is also differential – much of it is in English, with French and Spanish also important. It has also influenced the larger and more international companies rather more than small insular operations. Very few operators of small hotels, attractions, transport facilities and catering establishments have been exposed to management research on tourism. This is largely a problem of dissemination (and of training). A two-tier profession is emerging, with highly trained, aware up-to-date professional management in the large company transnational sector and traditional techniques prevailing in smaller companies. The focus of much research, also, has been on large companies. The role of management in the small company involved in international tourism is a research lacuna.

Within the management discipline, it is perhaps particularly the marketing area that has been most extensively developed. Comprehensive texts such as that of Middleton (1988) draw on a great deal of marketing research and provide a good vehicle for dissemination. There has been less of this kind of activity in finance, organizational behaviour, personnel and operations management. At the research level, though, the management disciplines have been active and, as funding for basic research from the industry itself increases, this research will feed into practice through more widespread dissemination in the near future.

Research on training in tourism

It is almost universally agreed that training is crucial to the competitiveness and indeed survival of the international tourism industry. As quality competition is so important to competitive strategy, the skills of the individuals in the component service industry (hotels, catering, transport) become key elements in the struggle for market position. In many countries, the lack of training in the industry has been identified as a key strategic weakness. Therefore, many countries have established or expanded their training programmes for the tourist sector. Because this is a relatively new phenomenon, there has been little analysis, as yet, of the efficiency or effectiveness of these programmes. Hence, there is little policy analysis to establish which training programmes produce the best results or what design the next generation of programmes should have. This is clearly an urgent task for the international tourism industry, its constituent bodies and national and regional governments.

Apart from overall policy and analysis, more micro-oriented research is required on the content of training programmes, teaching methods, curriculum development and access methods.

Research in hotel and catering studies

In some ways, work on the hotel and catering sector has been the poor relation of tourism research. Much of the work done has been teaching-related and this heuristic role has permeated research activity. Work that does exist takes a descriptive view of industry structure (Medlik, 1978) or methods of operation within the industry (Medlik, 1980; Greene, 1983). This type of work is aimed at the practitioner and is extremely valuable in raising standards and awareness.

There is a need to increase basic research on hotels and catering. Many of the fundamental and integrative concepts outlined above have yet to be applied to the hotel and catering sectors of the industry, and research remains almost entirely related to management operations.

Conclusion

This chapter has taken a wide remit in examining research and innovation in tourism. It is a fair criticism of what has been presented that research may be too grand a word for policy-oriented or descriptive or management-driven work. However, it is a major strength of research work in tourism that it has been and continues to be task-driven. There is more than a sense of partiality in much of the work. Indeed, tourism research is defined by its interest in a related cluster of industries rather than by a disciplinary, ethical or theoretical base. However, this bias, if bias there be, is not one-sided. Environmental groups have conducted research, showing the negative impact of tourism in the way that organizations in the tourist industry sponsor work that shows the good side of tourism. It is also a fair point that tourism research lacks a theoretical base, but it is perhaps unrealistic to expect such a variegated set of phenomena to have a single theoretical underpinning. Rather, we would expect the study of the international tourism industry (or industries) to be developing a number of theoretical underpinnings, and this is proving to be the case. In the forthcoming period we can expect a competition of paradigms and we should not expect any one research agenda to prevail. Tourism research, like tourism itself, will remain dynamic, variegated and at times internally conflictual. Its strengths of practicality, policy orientation and relevance are likely to be accentuated. It remains to be seen if its weaknesses can be ameliorated.

The research will continue to feed innovation to the industry and to be stimulated by it. There is a sense of closer community between those who work in the tourism industry and those who research it than is the case in almost any other field. However, many of the issues are new and it takes time to identify, describe, conceptualize and test hypotheses on new phenomena.

Research agenda in international tourism

The strengths of tourism research are its transdisciplinarity and its relevance to actual operation in the industry. Its weaknesses are its partiality and its lack of core theory. Key research issues are listed below:

- More comprehensive integration of tourism within a theoretical analysis of the services sector as a whole.
- A movement onwards from descriptive studies of destinations to analytical approaches to impact.
- More comprehensive cost-benefit analyses, based on a holistic

approach to the economic, sociological, environmental and political impact of international tourism.

- The integration of leisure and recreation, hotel and catering studies with tourism into a related framework of analysis.
- More fundamental understanding of the social psychology of tourists.
- Development from policy analysis to a political science of tourism.
- A feedback of concepts from management studies in tourism to tourism research.

Further reading

To encompass research and innovation in tourism in a few further readings can only be meaningful if the further readings lead into wider avenues of research. In several cases, examples of a genre are given.

1 On the international development of service industries as a whole, the UNCTC (1989) report, *Transnational Corporations in World Development: Trends and prospects*, has more than 100 pages devoted to transnational co-operations in services (Part 5). For the particular case of the United Kingdom, David Liston and Nigel Reeves (1988), *The Invisible Economy: A profile of Britain's invisible exports*, London: Pitman, is a comprehensive guide to international services, and Chung H. Lee and Seiji Naya (1988), *Trade and Investment in Services in the Asia–Pacific Region*, Boulder, Colo: Westview Press, does a similar job on a vitally important region.

2 For a review of research on multinationals in the service industries, see John H. Dunning (1989), 'Multinational enterprises and the growth of services: Some conceptual and theoretical issues', *Service Industries Journal*, vol. 9, no. 1.

3 Good examples of the role of tourism and development are given by John M. Bryden (1973) *Tourism and Development: A case study of the Commonwealth Caribbean*, Cambridge: Cambridge University Press, and Allan M. Williams and Gareth Shaw (eds) (1988), *Tourism and Economic Development: Western European experiences*, London: Belhaven Press, which shows that development issues are not confined to poor countries. Articles often appear on the development impact of tourism in journals such as *The Journal of Development Studies*.

4 The OECD's (1988) *Tourism Policy and International Tourism*, is a good sourcebook containing useful data.

5 A good, short summary on tourism multipliers is given by John Fletcher and Helena Snee (1989) in Stephen F. Witt and Luiz Moutinho (eds) (1989), *Tourism Marketing and Management Handbook*, Hemel-Hempstead: Prentice-Hall. A similar introduction to cost-benefit analysis is presented by Steve Curry in the same volume.

6 The sociology of tourism has a disparate and extensive scope. John Allcock's chapter ('Sociology of tourism') in Witt and Moutinho, op.

cit., allows an insight to be gained into the concern of sociologists. A dated but trenchant introduction to social problems of tourists is Louis Turner and J. Ash (1975), *The Golden Hordes: International Tourism and the Pleasure Periphery*, London: Constable.

7   On tourist motivation, see the short article by Kye-Sung Chon (1989) 'Understanding recreational traveler's motivation, attitude and satisfaction', in *The Tourist Review*, no. 1, 1989.

8   Tourism policies in the public sector are reviewed by G. P. Brown and S. J. Essex in the Witt and Moutinho volume; the further reading section of this chapter is very rewarding (pp. 537–9).

9   M. Withyman (1985) 'The ins and outs of international travel and tourism data', *International Tourism Quarterly*, no. 4, presents a criticism of data sources.

10 An example of a text that pulls together a great deal of management–related research is Victor T. C. Middleton (1988) *Marketing in Travel and Tourism*, London: Heinemann. Francis Buttle (1986), *Hotel and Food Service Marketing: A managerial approach*, London: Holt, Rinehart and Winston, also shows the application of research findings.

11 In order to keep up to date with tourism research, it is essential to read the key journals publishing refereed articles. These include *Tourism Management, Annals of Tourism Research, Journal of Travel Research, International Journal of Hospitality Management* and *The Services Industries Journal*. In addition, many applied economics, marketing, business, management, geography, transport (e.g. *The Journal of Transport Economics and Policy*) and other journals carry articles on tourism. There are also many non-refereed journals of high standing in the area, such as *The Tourist Review (Revue de Tourism)* and the *Travel and Tourism Analyst*.

Specialist publications, such as *International Tourism Quarterly* (Economist Publications), are also useful in tracking the latest contributions. The *Cornell Hotel and Restaurant Administration Quarterly*, New York: Cornell University, provides a more specialized review. Abstracting services can be most useful in identifying relevant pieces of research work.

The Travel and Tourism Research Association is devoted to improving the quality, scope and acceptability of travel research and marketing information. In addition to publishing the *Journal of Travel Research* it also publishes directories of information, conference proceedings and bibliographies, including the nine-volume biblio-graphy of tourism and travel research (Goeldner *et al.*, 1980), and a review of research in handbook form (Ritchie and Goeldner, 1986).

9

Corporate strategies for international tourism

Introduction

The practice of corporate strategy, strategic management or business policy is an integrative procedure, which attempts to draw together all aspects of the organization's decisions into a coherent whole. Although these decisions are often taken at different levels in the organization and, in practice, are often unco-ordinated, corporate planning is the responsibility of top management. It is only top management who can have the strategic vision necessary to take decisions on a company-wide long-term basis. This explains the difference between strategy that has a long-term aim and tactics that represent shorter-term contingent decisions aimed at implementing partial elements of the overall strategy.

Implementing corporate strategy is a process that take place over a discrete time period. The process should be iterative, with many stages of feedback. However, it is convenient (following Luffman *et al.* (1987)) to divide this process into setting objectives, appraisal (both internal and external), strategy choice and strategy implementation.

Setting corporate objectives

Any company faces a variety of corporate (internal) and environmental (external) pressures. Those pressures that impact on objectives may be termed stakeholders. These stakeholders, who can influence the firm, include: shareholders, management, suppliers, customers, employees and governments. In addition, objectives must take into account environmental change and, in particular, the actions of competitors. The outcome of the process of setting objectives will represent a balancing of these interest groups.

Stakeholders

SHAREHOLDERS

It is frequently stated that the only objective of the firm is to maximize profits. As a long-run objective it is essential for survival that the assets of the company in the broadest possible sense earn a rate of return superior to that which they could earn elsewhere. However, to give operational content to this and to achieve a balance between the very long-term and shorter-term objectives, it is essential to set sub-goals and to satisfy other stakeholders. This is the essence of the managerial theories of the firm, which propose a trade-off between profits and management satisfaction (for a survey, see Wildsmith, 1973). Despite this trade off, and others, it is essential that shareholders remain content to hold shares, which represent ownership of the firm. If shareholders become dissatisfied, then it is open to them to dispose of their shares and thus to precipitate a change in ownership, with possible serious consequences for policy, including a change of management. Indeed, it may be managers themselves who own the company or, in the case of 'management buy-outs', who acquire a company from its existing shareholders (Wright, 1987).

In many countries, institutional shareholders are very important. These may include financial institutions (Great Britain), banks (Germany) and intra-group holding (Japan). Where the proportion of shares held by powerful outside bodies is large, the influence of such bodies will be significant.

Similarly, the key form of ownership in many countries is the private company. This may be a family group, a cluster of related families or even a single individual. The owner/manager/entrepreneur will be a uniquely powerful figure in deciding corporate strategy, and 'the boss's word is final' may be a sufficient explanation of strategy in these cases. Because financial institutions and the corporate framework differ so much between countries, private ownership does not necessarily only apply to small companies. In Germany, for instance, the private company (Ag, Aktiengesellscaft) can be become very large before there is any necessity to consider change to a publicly quoted company (Gmbh, Gesellscaft mit beschränkter Haftung).

For all private companies, however, corporate strategy is influenced by the necessity to raise capital. This is particularly acute for rapidly growing private companies. The approach of private companies to the capital market is fraught with difficulties. The key problem is the need to raise capital without losing control. Often, the competitive advantage of smaller (private) firms rests in the possession of unique skills, products, technology or ideas. This compounds the problems when it becomes necessary to raise capital to exploit the idea without giving the idea away! Under these pressures many family-owned or closely held companies are constrained to issue shares, thus relinquishing total control.

The pressure then to earn a good (short-term) rate of return to prevent shareholder disquiet, take-over or buy-out provides a constraint on policy. Any policy that ignores the influence of the capital market in this way is bound to run into problems. Private companies are more able to withstand these pressures because they are insulated to some degree from the immediacy of returns required by a publicly quoted company. Indeed, in the leisure, tourism and travel field, it is noticeable that the entrepreneur Richard Branson brought his Virgin group of companies back into private ownership after being publicly quoted, so that they could concentrate on long-term policies by the exclusion of short-term earnings. The shareholder profile is thus a key influence on objectives.

MANAGERS

Managers are the most important decision-makers in a company. In many cases, they will not be owners of the firm but will be professionals implementing, in theory at least, the wishes of the owners. In practice, it is an increasing trend that managers are given shareholdings in the firm for which they work in order to secure their loyalty, ensure that they work on behalf of all shareholders and to reward them for performance. However, we can separate the pure motivations of managers from managers as shareholders.

Models of 'managerial discretion' (see the summary in Wildsmith, 1973) suggest that managerial remuneration and discretionary income ('perks') may well be traded off against increasing the net worth of the company (as measured, for instance, by the share price). In addition prestige, particularly among peer groups, may also be important. This may lead, for instance, to a desire for growth for its own sake or to becoming international (for prestige reasons). The objectives will be paid for by trading off other benefits.

The issue of ownership versus control has been a long-standing one in the corporate literature. The relationship between owners and managers is thus vitally important in the formulation of objectives.

SUPPLIERS

Suppliers will be dependent on the company through purchasing behaviour. They will have a vested interest in the company's success as a buyer of products or services. In situations where the company is reliant (even dependent) on its suppliers, then it is important to take their interests into account. Examples include hotels being dependent on catering supplies and the famous network of sub-contracting that characterizes Japanese business. There is, of course, a tendency for the large and powerful to take over the small in purchasing chains, and such internalization strategies are as characteristic of the tourism industry as elsewhere. However, control in a chain of supply can be exercised without ownership, as the retailing firm Marks and Spencers have shown. Excessive dependence on key suppliers may, however, bias strategy and objectives.

CUSTOMERS
Companies that forget customers in any part of the process of corporate planning, including the formulation of objectives, are doomed to failure. It is a truism that companies cannot ignore the market. It is through the medium of management that the impact of customers is felt. A key role of managers is to predict market demand. In an industry as fragmented, volatile and seasonal as tourism, this becomes an even more major task. Moreover, as a tourism company is involved in face-to-face transactions with people, contacts are vital and feedback is likely to be immediate.

EMPLOYEES
The goodwill of employees is a *sine qua non* of successful operation in which human contact and personal skills are as important as in tourism. Often it is possible to regard the role and influence of employees as a constraint on the objectives of companies. Much more satisfactory is the view that the role of employees can contribute in a positive way to the establishment and achievement of company goals.

In many countries, notably the Federal Republic of Germany, in certain circumstances employees will, by statute, be equivalent to shareholders in being represented on the management board of the company. Their objectives can thus, in theory at least, be converted into company policy. Although this relationship is not as direct in many other countries, an input from employees should certainly be considered in the formulation of objectives, as the employee perspective can be most valuable, derived as it is likely to be in tourism from a direct interface with customers.

GOVERNMENTS
In international tourism, dealing with governments in the plural is a key fact of operation. For all but the most multinational of companies, the most important influence will be the government of the home (or parent) country. Objectives will be constrained by the necessity to conform to the laws, directives, statutory requirements, exhortations and ad hoc mechanisms of the country. Complicity in

matters of taxation, anti-trust (anti-monopoly or cartel) legislation, accounting practices, trade regulation, product liability and the myriad other public policies of government is a crucial element of careful strategy formulation. However, when we deal with international operations, it is an unfortunate fact of life that the public policies of the host governments will conflict or at least not fully mesh with, those of the home government. This can involve heavy expenses, for example, in reconciling financial accounts of a conflict of objectives between different units of the firm and internal dissensions in management.

Setting objectives

It will be apparant from the review of stakeholder interests above that the process of setting objectives is essentially political in the sense of reconciling differences. The constraints on objectives are both internal and external, and the outcome will depend on the representation of those interests by the key actors, who will be in the main managers and owners. Despite these factors it is important that there should be a clear articulation of unambiguous objectives as a basis for policy choice, implementation and approval. Resistance to this process should not be ignored. It is essential to secure approval of objectives, and this can be done by consultation, attempting to achieve consensus, promotion of the objectives (propagandizing) and linking incentives to the achievement of objectives.

The role of top management is crucial. But the process should not be confined to top management. Corporate objectives are long term and planning too must be long term. The length of time over which objectives are defined will vary over industry segments. Many firms find it useful to have long-term objectives (10 years) within which five-year rolling plans are defined.

Strategic appraisal

It is essential that firms in international tourism should have a clear, unbiased view of their internal and external position. It is important to know where the firm is, and where it is going. Inevitably, this will involve a view of where the firm has been. Strategic appraisal has two main components: internal and external.

Internal appraisal

An analysis of where the company is – an appraisal of its strengths and weaknesses – is a vital and continuous process. It is necessary to cover all aspects of the firm's operations: marketing, finance, personnel, research and development, production, structure, and systems and procedures.

Several techniques of internal appraisal are available (Argenti, 1974). The appraisal can be conducted by insiders – executives and managers directly meeting and discussing the position – or via surveys. It may be useful to employ outsiders, whose views may be more objective and detached – but who may not have full access to information. Whoever conducts the analysis, it is important that it be systematic, unbiased and realistic. Evidence from comparable firms within and possibly outside the industry provides a benchmark against which the position of the firm can be judged. The coherence (even existence) of the firm's past and projected strategy can be judged against the (relative) position of the firm.

It is useful to place the information necessary for a strategic appraisal in a framework like the Strengths – Weaknesses – Opportunities – Threats (SWOT) approach discussed in chapter 5. Debate can then take place among the relevant managers (and possibly other stakeholders) regarding the realism and exactitude of the entries. 'Harder' information, such as profitability, market share, financial ratios and personnel audits, can then be brought to bear in giving coherence to the appraisal.

External appraisal

Two levels of external appraisal may be distinguished: one is the analysis of the macro environment of the firm; the other a more micro and localized approval of the firm's particular industries, market and competitive framework.

Analysis of the macro environment is important because the long-term and overall framework in which the firm operates is not static, and prediction of changes that have an immediate impact often depends on changes at the most fundamental level. For firms in international tourism, of particular importance will be: (1) changes in demand pattern, which depends on income levels, tastes and distribution of income; (2) changes in political circumstances, both in the firm's home country and worldwide; (3) changes in technology; (4) social changes, including the ageing (greying) of the population in most advanced countries.

Each of these key factors will influence the internal organization of the firm and the relative costs that face it in its own market and others that impinge on it (including suppliers and the labour market). Consequently, the scale and scope of the firm must adjust in order to accommodate these external changes. A change in taste from 'sea and sun' type holidays to 'cultural tourism' will affect the occupancy rates and, therefore, the profitability of hotels in different locations, the pattern of amenity provision and travel pattern. A revolution in Ruritania will deflect holidaymakers to countries that are close substitutes. Improvements in computer technology will allow worldwide centralized booking facilities for hotels and transport companies. Each of these changes will alter the size, scope and location of firms and their investment. They will also encourage or deter entry (and exit) into the industry. The firms that are most alert to changing opportunities will gain most.

Against this general backdrop, firms must attempt to appraise their more immediate environment. This will generally mean their competitors and potential competitors, their customers and suppliers and (potential) substitutes. Figure 9.1 shows the key pressures driving industry competition. The figure (from Porter, 1980) shows the necessity to consider relationships external to the firm and, in particular, those areas where significant dependencies exist. It also illustrates the necessity to keep in mind dynamics – the likely changes in the current environment through, for instance, potential entrants and substitute products. Rivalry between existing firms (within the box in Figure 9.1) is only one aspect of a complete external appraisal.

Congruence between internal and external appraisal

A crucial feature of a coherent corporate plan is that there must be congruence between the internal and external approval. If the internal appraisal has shown that a major strength exists in current product offerings, then we would expect this to be reflected in

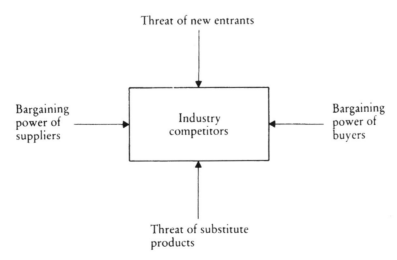

Figure 9.1 Forces driving industry competition.

current market share. Putting the two analyses together should reveal the extent to which internal perception is external reality.

Strategy choice

In examining the various frameworks available for strategy choice, several things should be borne in mind. First, these are merely frameworks. They enable choice to take place, based on the content put into the framework. If the content is wrong, the strategy will go wrong. If the internal and external appraisals contain errors of fact, perception and interpretation, no sophisticated framework of analysis will put it right. Second, the methods of structuring strategic choice will be more or less appropriate according to the strategic position and dynamics of the firm in its context. Some of these methods are appropriate to growing firms, others to firms wishing to arrest a decline. Some pay more attention to a rapidly changing environment, others are more suitable in situations closer to equilibrium. Third, none of the frameworks is a substitute for judgement. Managerial choice, entrepreneurial flair, careful planning are all required. The function of management is to adjust to change. These methods are an aid to that, not a substitute for it.

Several general tools of analysis are presented as examples of strategy choice: the Boston Consulting Group Matrix, General Electric Business Screen, Porter's Structural Analysis, Product Life Cycle Models and International Strategic Alternatives. For a more complete set, see Further Reading (p. 184).

The Boston consulting group matrix

The Boston Consulting Group Matrix, often referred to in shorthand terms as the 'Boston Box', is a device relating growth rate to relative competitive position at product level. Like many models in the strategic choice area, it presents a 2 by 2 matrix and reduction to two dimensions raises serious questions about its ability to handle complexity. It also suffers from a number of restrictive assumptions (Luffman *et al.*, 1987) that: the market can be defined, profitability and market share are positively related, there are no barriers to entry or exit in the market concerned, the stage of industry maturity can be defined and the market is still in the growth stage. Given these restrictions, however, the model still retains some heuristic value.

A representation of the matrix is shown in Figure 9.2. The two dimensions define four product categories – high-growth products where the firm has a strong relative competitive position ('stars'), lower-growth products with a strong market share ('cash cows'),

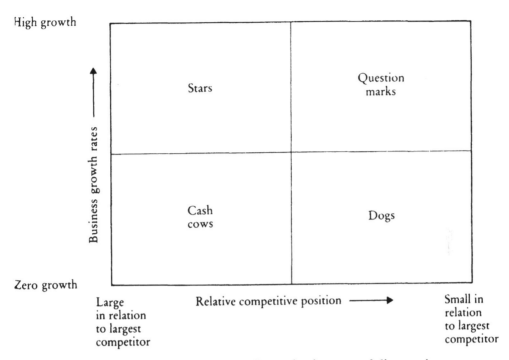

High growth

Business growth rates

Zero growth

Stars

Cash
cows

Question
marks

Dogs

Large
in relation
to largest
competitor

Relative competitive position ⟶

Small in
relation
to largest
competitor

Figure 9.2 The Boston Consulting Group business portfolio matrix.

high-growth products without a strong market share (question marks) and low-growth products with a weak market share (dogs). By mapping products according to their business growth rate and relative market share a current audit can be obtained. Strategy choice should then proceed by exiting from 'dogs' unless there is a powerful reason not to and by converting question marks into stars by increasing market share. Stars will eventually become cash cows as the market rate of growth slows and then these can be reinvigorated by using the cash flow for reinvestment. The matrix points to the need for balance between high-growth stars, which are unlikely to generate cash flow, and cash cows, which provide the wherewithal to generate new products and find investment. The approach assumes that a portfolio of products can be generated. It is difficult to apply the concept to a narrowly focused single-product company.

General Electric business screen

As a contrast to the over-simplistic approach of the Boston Box, the GE Matrix can become over-complicated. It includes, again, only two variables, but as these are industry attractiveness and competitive position, they break down into as many subvariables as can

Competitive Position

		Strong	Average	Weak
	High	Maximize investment Seek dominance seek		
Industry Attractiveness	Medium			Specialize Seek niche markets Consider exit
	Low			

Figure 9.3 The GE matrix analysis of strategy choice.

be suggested to affect a firm's profitability. In truth, the blank framework as presented in Figure 9.3 allows many interpretations. Essentially, the positioning of a firm's business units can begin only a preliminary screening of its choices.

It is essential in these approaches to pay particular attention to constraints on movement. It is costly both to enter and to exit from an industry and an industry segment. Attention to these costs is necessary to augment the analysis of strategic moves as presented by these frameworks.

Strategic growth vectors

It is often appropriate to analyse strategies around the issue of directions of growth of the company. Growth vector components as presented by Ansoff (1965) enable this to occur. Take first the simple division between existing and new products, existing and new missions. Thus, by examining the product market position it is possible to delineate generic growth strategies. As Figure 9.4 shows, the 2 by 2 matrix shows growth existing products in existing markets as market penetration, new products in existing markets as product development, new markets for existing products as market development, and new products and markets as diversification. This can be developed as Figure 9.5 shows, by including technology and the

Mission/Product	Present	New
Present	Market penetration	Product development
New	Market	Diversification

Figure 9.4 Growth vector components.

nature of integration to give a much richer pattern of growth strategies.

A matching of the perceived internal strengths and external opportunities can give a clear grasp of the important growth vectors likely to lead to success for the firm.

Product cycle models

The product cycle model (Vernon, 1966, 1979) makes four basic assertions: (1) Products undergo predictable changes in production and marketing. (2) There is restricted information available on

Products Customers	New Products Related technology	Unrelated technology
Some type	Horizontal diversification	
Firm its own customer	Vertical diversification	
Similar type	CD: Marketing and technology related	CD: Marketing related
New type	CD: Technology related	Conglomerate diversification

New missions

CD = Concentric diversification

Figure 9.5 Growth vectors in diversification.

products and technology; in particular proprietary knowledge, owned and controlled by firms, is crucial in attaining competitive leadership. (3) The production of goods and provision of services change over time and economies of scale are prevalent. (4) Tastes differ, so patterns of demand can vary. In particular, tastes differ according to income. This provides an opportunity for firms to standardize their offerings according to income levels. Segmentation of the market thus occurs as products travel through a life-cycle.

A 'typical' product cycle is depicted in Figure 9.6. The process has four stages, development, growth, maturity and decline. It is a notable weakness of product cycle analysis that the cycle is programmatic, not dynamic (Buckley and Casson, 1976). In other words, the programme is set (stage I→II→III), but there is insufficient explanation of the critical variables that drive this development and their relationship with elapsed time.

Stage I of the cycle is the innovation stage where a new product is created. This new product (for example, a Mediterranean 'sun and sea' holiday 'package' in the early postwar period) will tend to be unstandardized, high-priced and the province of one or a few innovative firms. These firms will receive quasi-monopoly returns to reward the innovation. In Stage II, the product becomes more standardized on both the demand side (as holidaymakers begin to follow the trend) and on the suply side (as the logistics become routine). New competitors enter the market and drive the price down. The possibility of economies of scale (block booking, purchase of aircraft and hotels with assured full occupation) also drive down costs. Investment by established firms in this stage may well occur to forestall entry. In State II the product becomes mature

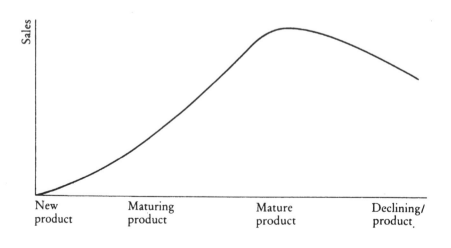

Figure 9.6   A typical product cycle.

and sells almost entirely on the basis of price. Attempts are made to secure niches within the market, but the primary imperative is to reduce costs. The product becomes susceptible to mass-marketing techniques. There is a tendency for the market to become dominated by a few large oligopolists. In the decline phase, substitute 'new products' (for example, long-haul packages to exotic destinations) begin to erode market share. The necessary capacity begins to decline and the product becomes much more like a commodity. This is not to say that the correct strategy is to leave mature product segments, because they are often capable of generating large cash flows. Strategies of product regeneration and segmentation can still earn a good return in such an industry. There is an imperative, however, to maintain strict cost control and this discipline may be beyond the capability of many operators.

Needless to say, there are many criticisms of the product cycle model as the basis for international corporate planning. It is over-deterministic and clearly does not apply to all products. It is also difficult to pin down exactly what constitutes a product (package holidays, Mediterranean package holidays, packages to Spain, the Costa del Sol?). In many ways the model is an industry cycle rather than a product cycle. There is also a great deal of evidence that product cycles are shortening, in many cases to the point where products are innovated, standardized and differentiated almost instantaneously rather than sequentially (air fares may be considered to be an example). The use of the product cycle model in international tourism may still have validity. However, it should be borne in mind that it splits three strategic decisions which are interdependent: investment in product development and innovation, the method of approaching foreign markets and the optimum way of competing with (potential) new entrants. The major criticism that the model is outdated must be judged in the context of product development in particular industry segments. The faster the speed of change, the less relevant is the model.

Structured analysis and generic strategies

The analysis of industry structure, competitive behaviour and relative competitive advantages can be key factors in strategic choice. Porter's work (1980, 1985) has suggested three key generic strategies: differentiation, overall cost leadership and focus. The choice, determined by strategic target and strategic advantage, is driven by the degree of uniqueness as perceived by the customer and the cost position of the company (see Figure 9.7).

Overall cost leadership rests on the ability of the firm to control costs. This means achieving economies of scale, gaining cost

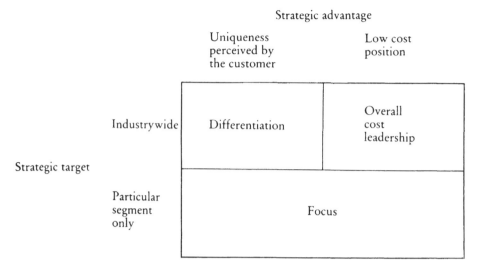

Figure 9.7   Porter's three generic strategies.

reduction through learning effects, tight control of overheads and reducing spending on sales costs. This strategy will tend to be linked to the achievement of high market share and maintaining a ruthless view of the product portfolio, eliminating products that do not conform to the strategy. Standardization of product and service is often the key to success in this strategy with mass marketing and advertising to maintain throughout. Examples in the tourist industry are basic package holidays and budget hotels.

A strategy based on differentiation requires that the firm's product be perceived as unique in the industry. This is usually but not necessarily a high-quality 'aim at the top of the market' type of strategy. The firm thus attains a defensible position by creating an area of quasi-monopoly, giving it some price leverage. A strategy of building consumer loyalty and quality superiority are adjuncts to the strategy. Some airlines, such as Cathay Pacific and Singapore Airlines, are in the enviable position of successfully following such a strategy. There is, however, often the necessity of sacrificing overall market share in order to differentiate successfully.

Finally, the strategy of focus is built on, aiming at a particular segment, geographical area or product line. The firm must be able to service this particular niche market more successfully than its broader-based competitors. It may, therefore, be lower cost or be perceived as superior by the key buyers in the niche. As there is an element of choice in this strategy, it can be used to secure niche positions that are least vulnerable to substitutes or where competitors are weak. Examples are companies specializing in safari holidays or specialists in particular destinations or hotels catering for minority needs.

Global planning – strategic alternatives

The issues of strategy choice do not differ when international aspects are considered, but the range of options and variables increase. Chapter 4 considered international modes of operation and entry strategy in detail, and this should be reviewed at this point. The mode of foreign market servicing is a critical aspect of international strategic planning and should be included in the choice of strategy. As Porter points out (Porter, 1986: Introduction), patterns of international competition vary widely across industries and a more flexible approach needs to be taken when planning on a global scale. This will require organizational innovations to deal with increased complexity (see chapter 7) and may involve coalitions with other firms. The firm will also have more, and often conflicting, government regulations with which to deal, and will have opportunities arising from its international scope to generate and exploit competitive advantages. Again, a two-dimensional table can be used to illustrate the key strategy choices in international competition. These are co-ordination of activities (those activities that are internally or externally managed) and configuration issues, which centre on the location of activities (Porter, 1986: chapter 1; Buckley, Pass and Prescott, 1989). This combination of internalization and location decisions across activities permits a great complexity of strategic choice (Figure 9.8). In

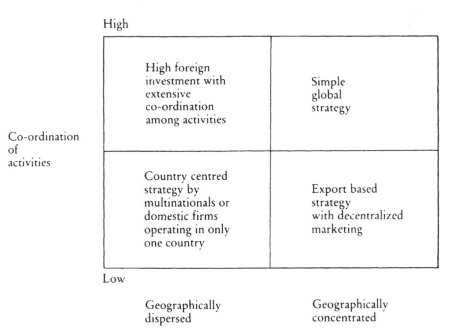

Figure 9.8 Types of international strategy.

practice, however, in the international tourism industry, many decisions will be constrained: for example, the location of the destination, integration of key activities. Exporting also is impossible with location-dependent services. Combining the international competitive framework with the generic strategies covered in the last section, Porter is able to define a small number of strategic alternatives where competition is global, as it is increasingly becoming in large segments of the international tourism industry. These alternatives are shown in Figure 9.9. It will rarely be the case that a firm follows one strategy exclusively and Figure 9.9 is best seen as a menu, from which the most appropriate strategy can be selected as internal circumstances and environmental constraints dictate.

Strategy implementation

A much neglected aspect of corporate planning is that of implementing the strategy. Implementation will be much easier if those whose role is crucial to achieving the strategy, which is likely to be every employee of the company, have been involved as much as is practically feasible in having an input into the strategy process. Widepsread consultation and consensus seeking may seem costly and time-consuming, but it may well pay dividends at the implementation stage. The Japanese have shown that competitive advantages can be gained by having the whole workforce moving in a single strategic direction. It has been shown that decisions take longer to reach in the Japanese firm, but, once reached, implementation is more efficient and effective. It should also be noted that conflict is an essential part of strategy implementation, because the strategy results from choice and choice involves taking decisions that will be

		Geographic scope	
	Many segments	Global strategy	Country-centred strategy
Segment scope		Global cost. Leadership or differentiation	Protected markets
	Few segments	Global segmentation	National responsiveness

Figure 9.9 Strategic alternatives in a global industry (*Source:* Porter, 1986, p. 46).

evaluated differently from different standpoints. Strategy involves making real resource decisions, thus depriving some members of the unit of resources in favour of others. It involves value judgements and predictions in an uncertain world. Conflict cannot be avoided, but it must be managed. The role of management in this context involves leadership, planning and control.

Leadership involves decision-taking, motivating others, monitoring outcomes and directing resources (giving orders). Leaders and managers are judged largely on the quality of their decision-taking, which is measured by the success of their outcomes. Decision-making often devolves on those with a track record of success. Successful entrepreneurs are those who are willing to back their judgement of the world against conventional wisdom (and the market) (Casson, 1987). Decision-taking within a company is also linked to motivating others, largely subordinates, to carry through the decision with the greatest possible effectiveness. Thus, employee motivation becomes important. Systems can be designed to encourage motivation, including payment by results. The creation of a positive company ethic is a major support in motivating employees. Effective leadership requires the constant monitoring of outcomes. Leaders will regularly adjust their decision-taking in order to improve outcome. Dogmatism should not be equated with leadership.

Planning, as Luffman *et al.* (1987) point out, is often relegated to budgeting (as marketing is relegated to selling). 'Systematic comprehensive corporate planning used to determine the future of a company is not widely in evidence in industrial organisations' (p. 144). This is even more true in service organizations and in the international tourism industry. Commitment to implementation of the plan, particularly by top management and the chief executive officer, is crucial. Plans do not implement themselves and, as this chapter advocates, planning must be seen as a process to which sufficient time has to be allocated.

Control mechanisms must be used within planning and its implementation. Usually these will be defined as financial controls (see chapter 6), but controls on the use of labour and management time are also clearly necessary. Naturally, there needs to be a careful balance between control and allowing innovation to take place. Controls that are too tight or require too much reporting are likely to be effective only in stifling enthusiasm. Organization design, which maximizes flexibility while ensuring effective reporting, will frequently emphasize decentralization into strategic business units (SBUs) with considerable autonomy (chapter 7).

Conclusion

As Luffman *et al.* (1987) says 'It should be emphasised that a highly formalised system of planning is no guarantee of success; but equally leaving things to chance constitutes the best possible guarantee of failure' (p. 5). It is crucial that firms in international tourism satisfy themselves that existing products and markets in which the firm operates are sufficient to satisfy future objectives. A continuous review is essential to secure this likelihood.

This chapter has provided the traditional role of strategy analyses in pulling together strands from the various functional areas of the business. It needs to feed off the analyses of marketing, finance and organization covered above. In the international context, the means of doing business abroad must be integrated with the corporate planning mechanism.

Further reading

1 Classic reviews of corporate planning are provided by H. Igor Ansoff (1965), *Corporate Strategy*, Harmondsworth: Penguin, and John Argenti (1974) *Systematic Corporate Planning*, London: Nelson. The more modern (and US-centred) approach of Michael Porter is contained in M. E. Porter (1980), *Competitive Strategy*, Oxford: Blackwell, and (1985), *Competitive Advantage*, New York: Free Press. For a concise and up-to-date review, see George Luffman *et al.* (1987), *Business Policy: An analytical introduction*, New York: Free Press.
2 Approaches to corporate planning on the international scale can be found in Michael Z. Brooke and M. Van Beusekom (1978), *International Corporate Planning*, London: Pitman, and Michael Z. Brooke (1986), *International Management*, London: Hutchinson. See also Michael Z. Brooke and Peter J. Buckley (eds) (1988), *Handbook of International Trade*, London: Macmillan, and Michael E. Porter (ed.) (1986) *Competition in Global Industries*, Boston, Mass.: Harvard Business School Press.
3 It is important not to ignore the international modes of operation covered in chapter 4. An examination of the further reading should also be carried out in conjunction with this material.

10

International tourism: the future

One thing can safely be said of tourism in the future: it will increase. Nothing but a global war can prevent that. Current forecasts suggest a 5 per cent yearly growth in international tourist flows through the 1990s, and that means a lot of tourists; expenditure is likely to grow even faster in real terms. But where will the increase occur? And where will there be a decline? These are more difficult questions. They will be answered partly by innovatory practices and new products, and the next question is – what will they look like? This chapter examines a number of issues that are likely to be landmarks of the future including:

directions of growth and decline;
products;
the role of government: intervention and market forces;
economic and social consequences of tourism;
working conditions;
ownership;
tourism backlash;
blockages and clearances including:
    currency exchange and frontier formalities;
    the transport infrastructure;
    nationalism and violence;
    pricing;
    health;
    the affairs of Eastern Europe.

Directions of growth and decline

Factors that influence the decision to journey abroad have already been identified. Overwhelmingly, tourism is related to personal expenditure, although international tourism is also influenced by exchange rates. A recent publication (Economist Intelligence Unit, 1988, p. 4) suggested that a 1 per cent growth in private consumption leads to a 0 per cent growth in tourism; but a 2.5 per cent increase leads to 4 per cent more tourism, while a 5 per cent figure adds up to a 10 per cent growth.

This accelerating relationship between economic and tourism growth rates leads to some interesting speculations for Europe, where the 2.5 per cent rate coincides exactly with forecasts for growth during the 1990s, which suggests that cross-border tourism both within and from Europe will increase rapidly; the increase will be assisted, no doubt, by the physical and psychological influences of the single market. The increase will be all the greater if the growth rates in the poorer countries of the Community, such as Spain, are higher.

Similar growth figures are anticipated for the other major industrial countries – United States, Canada, Japan and Australia – suggesting that for them also there will be considerable increases in tourist flows. The extra tourists generated will no doubt mainly follow conventional routes, although the numbers will certainly lead to an increasing popularity for destinations that are currently less popular. The 5 per cent figure leads to some even more intriguing speculations about countries outside Europe, because it is *below* the anticipated growth forecasts for the newly industrializing countries of South East Asia. This suggests a new source of tourism flows. It is possible, indeed, that even smaller growth rates than four or five per cent will increase the flow of tourists from developing countries. This arises from the unequal distribution of wealth in the poorer countries; where this applies, in a country like India, a relatively small growth in wealth could produce a larger increase in the demand for tourism. A growing middle class will be interested in foreign travel.

Growing wealth in Asia, and the move to use part of the growth in longer holidays, will help to change the directions of tourist travel, with an increase in holiday resorts in the Pacific. Japan will contribute to this when more of its wealth is translated into shorter working years by longer holidays. In that country, too, there is now government encouragement to travel abroad in order to reduce the balance of payments surplus.

But the increase in tourism from the newly industrializing countries and certain other developing countries is likely to be matched by an increase in tourism to those countries. This will happen because domestic tourism will also increase and with it the necessary facilities and infrastructure will emerge. The industry will then have stronger incentives to promote tourism from abroad. Aggressive marketing and a reduction in air fares in real terms will combine with a general growth in business to produce new directions of travel.

Traditional sunshine and seashore holiday resorts – such as the

Mediterranean coast – are near capacity already and some decline may be expected with the rising popularity of inland holidays. On the other hand, ageing populations in the industrial countries will lead to the promotion of more off-peak holidays.

A side-effect of the increase is that nations and would-be suppliers will read the statistics and be encouraged to enter the holiday market. As a result, it is likely that supply will move ahead of demand. This can be expected to increase competition and produce a general rise in standards.

Against all the pressure towards expansion stands the possibility of a world slump. A decline in the disposable income of the richer countries is unlikely to affect international tourism in the short term. The old (with enhanced pensions, including lump sum payments) and the young (with two incomes to a household) will retain some protection against setbacks and a propensity to use spare income on travel. But, in the longer term, the gearing effect that has rapidly increased tourist spending can work the other way – equally rapidly.

Demographic factors are often quoted, like the fact that the over 50s will outnumber the 25 to 50 year olds in Europe by the end of the century and that there will be less young people around – but those less will be much more prosperous. Also significant will be the general increase in the population, which continues against all the fluctuations in the birth rate.

Products

A major new product looms in the next century in the form of space travel.[1] This may be a long way off, although pressure to make possible a limited number of high-cost flights will build up as soon as techniques are devised to make capsules more inhabitable. Meanwhile, more mundane changes must be expected – nothing even as revolutionary as the package tour once was. Product innovation is more likely to be about unpackaging rather than packaging, providing more individual attention within a number of price bands. This means at the top level, more high luxury, individual, escorted tours with every possible need met. At a lower level, it will mean that tour operators exercise considerable ingenuity to combine individual arrangements in much the same way that freight is bulked now. The result will be an arrangement that appears personal to the tourist, but is less expensive than it would otherwise be because a block booking of facilities has been made. Even so, package holidays are not going to disappear. Indeed, they may increase in number as third world countries come into the market; they will make international tourism available to a wider population, one whose expectations have been raised. It is the relative importance of package tours that will decline.

Package tours and individual holidays

Some sectors of the inclusive tour market will continue to grow, but the core business of hotel-based summer tours is in decline. Air traffic control delays are one factor in this decline, as are health scares in the major Mediterranean resorts, but there does seem to be an underlying dissatisfaction with traditional packages. Clients have become tired of the increasingly developed and over-commercialized sun and sand resorts. Moreover, the price-based market share battle between the major operators has – in reality or in perception – lowered the quality of the holidays on offer. The traditional package holiday has become unfashionable, and the concern is that this is permanent rather than temporary.

Several factors have combined to depress the market in Britain. Short-term high interest rates have reduced discretionary spending and the price wars waged by competitors have reduced the quality of the product and profitability. Add to these the costs of congestion and bad publicity about overcrowding at destinations and there may be a long-term reaction against the package tour. This has not been the reaction in the rest of Europe, however – or at least not yet. Other package tour markets, such as West Germany, appear to have avoided the low price and low quality trap; as a consequence, they seem quite healthy. In Britain, despite the dramatic fall, there will still be 8–9 million package holidays sold in 1990, which, if not the hoped for 13 million, is still a large number. The accessibility of package holidays is still an attractive option for many. For the market to survive it has to maintain its quality. This means a higher price, because good accommodation and attendant support services do not come cheap. However, the general signs are that the traditional package holiday has become less popular in the industrial countries.

All tour operators are having to adjust to a market that demands independence but wants the advantages of bulk purchase as well as independence of action. In addition, the market for holidays specially tailored to specific segments (such as birdwatching and hiking) is large and growing rapidly. It will be in this market that the smaller operators will have good prospects.

Individual holidays are already increasing through the letting of individual accommodation (like the *gîtes* in France), the growth of timeshare and the purchase of holiday homes. There is scope for expansion in all three, especially for timeshare, in spite of recent setbacks in Britain. Reservation systems – especially those used by airlines – will increasingly be able to cope with customized arrangements.

The role of government

Governments generally favour tourism – unlike some of their subjects (see 'Tourism backlash', p. 192). The visitor brings foreign currency and assists the balance of payments; for countries with special problems, there is the bonus that a high proportion of the tourists bring hard currency. This situation is not going to change, but the forms of government intervention will. One likely change is from direct assistance to indirect.

Within limits imposed by government policies, investment incentives and grants for the development of tourism have become universal. The more interventionist-minded governments have given loans up to 100 per cent of the capital costs of new hotels on easy terms, sometimes interest free for an initial period. In countries with less interventionist governments, measures for encouraging new investment, at least, have been applied to tourism. In addition, the transport infrastructure is state-supported in most countries. Further local government assistance may well be available, even in countries where national governments do not provide support. The local promotion of tourism, even in areas previously not considered suitable, is a feature recorded earlier in this book.

In the future, however, direct aid by government or local government is likely to decline as tourism increases. A cycle, already evident, will become more pronounced. If we assume that the cycle starts with areas that are seen as having potential for tourism, such areas will attract direct aid, especially if there is also high unemployment. As direct aid becomes less necessary, other measures become more important such as attempts to relieve overcrowded areas or to help spread the season – by publicity or off-season entertainments and special events. Other forms of official assistance include aid to special groups, such as farmers, to enhance farm incomes by offering accommodation and farm tours. Help to the voluntary sector is yet another form of assistance. Not only has voluntary effort been the basis of tourism developments in many countries, but hard-pressed groups in the performing arts can find justification for official support by claiming that they encourage foreign visitors.

But the role of government is not likely to be confined to direct or indirect support for tourist facilities. Two controversial issues are safeguarding standards and training. On these issues, also, there seems to be a cycle of official support that waxes and wanes.

Countries such as Switzerland have a highly developed system for both standards and training, while the degree of acknowledged professionalism in the industry is higher in some countries than in others. It is doubtful whether any other country has equalled Swiss standards; it is certain that many aspire. The controversy is between state-sponsored or voluntary standards for facilities and for training. The climate of opinion in much of the world today is in favour of self-regulation and privatization. In a fragmented industry such as this, it may well turn out that some official control is necessary in view of the competition. As supply creeps ahead of demand, countries considered to have lax controls over, for instance, standards of accommodation may well find themselves losing out.

A controversy that has influenced official policies over the last twenty years is that between economic growth and the limits to growth. Once considered a minor issue that, in any case, was only of interest to the richest countries, the argument is rapidly becoming universal – stimulated by events like floods in Bangladesh, partly caused by agricultural changes in India. The argument is mainly concerned with the use of natural resources, in agriculture or in forestry, but it also affects road and rail building, and the use of fuel. A new road that may be economically desirable may not be wanted on social or environmental grounds. It may even open up sensitive areas to over-visiting.

Government initiatives aimed at improving the transport infra-structure will be more carefully scrutinized in the future; this can be expected to stimulate research into new technologies, which will themselves need assistance to become viable. Infrastructure problems are discussed below (see 'Blockages and clearances', pp. 192–4).

Economic and social consequences of tourism

International tourism has been credited with benefits such as improving the balance of payments, providing employment and helping citizens of different countries to understand one another. This last consideration has influenced the European Commission to arrange visits and educational programmes between member states and to launch a European Year of Tourism (1990) with, among its objectives, 'bringing Europeans still closer to one another.'

Inevitably, each of these advantages has its characteristic draw-back. The balance of payments is only benefited by inward tourism, the type of employment is sometimes considered undesirable – often as a last resort by local nationals – and hostility can arise as well as understanding.

European countries, such as Spain and Portugal, owe part of their success with foreign tourism to their prices. These are likely to increase rapidly, partly as a side-effect of a favourable balance of payments, which will also raise the value of the currency, and partly as a consequence of continuing industrialization causing wages to rise. As a result, the two countries are likely to experience strong competition from tourist facilities on the North African shores of the Mediterranean.

Working conditions

The professionalism of tourism staff, it has already been indicated, varies from country to country; it has also been suggested that competition will lead to upgrading in many countries. Continuing efforts will be made to dispel the image of low-paid workers in poor conditions. There will remain, however, a strong lure for providing employment for immigrants, legal and illegal, and for temporary workers who are themselves tourists. The increasing availability of international tourism will do nothing to lessen the ambitions of those who cannot afford it.

Rival pressures from demand for more professionalism and higher pay on the one hand (a pair of factors that do not necessarily support one another) and a continuing supply of cheap labour on the other are likely to increase the current trend towards a two-tier labour force. Ultimately, mechanization of the more menial tasks may reduce the lower tier. Currently, tourist facilities, like the service sector in general, are noted for being labour-intensive, but this is likely to change. One reason why hotels, for instance, have become more labour-intensive is because of the general move upmarket, which became apparent in the 1970s. In the 1990s, it is not improbable that self-service will move upmarket.

Ownership

The facilities sector, as opposed to transport, has always demonstrated in an exaggerated form an ownership structure common to other industries – concentration at one end and fragmentation at the other. The fact that catering and tourism facilities are an attractive way into a business of one's own is not going to change, nor are the opportunities for building empires in hotels or theme parks. In this sector the extremes support one another: major companies operate franchising arrangements for small firms as well as supporting tourism activities which it is not economic for them to own. The larger owners are likely to put much effort into anticipating or finding new tourist centres. This will extend large company ownership to regions that have not known it before.

Tourism backlash

Running through this chapter have been themes that are likely to intensify the backlash against tourism, first noted as a growing threat since the early 1970s (Turner and Ash, 1975). The industry is an easy target for criticism, and will become easier as it grows ever more universal, raising and dashing expectations in the process – and bringing more foreign ownership to overpower more local businesses. Perceptions about the character of tourism employment have already been mentioned: a major grievance is that the periodical influx of foreigners disturbs the calm and injures the culture of a locality. Whatever the economic benefits to the country or to the town, many local inhabitants do not benefit. They form a core of opposition, which may centre around local issues such as culture or care of the countryside. It is likely that environmentalism will be increasingly seen – whether justly or not – as opposed to tourism.

As this book was being prepared for the press (in the summer of 1990) campaigns were going on to restrict tourism in Goa (where a million visitors a year invade a region of 1,200,000 inhabitants) and in Thailand (where the government has protested against the publicity of the tourism companies); a campaign was also being mounted against the expected dangers of tourism in Antarctica. More is going to be heard of the backlash against tourism.

Blockages and clearances

The tourism backlash will probably spread, but will generally focus around local issues. Neither national nor international organizations are likely to treat it seriously as a world phenomenon; at the most, it will be looked upon as a curable problem of little relevance to policy-makers. The following factors, which are related to general world issues, are likely to feature more prominently on the agenda of world organizations in the years to come.

Currency exchange and frontier formalities

One of these factors is currency exchange. There can be little doubt that irresistible pressures towards a European currency are building up and that – give or take a hiccough or two – this will become a reality in the next few years. The next question is – how long before the adoption of a world currency comes on the agenda? A European currency, if successful, will surely stimulate a demand elsewhere. Back in 1988, *The Economist* forecast that a world currency (provisionally entitled 'The Phoenix') would come into existence in about thirty years' time.[2] Although a world currency would not take over all countries in the world at once, any more than a European currency would be acceptable to all Europeans at the same time, it would be a boon to tourists and tour operators.

The psychological boost, resulting from becoming accustomed to money that can be used almost anywhere, may well prove even more significant than overcoming the relatively minor inconvenience of exchanges and travellers' cheques. The change will obviously not be so welcome to banks and other organizations that provide exchange facilities, although they may benefit in other ways – money transfer will become less expensive.

Another probable change that will not be welcome to a number of interests, including the tourists themselves, is the abolition of 'duty free' goods. The demise in Europe of this survival from the days of sailing boats has been forecast for many years – and has yet to happen. If vested interests and public opinion are strong enough to retain in Europe a practice that is clearly incompatible with the principles of a common market, it must be a long time before duty free is brought to an end globally. Nevertheless, it is surely true that this special privilege to the traveller will be ended eventually.

A consequence of this abolition, at least in the short term, will be a tightening of frontier controls – there will be a temptation for travellers to become petty smugglers. In the longer term, there is the prospect of international agreements on excise duties and sales taxes that make smuggling less worth while. But this prospect has still not produced an agreement within the European Community, where excise duties vary widely. The difficulties of producing standard rates of value added tax and excise in the Community provide an idea of the problems likely to be encountered worldwide. Nevertheless, the growth of travel is going to persuade governments to look hard at the possibilities of reducing frontier formalities.

The transport infrastructure

Congestion is a word currently associated with all forms of transport. Airports and air routes are crowded, roads are at a standstill and trains are filled beyond capacity. For air transport, the next ten years appear to be a holding period. An anticipated growth rate of 4–6 per cent per year can just be supported by better management and improvements of the existing infrastructure and increases in aircraft size. Passengers will have to accept some penalties in less convenient scheduling and a greater use of differential pricing to encourage off-peak travel. Some relief will be provided by improvements in other forms of transport, but the growth of longer-distance travel for both business and leisure will wipe out the effects of many of the short-term measures.

In the next century, at least three important technical developments are likely to lead to a steep expansion in air travel. One is the emergence of a new generation of short-take-off aircraft and another is the finding of a solution to the noise problem. The latter development is needed to make the former acceptable. These developments could transform air transport early in the next century. Quieter aircraft could mean airports closer to city centres and to the relaxing of restrictions on night flights. Already, the existence of allegedly quieter planes has led operators to demand that airports remain open for longer hours. A third technical change will take longer: thirty years has been suggested as a likely period before space technology is applied to intercontinental travel. The possibility of travelling from Tokyo to Paris in an hour must surely stimulate research and investment.

Congestion in the air has stimulated investment in surface transport; rail – against all the expectations of a decade ago – is making the running with technical advances meaning that speed increases will make rail competitive for lengthening journeys. A further stimulus is being provided by the growth of fixed links, such as the Channel Tunnel between Britain and France, the series of bridges and tunnels that will link Scandinavia to the rest of Europe by the end of the decade and the routes joining the islands in Japan. These links have also stimulated road building. Evidently the car is going to be the principal means of transport for the foreseeable future, but a greater use of multiple modes of transport is a possibility. The current low technology version – loading cars on to trains – currently accounts for a very minor part of the industry. Indeed, cheaper and more efficient car hire blocked growth in car-by-rail systems many years ago. The revival of the multimode transport for freight, especially in North America, may well stimulate new inventions that will affect road and rail transport – but never to a great extent. A bigger change will come with the development of a form of transport that combines the advantages of both. Indeed, when railways were first invented, they experimented with attaching private carriages to trains. Intermodal transport is a major topic of discussion nowadays. Motorail (carriage of cars by train) has long been used to a limited extent in many countries. More efficient means of intermodal transport – similar to those being developed for freight – are likely to be used to reduce road congestion in the twenty-first century.

Nationalism and violence

Uprisings and riots are much publicized, but have little effect on tourism in the longer term. A few years ago violence in Greece caused a decrease in tourism to that country, but the decrease only lasted a short time and is now forgotten. Similarly, a bomb on a plane causes cancellation during the following twelve months, but bookings revive after that. In some circumstances, violence can be an attraction. Tourism to Fiji increased after the revolution there, because pictures of the violence also showed the beauty of the islands.

Pricing

A considerable stimulus to international tourism has been the price. For a richer country a combination of weak currencies and low wages has made holidays in even distant poor countries attractive. This combination changes, sometimes quickly. Relative exchange rates change and wages increase. For the foreseeable future, there will always be poorer countries to take the place of those that raise their prices unduly – and this will further the trend towards long-distance travel.

Health

Long-established threats to health, such as contaminated water or infectious diseases, have been much reduced; malaria, once a strong disincentive to travel in both Africa and Asia, has been largely overcome by readily available tablets that are also easy to take – although the emergence of fresh strains immune to existing drugs may still cause scares. One infectious disease – AIDS – has caused a setback in some areas, or at least a rethink of certain tourist attractions. A possible influence on future attitudes is the danger of skin cancer from over-exposure to the sun. This is hardly likely to be more than a passing scare for a fortnight's holiday; but health consciousness is still likely to affect tourism patterns.

The affairs of Eastern Europe

The opening up of Eastern Europe can be regarded as yet another factor that will increase the numbers of international tourists. Inward tourism has long been possible ('encouraged' might be considered too strong a word), but outward tourism has been more difficult. Does this mean that established tourism areas should be looking to yet another increase in their markets? At present, it looks as if they are more likely to be looking at some determined competitors.[3] A desperate need for hard currency will surely produce strong efforts to promote foreign tourism in Eastern Europe. For companies who build or operate facilities, there is likely to be a boom in business, from straightforward contracts to more elaborate joint venture arrangements.

Conclusion

Increases in international tourism

Especially in fast-growing areas like South East Asia, increases in international tourism have been confidently forecast. In addition to changing directions of travel, there will be changes in the segmentation of the market. More invidivual and more expensive holidays are expected, with new markets opening up, especially for those without family – whether old or young. Demographic change will combine with growing wealth to mean that the old will be increasingly targeted by the tourism and travel industry. The more traditional targets (35 to 55 year olds) will increase with growing prosperity, but will continue to be sensitive to price changes and economic conditions at home and abroad.

The figures suggesting a steep increase in international tourism will be widely read and produce an over-supply of opportunities. This, in its turn, will increase competition, which may lead to a general raising of standards; but this may be frustrated if the competition is mainly on price.

Notes

1   As long ago as 1987, space travel was being offered. 'But the ultimate yuppie long-haul holiday must be that offered by the Twickers World travel agency. From October 1992, short space flights in the US space shuttle are being offered for sale at a mere £31,000 a person.' (*Financial Times*, 1 August 1987).
2   See *The Economist*, 9 January 1988.
3   This view was neatly expressed in a recent article in *The Guardian*. See: Daniel John, 'Making sure the tourist bus hasn't left Europe behind', *The Guardian*, 3 February 1990, p. 9.

Further reading

Hawkins, D. E. (1989), 'Impact of World Events on Tourism', in Witt, S. F. and Moutinho, L. (eds), *Tourism Marketing and Management Handbook*, Hemel Hempstead: Prentice Hall, pp. 219–22.
Schwaninger, M. (1989), 'Trends in Leisure and Tourism for 2000–2010: Scenario with Consequences for Planners', in Witt, S. F. and Moutinho, L., op. cit., pp. 599–605.
Shafer, E. L. and Moeller, G. (1989), 'Science and Technology in Tourism', in Witt, S. F. and Moutinho, L., op. cit., 381–6.

Wheatcroft, S. (1989), 'Present and Future Demand for Transport', in Witt, S. F. and Moutinho, L., op. cit., pp. 299–304.

References

Allard, L. (1989), 'Statistical measurement in tourism', in Witt, S. F. and Moutinho, L. (eds), *Tourism Marketing and Management Handbook*, Hemel Hempstead: Prentice-Hall, pp. 419–24.

Allcock, J. B. (1989a), 'Sociology of tourism', in Witt, S. F. and Moutinho, L., op. cit., pp. 407–14.

Allcock, J. B. (1989b), 'Seasonality', in Witt, S. F. and Moutinho, L., op. cit., pp. 387–92.

Ansoff, H. I. (1965), *Corporate Strategy*, Harmondsworth: Penguin.

Archer, B. H. (1977), *Multipliers: The state of the art*, Bangor Occasional Papers No. 11, Cardiff: University of Wales Press.

Archer, B. H. (1987), 'Demand forecasting and estimation', in Ritchie, J. R. B. and Goeldner, C. R. (eds), *Travel, Tourism and Hospitality Research*, New York: Wiley, pp. 77–85.

Archer, B. H. (1989), 'Trends in international tourism', in Witt, S. F. and Moutinho, L., op. cit., pp. 593–7.

Argenti, J. (1974), *Systematic Corporate Planning*, London: Nelson.

Ashworth, G. and Goodall, B. (eds) (1990), *Marketing Tourism Places*, London: Routledge and Kegan Paul.

Association International d'Experts, Scientifiques du Tourisme (1988), *Day Trips and their Impacts*, St-Gall, Switzerland: AIEST.

Balasubramanyam, V. N. (1973), *International Transfer of Technology to India*, New York: Praeger.

Baron, R. R. V. (1975), *Seasonality in Tourism*, Technical Series No. 2, London: Economist Intelligence Unit, pp. 45–55.

Baron, R. R. V. (1989), *Travel and Tourism Data*, London: Euromonitor.

Boddewyn, J. J., Halbrich, M. B. and Perry, A. C. (1986), 'Service multinationals: Conceptualisation, measurement and theory', *Journal of International Business Studies*, vol. 17, no. 3, pp. 41–58.

Bodlender, J. A. and Ward, T. J. (1989), 'Profile of investment incentives', in Witt, S. F. and Moutinho, L., op. cit., pp. 325–8.

Bouquet, M. and Winter, M. (eds) (1987), *Who From Their Labours Rest? Conflict and practice in rural tourism*, Aldershot: Avebury.

Brooke, M. Z. (1985), *Selling Management Services Contracts in International Business*, Eastbourne: Holt, Rinehart and Winston.

Brown, G. P. and Essex, S. J. (1989), 'Tourism policies in the public sector', in Witt, S. F. and Moutinho, L., op. cit., pp. 53–9.

Bryden, J. M. (1973), *Tourism and Development: A case study of the Commonwealth Caribbean*, Cambridge: Cambridge University Press.

Bryden, J. M. and Faber, M. (1971), 'Multiplying the tourist multiplier', *Social and Economic Studies*, vol. 20, no. 1, pp. 61–82.

Buckley, P. J. (1982), 'The role of exporting in the market servicing policies of multinational manufacturing enterprises', in Czinkota, M. and Tesor, G. (eds), *Export Management: An International Context*, New York: Praeger.

Buckley, P. J. (1985), 'New forms of international industrial cooperation', in Buckley, P. J. and Casson, M. (eds), *The Economic Theory of the Multinational Enterprise*, London: Macmillan.

Buckley, P. J. (1987), 'Tourism – An economic transactions analysis', *Tourism Management*, vol. 8, no. 3, pp. 190–4.

Buckley, P. J. (1989), 'Foreign market servicing strategies and competitiveness: A theoretical framework', in Negandhi, A. R. and Savara, A. (eds), *International Strategic Management*, Lexington, Mass.: D. C. Heath.

Buckley, P. J. and Casson, M. (1976), *The Future of the Multinational Enterprise*, London: Macmillan.

Buckley, P. J. and Casson, M. (1985), *The Economic Theory of the Multinational Enterprise*, London: Macmillan.

Buckley, P. J. and Casson, M. (1988), 'A theory of international corporation cooperation', in Contractor, F. J. and Lorange, P. (eds), *Cooperative Strategies in International Business*, Lexington, Mass.: D. C. Heath.

Buckley, P. J., Mirza, H. and Witt, S. F. (1989), 'Japan's international tourism in the context of its international economic relations', *Service Industries Journal*, vol. 9, no. 3, pp. 357–83.

Buckley, P. J., Newbould, G. D. and Thurwell, J. (1988), *Foreign Direct Investment by Smaller UK Firms*, London: Macmillan.

Buckley, P. J. and Papadopoulos, S. I. (1986), 'Marketing Greek tourism – the planning process', *Tourism Management*, vol. 7, no. 2, pp. 86–100.

Buckley, P. J., Pass, C. L. and Prescott, P. (1990), 'Foreign marketing servicing by multinationals: An integrated approach', *International Marketing Review*, vol. 7, no. 2.

Buckley, P. J. and Witt, S. F. (1985), 'Tourism in difficult areas: Case studies of Bradford, Bristol, Glasgow and Hamm', *Tourism Management*, vol. 7, no. 2, pp. 86–100.

Buckley, P. J. and Witt, S. F. (1989), 'Tourism in difficult areas II: Four North of England case studies', *Tourism Management*, vol. 10, no. 2, pp. 138–52.

Burkart, A. J. (1975), 'The role of the large tour operator in the development and promotion of tourism', in Burkart, A. J. and Medlik, S. (eds), *The Management of Tourism: A selection of readings*, London: Heinemann.

Burkart, A. J. and Medlik, S. (1981), *Tourism: Past, present and future*, 2nd edn, Oxford: Heinemann.

Buttle, F. (1986), *Hotel and Food Service Marketing*, London: Holt, Rinehart and Winston.

Casson, M. (1982), *The Entrepreneur: An Economic Theory*, Oxford: Martin Robertson.

Casson, M. (1985), 'Transaction costs and the theory of the multinational enterprise', in Buckley, P. J. and Casson, M., *The Economic Analysis of the Multinational Enterprise*, London: Macmillan.

Chisman, N. R. (1989), 'Financial planning and control in tourism', in Witt, S. F. and Moutinho, L., op. cit., pp. 157–62.

Chon, K. (1989), 'Understanding recreational traveler's motivation, attitude and satisfaction', *The Tourist Review*, no. 1, pp. 3–6.

Coase, R. (1937), 'The nature of the firm', *Economica* (new series), no. 4, pp. 386–405.

Cohen, E. (1972), 'Towards a sociology of international tourism', *Social Research*, vol. 39, no. 1, pp. 164–82.

Commission of the European Communities (1985), *The Tourism Sector in the Community: A study of concentration, competition, and competitiveness*, Luxembourg: European Communities.

Croizé, J. C. (1989), 'Theme and leisure parks', in Witt, S. F. and Moutinho, L., op. cit., pp. 459–62.

Curry, S. (1989), 'Cost-benefit analysis', in Witt, S. F. and Moutinho, L., op. cit., pp. 83–7.

Davies, H. (1977), 'Technology transfer through commercial transactions', *Journal of Industrial Economics*, vol. 26, pp. 161–75.

De Kadt, E. (ed.) (1979), *Tourism: Passport to development?* Oxford: Oxford University Press.

Dobbins, R. and Witt, S. F. (1983), *Portfolio Theory and Investment Management*, Oxford: Blackwell.

Dobbins, R. and Witt, S. F. (1988), *Practical Financial Management*, Oxford: Blackwell.

Dunning, J. H. (1988), *Explaining International Production*, London: Unwin Hyman.

Dunning, J. H. (1989), 'Multinational enterprises and the growth of services: Some conceptual and theoretical issues', *Service Industries Journal*, vol. 9, no. 1, pp. 5–39.

Dunning, J. H. and McQueen, M. (1981), *Transnational Corporations in International Tourism*, New York: United Nations Centre on Transnational Corporations.

Dunning, J. H. and McQueen, M. (1982), 'The eclectic theory of the multinational enterprise and the international hotel industry', in Alan M. Rugman (ed.), *New Theories of the Multinational Enterprise*, London: Croom Helm.

Economist Intelligence Unit (1988), *International Tourism Forecasts*, London: EIU.

Elias, N. and Dunning, E. (1986), *The Quest for Excitement: Sport and leisure in the civilising process*, Oxford: Blackwell.

English Tourist Board (1980), *Tourism and the Inner City*, Planning Advisory Note 3, London: English Tourist Board.

Etzel, M. J. and Swensen, P. R. (1981), 'Taking the mystery out of travel investment decisions', *Journal of Travel Research*, vol. XX, no. 2, pp. 24–8.

Falk, N. (1986), 'Baltimore and Lowell: Two American approaches', *Built Environment*, vol. 12, no. 2, pp. 142–52.

Finnegan, M. B. (1976), *Current Trends in Domestic and International Licensing*, New York: Practising Law Institute.

Fletcher, J. E. and Snee, H. R. (1989a), 'Impact of tourism', in Witt, S. F. and Moutinho, L., op. cit., pp. 215–17.

Fletcher, J. E. and Snee, H. R. (1989b), 'Tourism multiplier effects', in Witt, S. F. and Moutinho, L., op. cit., pp. 529–31.

Fletcher, J. E., Snee, H. R. and Macleod, B. (1981), *An Input–Output Study of Gibraltar*, Bangor: University College of North Wales, Institute of Economic Research.

Foster, D. (1985), *Travel and Tourism Management*, London: Macmillan.
Friel, E. J. (1989), 'Convention market', in Witt, S. F. and Moutinho, L., op cit., pp. 75–7.

Gilbert, D. (1990), 'Strategic marketing planning for national tourism', *The Tourist Review*, vol. 45, no. 1, pp. 18–26.
Glueck, W. F. (1976), *Business Policy: Strategy formulation and management action*, Tokyo: McGraw-Hill.
Goeldner, C. R. *et al.* (1980), *Bibliography of Tourism and Travel Research Studies, Reports and Articles*. Nine volumes: I Information Sources, II Economics, III International, IV Lodging, V Recreation, VI Transportation, VII Advertising–Planning, VIII Statistics–Visitors, IX Index. Salt Lake City, Utah: Travel and Tourism Research Association.
Goodall, B. and Ashworth, G. (eds) (1988), *Marketing in the Tourism Industry: The promotion of destination regions*, London: Croom Helm.
Gratton, C. and Taylor, P. (1988), *Economics of Leisure Services Management*, London: Longman.
Greene, M. (1983), *Marketing Hotels into the 90s*, London: Heinemann.
Gunn, C. A. (1979), *Tourism Planning*, New York: Crane Russak.

Habermas, J. (1976), *Legitimation Crisis*, London: Heinemann.
Hall, G. R. and Johnson, R. E. (1970), 'Transfers of United States Aerospace Technology to Japan', in Vernon, R. (ed.), *The Technology Factor in International Trade*, New York: National Bureau of Economic Research, Columbia University Press.
Hampton, A. (1989), 'Business travel', in Witt, S. F. and Moutinho, L., op. cit., pp. 27–33.
Hartley, J. S. and Witt, S. F. (1990), 'Cancelling conferences and functions: How should hotels respond?', in Muhlbacher, H. and Jochum, C. (eds), *Advanced Research in Marketing: Proceedings of European Marketing Academy (EMAC) 19th Annual Conference*, Innsbruck: EMAC, pp. 1855–69.
Hawkins, D. E. (1989), 'Impact of world events on tourism', in Witt, S. F. and Moutinho, L., op. cit., pp. 219–22.
Hennart, J. F. (1982), *A Theory of Multinational Enterprise*, Ann Arbor, Mich.: University of Michigan Press.
Heraty, M. J. (ed.) (1989a), *Developing World Transport*, London: Grosvenor Press International.
Heraty, M. J. (1989b), 'Tourism transport – Implications for developing countries, *Tourism Management*, vol. 10, no. 4, pp. 288–92.
Holloway, J. C. (1985), *The Business of Tourism*, 2nd edn, London: Pitman.
Hood, N. and Young, S. (1979), *The Economics of Multinational Enterprise*, London: Allen & Unwin.

International Monetary Fund (1989), *International Financial Statistics*, Washington, DC: IMF.
Izreali, D. (1972), *Franchising and the Total Distribution System*, London: Longman.

Jansen-Verbeke, M. (1986), 'Inner city tourism: Resources, tourists and promoters', *Annals of Tourism Research*, vol. 13, no. 1, pp. 79–100.
Jefferson, A. and Lickorish, L. (1988), *Marketing Tourism: A practical guide*, London: Longman.
Joppe, M. (1989), 'Government controls on and support for tourism', in Witt, S. F. and Moutinho, L., op. cit., pp. 183–7.

Kaynak, E. and Yavas, U. (1981), 'Segmenting the tourism market by purpose of trip', *Tourism Management*, vol. 2, no. 2, pp. 105–12.

Lee, C. H. and Naya, S. (eds) (1988), *Trade and Investment in Services in the Asia–Pacific Region*, Boulder, Colo.: Westview Press.
Liston, D. and Reeves, N. (1988), *The Invisible Economy: A profile of Britain's invisible exports*, London: Pitman.
Little, I. M. D. and Mirrlees, J. A. (1968), *Manual of Industrial Project Analysis in Developing Countries*, Paris: Development Centre, OECD.
Lockwood, R. D. (1989), 'Foreign exchange management', in Witt, S. F. and Moutinho, L., op. cit., pp. 175–8.
Luffman, G. et al. (1987), *Business Policy: An analytical introduction*, Oxford: Blackwell.

MacCannel, D. (1976), *The Tourist*, New York: Schocken Books.
McIntosh, R. W. and Goeldner, C. R. (1986), *Tourism: Principles, practices, philosophies*, 5th edn, New York: Wiley.
McQueen, M. (1989), 'Multinationals in tourism', in Witt, S. F. and Moutinho, L., op. cit., pp. 285–9.
Majaro, S. (1980), 'The best way to mix success', *Marketing*, 22 October 1980, pp. 28–30.
Mak, J. and White, K. (1988), 'Tourism in Asia and the Pacific', in Lee, C. H., and Naya, S. (eds), *Trade and Investment in Service in the Asia Pacific Region*, Boulder, Colo.: Westview Press.
Martin, C. A. and Witt, S. F. (1987), 'Tourism demand forecasting models: Choice of appropriate variable to represent tourists' cost of living', *Tourism Management*, vol. 8, no. 3, pp. 233–46.
Martin, C. A. and Witt, S. F. (1988a), 'Substitute prices in models of tourism demand', *Annals of Tourism Research*, vol. 15, no. 2, pp. 255–68.
Martin, C. A. and Witt, S. F. (1988b), 'Forecasting performance', *Tourism Management*, vol. 9, no. 4, pp. 326–9.
Martin, C. A. and Witt, S. F. (1989), 'Accuracy of econometric forecasts of tourism', *Annals of Tourism Research*, vol. 16, no. 3, pp. 407–28.
Martin, M. (1989), 'Tourism marketing management', in Witt, S. F. and Moutinho, L., op. cit., pp. 511–16.
Mathieson, A. and Wall, G. (1982), *Tourism: Economic, physical and social impacts*, London and New York: Longman.
Mazenec, J. A. (1989), 'Consumer behaviour in tourism', in Witt, S. F. and Moutinho, L., op. cit., pp. 63–8.
Medlik, S. (with Airey, D. W.) (1978), *Profile of the Hotel and Catering Industry*, 2nd edn, London: Heinemann.
Medlik, S. (1980), *The Business of Hotels*, London: Heinemann.

Medlik, S. (1988a), *Tourism and Productivity*, London: British Tourist Authority/English Tourist Board.

Medlik, S. (1988b), 'What is tourism?', *Tourism Teaching into the 1990s Conference*, Guildford: University of Surrey.

Middleton, V. T. C. (1988), *Marketing in Travel and Tourism*, London: Heinemann.

Mill, R. C. and Morrison, A. M. (1985), *The Tourism System: An introductory text*, Englewood Cliffs, NJ: Prentice-Hall.

Murphy, M. F. (1985), 'Positioning the tour operator on the international market', *Journal of Irish Business and Administrative Research*, vol. 7, no. 2, pp. 55–67.

Murphy, P. E. (1985), *Tourism: A community approach*, London and New York: Methuen.

Oman, C. (1980), *Research Project on Changing International Investment Strategies: The new forms of investment in developing countries – a 'state of the art'*, Paris: OECD Development Centre.

Organisation for Economic Co-operation and Development (1987, 1988), *Tourism Policy and International Tourism*, Paris: OECD.

Pallard, H. J. (1976), 'Antigua, West Indies: An example of the operation of the multiplier process arising from tourism', *The Tourist Review*, no. 3, pp. 30–4.

Papadopoulos, S. I. and Witt, S. F. (1985), 'A marketing analysis of foreign tourism in Greece', in Shaw, S., Sparks, L. and Kaynak, E. (eds), *Proceedings of Second World Marketing Congress*, Stirling: University of Stirling, pp. 682–93.

Pearce, D. (1989), *Tourist Development*, 2nd edn, Harlow: Longman.

Porter, M. E. (1980), *Competitive Strategy*, New York: Free Press.

Porter, M. E. (1985), *Competitive Advantage*, New York: Free Press.

Porter, M. E. (ed.) (1986), *Competition in Global Industries*, Boston, Mass.: Harvard Business School Press.

Prasad, A. J. (1981), 'Technology transfer to developing countries through multinational corporations', in Hawkins, R. G. and Prasad, A. J. (eds), *Technology Transfer and Economic Development*, Greenwich, Conn.: J. A. I. Press.

Prentice, R. (1989), 'Environmental analysis in tourism', in Witt, S. F. and Moutinho, L., op. cit., pp. 131–6.

Ritchie, J. R. B. and Goeldner, C. (eds) (1986), *Travel, Tourism and Hospitality Research: A handbook for managers and researchers*, Travel and Tourism Research Association, New York: John Wiley.

Sadler, P. G., Archer, B. H. and Owen, C. B. (1973), *Regional Income Multipliers: The Anglesey study*, Bangor Occasional Papers No. 1, Cardiff: University of Wales Press.

Salem, S. and Sansom, M. A. (1979), *Les Contrats 'Clés en Main' et les Contrats 'Produits en Main'*, Paris: Libraries Techniques.

Sikorski, D. (1990), 'A comparative evaluation of the governments' role in national airlines', *Asia-Pacific Journal of Management*, vol. 7, no. 1, pp. 97–120.

Sternquist, B., Davis, B. and Pysarchik, D. (1989), 'Financial Analysis in Tourism', in Witt, S. F. and Moutinho, L., op. cit., pp. 151–5.

Taylor, G. D. (1989), 'The United States pleasure travel market', *Journal of Business*, vol. 18, no. 1, pp. 1–79.

Telesio, P. (1979), *Technology, Licensing and Multinational Enterprise*, New York: Praeger.

Travis, A. S. (1984), *Realizing the Tourism Potential of the South Wales Valleys*, Cardiff: Wales Tourist Board.

Travis, A. S. (1989), 'Tourism destination area development (from theory into practice)', in Witt, S. F. and Moutinho, L., op. cit., pp. 487–98.

Turner, L. and Ash, J. (1975), *The Golden Hordes: International tourism and the pleasure periphery*, London: Constable.

United Nations Centre on Transnational Corporations (1982), *Transnational Corporations in International Tourism*, by Dunning, J. H. and McQueen, M., New York: UNCTC.

United Nations Centre on Transnational Corporations (1989), *Transnational Corporations in World Development: Trends and prospects*, New York: UNCTC.

Vandermey, A. (1984), 'Assessing the importance of urban tourism', *Tourism Management*, vol. 5, no. 2, pp. 123–35.

Vaughan, D. R. (1986), *Estimating the Level of Tourism Related Employment: An assessment of two non-survey techniques*, London: British Tourist Authority/English Tourist Board.

Vaughn, C. L. (1979), *Franchising*, 2nd edn, Lexington, Mass.: D. C. Heath.

Vernon, R. (1966), 'International investment and international trade in the product cycle', *Quarterly Journal of Economics*, vol. 80, pp. 190–207.

Vernon, R. (1979), 'The product cycle hypothesis in a new international environment', *Oxford Bulletin of Economics and Statistics*, vol. 41, pp. 255–67.

Wahab, S. E. A. (1973), 'Elements of macro-planning in tourism development, *The Tourist Review*, no. 2, pp. 50–9.

Walsh, R. G. (1986), *Recreation Economic Decisions: Comparing benefits and costs*, State College, Pennsylvania: Venture Publishing Inc.

Wandner, S. A. and Van Erden, J. D. (1980), 'Estimating the demand for international tourism using time series analysis', in Hawkins, D. E., Shafer, E. L. and Rovelstad, J. M. (eds), *Tourism Planning and Development Issues*, Washington, DC: George Washington University, pp. 381–92.

Wanhill, S. (1988), 'Tourism statistics to 2000', *Proceedings of Current Issues in Services Research Conference*, Poole: Dorset Institute.

Wanhill, S. (1989), 'Development and investment policy in tourism', in Witt, S. F. and Moutinho, L., op. cit., pp. 103–5.

Weigand, R. E. (1980), 'Barters and buy-backs – let Western firms beware!', *Business Mergers*, June 1980, pp. 54–61.

Wildsmith, J. R. (1973), *Managerial Theories of the Firm*, London: Martin Robertson.

Williams, A. M. and Shaw, G. (eds) (1988), *Tourism and Economic Development: Western European experience*, London: Belhaven Press.

Williamson, O. E. (1975), *Markets and Hierarchies: Analysis and anti-trust implications*, New York: Free Press.

Wing, P. C. L. (1989), 'Marketing of tourism in small island states', in Witt, S. F. and Moutinho, L., op. cit., pp. 269–73.

Withyman, M. (1985), 'The ins and outs of international travel and tourism data', *International Tourism Quarterly*, no. 4, London: Economist Publications.

Witt, S. F. (1980a), 'An abstract mode – abstract (destination) node model of foreign holiday demand', *Applied Economics*, vol. 12, no. 2, pp. 163–80.

Witt, S. F. (1980b), 'An econometric comparison of U.K. and German foreign holiday behaviour', *Managerial and Decision Economics*, vol. 1, no. 3, pp. 123–31.

Witt, S. F. (1989a), 'Forecasting international tourism demand: The econometric approach', in Witt, S. F. and Moutinho, L., op. cit., pp. 163–7.

Witt, S. F. (1989b), 'Forecasting international tourism demand: Univariate time series methods (noncausal quantitative techniques)', in Witt, S. F. and Moutinho, L., op. cit., pp. 169–74.

Witt, S. F. and Martin, C. A. (1987a), 'Deriving a relative price index for inclusion in international tourism demand estimation models: Comment', *Journal of Travel Research*, vol. XXV, no. 3, pp. 38–40.

Witt, S. F. and Martin, C. A. (1987b), 'International tourism demand models – inclusion of marketing variables', *Tourism Management*, vol. 8, no. 1, pp. 33–40.

Witt, S. F. and Martin, C. A. (1987c), 'Measuring the impacts of mega-events on tourism flows', in AIEST publication vol. 28, *The Role and Impact of Mega-Events and Attractions on Regional and National Tourism Development*, St Gallen: AIEST, pp. 213–21.

Witt, S. F. and Martin, C. A. (1989), 'Demand forecasting in tourism and recreation', *Progress in Tourism, Recreation and Hospitality Management*, vol. 1, pp. 4–32.

Witt, S. F. and Moutinho, L. (eds) (1989), *Tourism Marketing and Management Handbook*, Hemel Hempstead: Prentice-Hall.

World Tourism Organization (1990), *Yearbook of Tourism Statistics*, Madrid: WTO.

World Tourism Organization/Horwath and Horwath (1981), *Tourism Multipliers Explained*, London: Horwath and Horwath.

Wright, M. and Coyne, J. (1985), *Management Buyouts in British Industry*, London: Croom Helm.

Wright, P. *et al.* (1981), 'The developing world to 1990: Trends and implications for multinational business', *Long Range Planning*, vol. 15, pp. 116–25.

Yavas, V. (1987), 'Foreign travel behaviour in a growing vacation market: Implications for tourism marketers', *European Journal of Marketing*, vol. 21, no. 5, pp. 56–69.

Index: topics

Index: names